Modernity, Memory and Identity in South-East Europe

Series Editor
Catharina Raudvere, Department of Cross-Cultural and Regional Studies, University of Copenhagen, Copenhagen, Denmark

This series explores the relationship between the modern history and present of South-East Europe and the long imperial past of the region. This approach aspires to offer a more nuanced understanding of the concepts of modernity and change in this region, from the nineteenth century to the present day. Titles focus on changes in identity, self-representation and cultural expressions in light of the huge pressures triggered by the interaction between external influences and local and regional practices. The books cover three significant chronological units: the decline of empires and their immediate aftermath, authoritarian governance during the twentieth century, and recent uses of history in changing societies in South-East Europe today.

Abdullah Simsek

Ottoman Nationalism in Transition from Empire to Republic, 1908–1931

palgrave
macmillan

Abdullah Simsek
The Many Roads in Modernity
University of Copenhagen
Copenhagen, Denmark

ISSN 2523-7985   ISSN 2523-7993   (electronic)
Modernity, Memory and Identity in South-East Europe
ISBN 978-3-031-56927-2   ISBN 978-3-031-56928-9   (eBook)
https://doi.org/10.1007/978-3-031-56928-9

© The Editor(s) (if applicable) and The Author(s), under exclusive license to Springer Nature Switzerland AG 2024

This work is subject to copyright. All rights are solely and exclusively licensed by the Publisher, whether the whole or part of the material is concerned, specifically the rights of translation, reprinting, reuse of illustrations, recitation, broadcasting, reproduction on microfilms or in any other physical way, and transmission or information storage and retrieval, electronic adaptation, computer software, or by similar or dissimilar methodology now known or hereafter developed.

The use of general descriptive names, registered names, trademarks, service marks, etc. in this publication does not imply, even in the absence of a specific statement, that such names are exempt from the relevant protective laws and regulations and therefore free for general use.

The publisher, the authors and the editors are safe to assume that the advice and information in this book are believed to be true and accurate at the date of publication. Neither the publisher nor the authors or the editors give a warranty, expressed or implied, with respect to the material contained herein or for any errors or omissions that may have been made. The publisher remains neutral with regard to jurisdictional claims in published maps and institutional affiliations.

This Palgrave Macmillan imprint is published by the registered company Springer Nature Switzerland AG
The registered company address is: Gewerbestrasse 11, 6330 Cham, Switzerland

Paper in this product is recyclable.

To Emine

Acknowledgements

I am indebted to all those individuals and organizations involved in the creation of this book, which originated from my postdoctoral project at the University of Copenhagen.

First of all, I extend my special thanks to the Carlsberg Foundation for its funding, as well as to the research centre, Many Roads in Modernity (https://modernity.ku.dk), of which this project is a part. Many thanks to the members of the research group at the centre, particularly Professor Catharina Raudvere, whose continual support, encouragement, and patience kept me on track and made this book possible.

I would also like to thank the Palgrave Macmillan team for their invaluable support and guidance during the publication process and their much-appreciated commitment towards this project.

And finally, endless gratitude to my heart and soul, my beloved wife Emine, not only for her unwavering support throughout this project, despite all hardships encountered, but also for her very being.

Contents

1	**Introduction**	1
	Historiography and Theory	9
	The Source Material	17
	The Structure of the Book	18
2	**Framing the Ottoman Nation**	23
	Tanzimat Reformers and Nation-Building	29
	The Constitution and the Ottoman Citizen	35
	Abdulhamid II and Ottoman Muslim Nationalism	39
3	**Ottomanism Between Ideology and *Realpolitik***	43
	The Response: Ali Kemal and the Liberal Critique	54
	Ahmet Ferit's Realism	55
4	**Revolution and Disillusion**	63
	The Reception	70
	Freedom of the "People"?	77
	Early Disappointments and the End of Euphoria	80
	The Politics of Revolution	82
	The Counterrevolution Attempt	86
5	**Identity Policies in Action**	91
	Centralization and the Nationalities	96
	Ottoman Unity Through Education	104
	Reactions to Centralization and Homogenization	107

Return to Ottoman Muslim Nationalism   112
The Balkan Wars   115
World War I   119

6 **Claiming the Homeland?**   125
    A "Nationalist" Movement?   127
    Armistice and the New Ottoman Realities   129
    The Political Situation: Unionists and Resistance   131
    The Officers Make Their Move   136
    Wilson and National Self-Determination   139
    From Population to Nation   144
    The Ottoman non-Muslims and the Resistance Movement   146
    Kurds, Turks and Ottoman Muslim Unity   148
    The Central Government and the Resistance Movement   153
    The Last Assembly of Deputies and the New Assembly in Ankara   155
    Ottoman to Turk or Ottoman as Turk?   158

7 **Reframing the Nation**   165
    A (Partial) Farewell to Ottomanness?   167
    "National" Territory and Its "Nation"   170
    Non-Muslims and the Nation   175
    Mosul or the "Homeland"?   181
    The Halkists and the Turkists—Power Politics and Nationalism   187
    The Political Process and Muslim Unity   193
    A Question of Saying or Not Saying?   208

8 **Conclusion**   217

Bibliography   229

Index   249

CHAPTER 1

Introduction

millet, s . (pl. milel) 1. One's belief, faith, religion. 2. A nationality, a people; especially, a people united by a common faith; a sect. *Millet-i Islam* 1. The faith of Islam. 2. The whole body of believers of Islam. *Millet-i Beyza* s. The Muslims as a whole. *Millet-i Mesihiye* The whole body of Christians. *Frenk Milleti* The whole body of Europeans, The Franks.[1]

millet : Religion and sharia: "To us, religion and nation are one". A group sharing the same religion: *Millet-i Islamiyye* [the Islamic millet]. It is better not to use the word in the meaning of *nation* which signifies a community of individuals born in the same country, or made it a homeland by settlement, and live under the same government. For the latter should be used the terms *kavim* or *ümmet* [ummah].[2]

millet : A group of people who live on the same soil and share the same origin and language or who have had common

---

[1] Redhouse. (1890). *A Turkish and English Lexicon.* Emphases mine. In the original text, the emphasized words are written in the Ottoman Arabic script.

[2] Muallim Naci. (1318 [1902]). *Lugat-ı Naci.* In the original text, the word "nation" is written in Latin letters, whereby the author makes a direct comparison between "nation" and "millet", thus between a Western European and Ottoman concept respectively.

interests for a very long time; a nation [kavim], who live in the same country and is ruled by the same government; a people [halk], an ummah [ümmet], a race [cins], a tribe [taife]. In Arabic, the term originally means sect or religion.[3]

millet : religion, sect, sharia ... The whole community of those who belong to the same religion ... *Millet-i Islamiye* [the Islamic millet].[4]

"Nation" (*millet*), from which modern Turkish derives its words for "nationality" (*milliyet*) and nationalism (*milliyetçilik*), is a key concept in Turkish history.[5] As indicated by the lexical excerpts above, its metamorphoses along the way tell the story of a highly complex, fluid, and ambivalent process of nation formation and national identity construction. Still ongoing with varying intensity, this process of nation-building with its twin concepts of "nation" and "modernity" has constituted the centrepiece of Turkish politics and state ideology, which, however, often conflicts with alternative modes of identity, including those related to religion, ethnicity, culture, and gender. The sensitivity of the topic in contemporary Turkey, evident not only in the heated public debates it generates but also in the violent encounters of various magnitudes involving state security forces and non-state groups, shows that the national question is still very much alive. Gaining a clearer understanding of the origins and formative phases of the nation-building process is therefore crucial to uncovering its components, characteristics, and unresolved issues, especially those related to national unity and societal coherence, or the lack thereof.[6] The field generates a number of important questions, including how to construct a well-integrated society and what constitutes a coherent nation, an enduring issue since the late Ottoman period.

---

[3] Toven. (1346 [1927]). *Yeni Türkçe Lugat*.

[4] Hüseyin Kazım Kadri. (1943). *Türk lugatı*, Dördüncü Cilt.

[5] According to Ziya Gökalp, a highly influential thinker of Turkey in the 20th century and one of the main figures of Turkish nationalism, the most important themes of Ottoman history were Turkification, Islamization, and modernization (*Türkleşmek, Islamlaşmak, Muasırlaşmak*), from which Ottomans had to choose.

[6] Feroz Ahmad for instance describes Turkey as a torn country with a serious identity crisis in his *Turkey: A Quest for Identity*.

Meanwhile, as the Turkish public debates the reasons for its lack of unity and calls for stronger national integration—especially when faced with challenges posed by the "Kurdish problem" (*Kürt sorunu*)—on the agenda is a new beginning with a new constitution in a "new" Turkey.[7] The polarizing policies and rhetoric along ethnic, cultural, and religious lines of the Turkish government under the authoritarian leadership of R.T. Erdogan seem, however, to point in a different, historically well-known, and well-worn direction rather than towards something new. The issue is further complicated and the contradictions even more evident when the president, while citing the all too familiar, state-centred nationalist slogans like "one nation, one state, one flag, one fatherland", also makes use of symbolism and vocabulary assumed to relate to the Ottoman past, often approached as a monolith, giving impressions of a state-sponsored Ottoman turn.[8]

While a "new Turkey" is in the making, at least on the rhetorical level, the challenges appear old, with questions of democracy, rights and freedoms, pluralism, constitutionalism, modernization, and Islam remaining pivotal. Furthermore, deep-rooted conflicts on national identity and the need for societal peace are important reminders of the fragile nature of Turkey's national unity. Indeed, the issue of the results of the nation-building process under the republic becomes highly relevant, considering that Turkey is a country still trying to mould its society into one nation, find societal common ground, and lay down fundamental rules for a political and legal system.[9]

This problem is particularly interesting, as Turkey has been classified as a "nation-state" for nearly a century, since the foundation of the Republic of Turkey under the leadership of the Ottoman general, Mustafa Kemal Atatürk.[10] Head of the remaining Ottoman military forces, Atatürk turned Turkey's catastrophic defeat in WWI into victory in 1919–22 and, as the figurehead of the new parliament in Ankara, put an end to the sultanate, then the caliphate, and situated the "nation" as the sole source of power, heralding brand new times for "modern" Turkey. This image

---

[7] http://www.bbm.gov.tr/Forms/pgNews.aspx?Type=4.

[8] Çağaptay, *The New Sultan*, 185–187.

[9] Özbudun, *The Constitutional System of Turkey*, 151–156. See also Petersen & Yanaşmayan, *The Failure of Popular Constitution Making in Turkey*.

[10] Bayar, *Formation of the Turkish Nation-State*.

was taken up and elaborated further by European observers and scholars alike, who for decades to come praised the impressive transformation of Turkey under Atatürk and the Kemalists. The republican nation-state and Western-influenced secularism were particularly highlighted as markers of the "modernity" of the new Turkey, and the success story and irreversible fact of "modern" Turkey's transformation continued to produce such famous works as that by B. Lewis and D. Lerner, even during the post-World War II era.[11]

Subsequent events and the picture since then, however, tell a different story. Although Turkish nationalism—included in the Turkish constitution since 1937 as its fundamental principle—is one of the ideological pillars of the Turkish republican state, which has invested vast energies into moulding the population into "Turks", the challenge has grave difficulties, evidenced by the fact that Turkey still struggles with national cohesion and polarization along ethnic, cultural, and religious lines. One of the most prominent scholars of Ottoman Turkish history, Sükrü Hanioglu, criticizing the very structure that Lewis and Lerner had praised so highly, argues that the reason lies in the founding of the Republic of Turkey. In his words, the shirt was buttoned up wrongly from the first button, affecting the rest all the way down.[12] The "wrong button", according to Hanioglu, was the lack of societal reconciliation, negotiation, and agreement: a new social contract, so to speak, between the remaining elements of the population in Turkey after the demise of the empire. Rather than seeking social agreement through open negotiation, however, the Kemalist regime chose a more authoritarian way to reform and rebuild society. This in turn had a negative impact on the future of Turkish society as a whole, and the viability of the Kemalist reform project in particular. As a result, societal and national cohesion never materialized, leaving the problem of national unity an enduring source of instability.

It is, however, highly debatable whether all these ills mentioned by Hanioglu were due to Kemalist policies or even if the so-called "wrong button" can be narrowed down to that particular period; the problem of sociopolitical cohesiveness, or "unity" (*ittihat*) to use the general word in Ottoman historical discourse, and attempts to remedy it, have had a long lifespan and there were many "buttonholes" before the republic.

---

[11] Lewis, *The Emergence of Modern Turkey*; Lerner, *The Passing of Traditional Society*.
[12] Hanioğlu, M.Ş., "Neden demokratikleşemiyoruz?" *Sabah*, (6 October 2013).

Yet what is beyond doubt is the paramount importance of the transition from the Ottoman Empire to the Turkish Republic, with its vast impact on Turkish society and the state, and, not least, its lasting effects on the subsequent process of nation-building in Turkey. Many of the societal structures—political, institutional, and ideological—were built or solidified in this period. Likewise, some of the crucial topics and debates of the late Ottoman and early republican periods are resurfacing at an increasing pace, which in turn puts greater emphasis on the implications of unsolved issues in the late Ottoman and early republican periods.

This study suggests an alternate periodization to the traditional 1923 divide that revolves around the republican Turkish state's phoenix-like "emergence". It analyses the subject matter as a continuous process within the period, 1908–1931. It takes the Young Turk revolution as its point of departure, as it heralded a radically new phase of Ottoman nation-building, with the introduction of new symbols, imaginaries and vocabulary of Ottomanness along with the reinstatement of the constitution, parliamentary representation, party politics, and a vibrant Ottoman public and press. As the endpoint, the year 1931 is chosen because it marks the establishment of the Kemalist one-party state, ushering in another stage of nation-building policies and rhetoric significantly differing from the previous period. This development in the 1930s, partly a reflection of the authoritarian political system, partly influenced by ideological tendencies in Italy and Germany at the time, as well as the severe socioeconomic repercussions of the world economic crises, led to what Ahmet Yıldız has characterized as a new "ethnic-racial dimension" (*etnikırki boyut*) in Kemalist nationalism.[13] This periodization is arguably more suitable for analysing and providing a better understanding of the transition from empire to the republic in terms of the development of national identity formation and the shifting policies, rhetoric, and positioning of the actors involved.

Since its inception, the Young Turk Revolution has been regarded by both contemporary observers and the generations thereafter as a watershed event. July 10, the day of the "proclamation of Liberty" became a national holiday, which continued to do so during the Kemalist republic under Atatürk (1881–1938), until it was abolished by "the law on

---

[13] Yıldız, *Ne Mutlu Türküm Diyebilene*, 159.

national holidays" adopted on 27 May 1935.[14] This continuation was hardly surprising as, despite the outward rhetoric of the Kemalist regime to eradicate everything "Ottoman" from collective memory, the founders of the republic, as former Young Turks, or more specifically Unionists, had themselves participated in the revolution and were, for good or worse, the bearers of its legacy.

The revolution was orchestrated by the Young Turks, a loosely connected group unified by their opposition to Abdulhamid II's regime. Ironically, the core of this movement consisted mainly of young officers and civil servants who had received education in Abdulhamid's European-inspired educational institutions, which in turn was a consequence of the significant transformations that took place in the late nineteenth century within Ottoman state and society. These complex modernization processes had opened up new rights, relations, and opportunities for different segments of the Ottoman population. More importantly, the revolution had a profound and long-lasting impact on the Ottoman power structure and the composition of political elites, as the Young Turks successfully assumed control over both the central government and communal organizations. The political cadres associated with the Hamidian regime, unable to maintain their positions, were subsequently purged.

At this point, finding in the revolution an opportune moment for a national revival, the Young Turks rallied around an old project, "the unity of elements" (*ittihad-ı anasır*), otherwise known in historiography as "Ottomanism" with the declared aim to unify the "Ottoman nation" (*millet-i osmaniyye*).[15] It entailed a commonality among all Ottomans, based on a selectively constructed model grounded in the ideas of constitutional government, equality before the law, and equal citizenship, regardless of ethnicity and religious affiliation.

At the heart of this principle lay the notion that the state should be able to garner support from its population in order to mobilize

---

[14] The "Law on National Holidays", made 29 October, the proclamation of the republic in 1923, the most important holiday, with the reason given that: "Because on that day, the Turkish nation has found its identity and Turkey began its period of progress and rise". TBMM ZC, D: 5, Cilt 3, S. Sayısı: 130, 1–4.

[15] Not surprisingly, the Ottomanist principle found its way into the very name of the most powerful faction within the Young Turk movement, the *Unionists*, and their organisation "*Union* and Progress".

men and resources for the preservation and well-being of the empire. In order for this to occur, however, the subjects of the empire had to be transformed into Ottoman citizens who identified with and rallied behind the Ottoman state and country. The approaches proposed to attain this, however, varied significantly. The initial spirit and rhetoric of the revolution declared that it could be accomplished through a process of negotiations, ensuring that all population elements within the empire had a voice in the governance of the state through instruments such as parliament, a constitution, a free press, and a pluralistic environment for differing opinions.

Indeed, initially at least, in the new constitutional framework, and the ensuing pluralist political atmosphere, a wider range of people and groups gained the opportunity to express themselves and seek political influence and positions within the state apparatus. As such, this process had the potential to better reflect the ethnic diversity and multi-religious composition of the empire. However, the success of this inclusive approach relied heavily on the relations between the central state and local groups, the outcome of the political process, and the events and circumstances facing the empire.

This experiment with Ottomanism[16] as a particular form of nation-building constitutes the subject matter of this book. Within this framework, I examine the evolving strategies and rhetoric adopted by the political elites in their efforts towards nation-building and national identity formation in the Ottoman Empire and Turkey during the defining years of 1908–1931. With Ottoman nationalism as the primary focus, I investigate its characteristics and development during this period. How

---

[16] It should be pointed out here that there is an important difference between what in historiography has been termed "Ottomanism" and the nearest concepts used in Ottoman source material, *osmanlılık* ("Ottomanness"). In Ottoman vocabulary, the term was expressed as a –ness rather than an –ism, meaning identity rather than ideology. Hence, "Ottomanism" appears more clear-cut in English than in Ottoman Turkish. In what appears to be an attempt to bring greater alignment between "Ottomanism" with modern Turkish, another term was coined, *osmanlıcılık* (in which case the concept is reframed as an –ism in Turkish as well). This has created a peculiar problem of reference when speaking of Ottomanism in Turkish. Sometimes *osmanlıcılık* is used and other times *osmanlılık*, or "Ottomanness", making it arguably even more confusing in modern Turkish than English. Hence, in this study "Ottomanism" is used as a designation for Ottoman state policies, and the related conceptual framework, to promote an Ottoman national identity among the empire's population elements as a whole.

were the principles of Ottomanism and the boundaries of the nation reinterpreted and reconceptualized according to the changing circumstances? What were the elements of continuity and change in that regard? To what extent did the elements of Ottoman nationalism survive in the Kemalist republic? What was retained and what was discarded in the process of adaptation? How did the inclusion and exclusion occur, and why? The goal here is to show how Ottoman national identity was constructed and its related concepts changed over time during this period.

The framework of this study comprises four major analytical focal points: demography, territory, hegemony, and security. The first, demography, has enabled analysis and understanding of the most notable aspects of change and continuity, and their impact on identity construction. As the demographic makeup of the country changed drastically in this transitional period from empire to republic, so did the demarcations and definitions of the characteristics and composition of the nation. Concepts and imaginings also changed, especially with the demise of the non-Muslim population and the radical reduction of non-Turk elements at the end of the empire, although some well-established habits and methods of inclusion and exclusion remained.

The territory was another aspect that drastically altered, with far-reaching implications for the nation-building process. As the vast territory of the Ottoman Empire shrank into what is now Anatolia and a small portion of Thrace within a period of ten years, imagining and defining a new version of a "homeland" and its boundaries became of utmost urgency. Of particular interest here is the way this radical territorial reduction shaped national identity construction.

Hegemony involves issues of power, both of and within the governing elite: who had the power to define the nation and how, and with what results on the discursive level? It is also relevant to power as it was distributed between elements of the population. As the dominant Ottoman discourse operated with the notion of *millet-i hakime* (the ruling nation)—that is, the Muslim element—power functioned in various ways in the production of meaning, undergoing great shifts alongside those within the demographic makeup and the radically diminished territory. Thus, as the *millet-i mahkume* (the ruled nation)—traditionally the non-Muslim elements—gradually disappeared, new divides and subcategorizations came into existence within the remaining Muslim population.

Finally, the issue of security has to do with aspects of war and peace. Conceptualizations of Ottoman identity and unity were closely connected with national security and survival, intensified at times of immense crisis, such as Austria-Hungary's annexation of Bosnia-Herzegovina in 1908, the Ottoman-Italian War in 1911, and the Balkan Wars in 1912–13. Times of war being especially well suited to patriotic rhetoric and defining the national self and the other, parliamentary and public discussions on these issues give valuable insights into perceptions and definitions of Ottoman nationality, and the Ottomans' sense of belonging. Thus, the characteristics and discursive content of national identity construction in times of peace and war are of considerable interest, especially notions of loyalty, survival, and threats to national existence.

HISTORIOGRAPHY AND THEORY

The historiography of the Late Ottoman Empire and the early Turkish Republic has undergone significant developments since the 1950s, with three major currents emerging in the process. The first trend coincided with the end of the Kemalist one-party rule, leading to a multi-party system, liberalization of the economy, and, more decisively, Turkey's entrance into the NATO alliance against the Soviet bloc. In this context, Western perceptions of Turkey's "modernity" were significantly heightened, and its historical trajectory drew considerable scholarly attention during the 1950s and 60s, a period dominated by the modernization paradigm. The latter sought to explain the course of Ottoman Turkish history in terms of ongoing westernizing reforms and a continual conflict between the reform-minded and the reactionary forces.[17] Scholars such as Bernard Lewis and Daniel Lerner played key roles in this regard, epitomized by Lewis' *Emergence of Modern Turkey* (1961) and Lerner's *Passing of Traditional Society* (1958) which narrated the national birth of a "modern" Turkey rising out of the ashes of a backward empire. Lerner, in particular, emphasized the demise of "tradition" as Kemalist secularization and Westernization had finally borne fruit, liberating Turkish society from the constraints of Islam and ultimately achieving modernity. Presented

---

[17] Lewis, *The Emergence of Modern Turkey*; Lerner, *The Passing of Traditional Society*; Ward & Rustow, *Political Modernization in Japan and Turkey*. See also a later version of this approach in Ahmad (1993), *The Making of Modern Turkey*.

as a one-way track from the "traditional" to the "modern", this narrative focused on the end results of history, highlighting the triumph of modernity over tradition, secularism over religion, reform over reaction, civilization over backwardness, etc.

A central tenet of this model was the significance attributed to the nation-state as another end result of modernity. While Ottoman history was divided into three distinct periods—rise, decline, and demise—the final phase, marked by the Republic under Atatürk, was characterized as a contrast between ruin and national rebirth, as the processes of westernization would finally lead the empire into the modern Turkish nation-state.[18] Thus, considering the Ottoman Empire ultimately as a failure, the extensive efforts invested in reforming the imperial state and society, along with the highly complex processes of transformation that ensued, were deemed significant only insofar as they contributed to the presumed end result.

This version, in fact, largely reflected the original Kemalist history thesis, itself a product of the nation-state environment in the post-Ottoman era.[19] Similar to the modernization paradigm, the Kemalist version of history portrayed the Ottoman Empire and the Republic of Turkey as direct opposites. Behind this rationale was the notion that the imperial context was incompatible with post-war projects of imagining and constructing political communities, namely nation-states. As a result, the official history narrative in Turkey retrospectively presented the late Ottoman period as one marked by conflict and division, towards which Turkish nationalism had already established itself as the sole viable solution. Together, the Kemalist version on the one hand, and Western scholarship on the other, produced a highly robust Turkish nationalism thesis, according to which the course of Turkish history was clear, and already unfolding during the last decade of the empire, towards a modern Turkish nation-state.[20] Furthermore, considering Ottomanism and Islamic national identity as non-modern, unlike Turkish nationalism, the envisioned path to Turkish modernity was to transition from the multiethnic, multi-religious, and perceived backward Ottomanness

---

[18] Lewis, *The Emergence of Modern Turkey*; Berkes, *Development of Secularism*.

[19] Türkiye Cumhuriyeti Maarif Vekaleti, *Türk Tarihinin Ana Hatları* (1931); Türk Tarihi Tetkik Cemiyeti, *Tarih IV*. (1934); Şapolyo, *Atatürk* (1943); Tekinalp, *Kemalizm* (1936).

[20] Berkes, *Development of Secularism;* Kili, *Türk Devrim Tarihi*; Afetinan, *Türkiye Cumhuriyeti ve Türk Devrimi*.

to a nationally awakened, secularist Turkishness. Consequently, Turkish modernity was closely associated with national consciousness, meaning the embrace of Turkish identity. In contrast, the Ottoman multiethnic imperial setting was believed to have suppressed or laid dormant this national consciousness.

Although this interpretation brought order to an immense, complex reality, its reductionism and narrow approach presented serious impediments to grasping events and circumstances from different angles. Furthermore, the rather dichotomous modernization and Kemalist approaches had profound implications. For instance, it seems problematic to regard nation-state formation as the end result of history, and thus Turkish nationalism as the only viable, and therefore inevitable, course of action. Further, both suggest that Ottomanism, another perspective on nationhood, was "out of date" or mere fantasy,[21] although it presented alternative visions of nationhood which in many respects represented a more inclusive and pluralistic line.

The modernization paradigm faced its first significant challenge during the 1970s, influenced by the Marxist camp and the world system theory developed by scholars like Immanuel Wallerstein and Andre Gunder Frank,[22] who, employing a macro-scale understanding of world history and social change, redirected the focus to structures of development across extended time spans and broader regional spaces beyond nation-state borders. These perspectives offered an alternative interpretation of the inner workings of the global economic system and the diverse paths of development in countries and regions, which could not be reduced to the "modern-backward" dichotomy. The world system theory further criticized the modernization model for its rather Eurocentric and teleological approach, which, it pointed out, was too narrow to be able to capture the complexities and multifaceted processes of socioeconomic historical change. Within Ottoman historiography, this approach found its most notable expression in Kemal Karpat's *The Ottoman State and its Place*

---

[21] Kili, *Türk Devrim Tarihi*, 177–186.

[22] Wallerstein, I. (1974). *The Modern World-System: Mercantilism and the Consolidation of the European World-Economy, 1600–1750*. New York: Academic Press; Frank, A.G. (1967). *Capitalism and Underdevelopment in Latin America: Historical Studies of Chile and Brazil*. Monthly Review Press.

in World History (1974),[23] which challenged the nation-centred historical perspective hitherto dominating the field. By situating the Ottoman Empire within the context of world and regional history and seeking to trace its history across a longer time span—for instance, exploring the influence of the Ottoman past in the successor states in the Middle East—this work significantly shifted the focus away from particular state boundaries and national histories.

Since the 1990s, Ottoman historiography has experienced formidable productivity and development, marked by an impressive number of innovative in-depth studies that cast new light on various aspects of Ottoman history. Within this context, a third theoretical current has emerged, adopting an approach that places greater emphasis on local dynamics and processes of connectivity among diverse actors, forces, and places. This approach also considers transformations on multiple levels—social, economic, cultural, ideological, and political - that swept through late Ottoman society.[24] In this regard, particularly noteworthy for this study, are the contributions that sought to transcend the imperial nation-state divides. Early influential examples include L.C. Brown's (1996) and Karen Barkey's (1997) edited works,[25] which, focusing on the "legacy" and "consequences" of empire, respectively, investigated different empires and post-empire experiences, gathering perspectives from historians of various countries and regions, including Turkey, Balkans, the Middle East, and more.

Since then, many other collections have charted the path of revisionist histories, showing a trend towards departing from the notion of a drastic and revolutionary split in 1923 and instead highlighting the similarities between the late Ottoman and early republican periods.[26] In this regard,

---

[23] An edited work, *The Ottoman State and Its Place in World History* consisted of contributions from highly influential scholars such as H. Inalcık, A. Hourani, C. Issawi, and S. J. Shaw, among others.

[24] See esp. Kayalı, *Arabs and Young Turks;* Faroqhi, *Subjects of the Sultan;* Göçek, *Transformation;* Fortna, *Imperial Classroom;* Quataert, *The Ottoman Empire*.

[25] Brown, *Imperial Legacy: The Ottoman Imprint on the Balkans and the Middle East;* Barkey & Hagen, *After Empire*.

[26] Among these revisionist histories are especially important works such as S. Çağaptay *Islam, Secularism, and Nationalism in Modern Turkey;* S. Deringil, *The Well-protected Domains: Ideology and the Legitimation of Power in the Ottoman Empire 1876–1909;* H. Kayalı, *Arabs and Young Turks: Ottomanism, Arabism and Islamism in the Ottoman Empire, 1908–1918,* K. Barkey & M. von Hagen, *After Empire: Multiethnic Societies and*

Erik J. Zürcher's work stands out as the most influential pioneering contribution, especially with his proposition of a revised periodization, presenting 1908–1950 as a singular "Young Turk" era, and while so doing highlighting the continuity of networks, concepts, and motivations during the transition from the Ottoman Empire to the Turkish Republic.[27] Furthermore, he traces greater continuity than rupture between the Young Turk and the early republican regime in terms of leadership cadres, institutions, ideology, political outlook, nation-building policies, etc.[28]

While acknowledging Zürcher's premise that the policies of the Unionist regime were driven by action and pragmatism, rather than ideology, however this study further aims at examining the effect of these actions on ideas, concepts, rhetoric, and worldview. For the policies of the Unionists/Kemalists were not merely transient responses to changing circumstances, only to disappear afterwards. These actions and consequences not only shaped experiences and understanding, but they also left their unmistakeable mark on the discursive field. Thus, these actions and concrete policies during the second constitutional period (1908–1918), particularly in WWI, and the Armistice period (1918–1922), had a profound impact on the perceptions, themes, and rhetoric related to the ways of framing the national question, including key concepts, such as "nation" (*millet*), "people" (*halk*), "culture" (*hars*), "citizen" (*vatandaş*), "religion" (*din*), "state" (*devlet*), etc. Hence, rather than representing the reasoning behind the policies of the governing elite, the parliamentary minutes—the main source material used in this book—should be read as reflections of these very actions and the ongoing process of conceptualizing, interpreting, rationalizing, redefining, and legitimizing them. This is especially evident in the debates of the assemblies of 1908–12, 1920–23, and 1923–27, which introduced formative discourses and attitudes that influenced subsequent policies and ideas.

Nation-building; K. Karpat, *Politicization of Islam*; F. Göçek, *Rise of the Bourgeoisie, Demise of Empire*; E. Boyar, *Ottomans, Turks and the Balkans: Empire Lost, Relations Altered*; I. Blumi, *Reinstating the Ottomans: Alternative Balkan Modernities, 1800–1912*; B.C. Fortna, *State-Nationalisms in the Ottoman Empire, Greece and Turkey*; U. U. Üngör, *The Making of Modern Turkey: Nation and State in Eastern Anatolia, 1913-1950*; D. Gürpınar, *Ottoman Turkish Visions of the Nation, 1860–1950*.

[27] Zürcher, *Turkey: A Modern History*.

[28] Zürcher, *The Young Turk Legacy*.

Furthermore, this study also benefits immensely from recent scholarship in the field, such as Howard Eissenstat, Yeşim Bayar, Virginia Aksan, Erol Ülker, and Michael E. Meeker.[29] Eissenstat utilizing the concept of Ottoman nationalism, highlights the contingent and ambiguous nature of Ottoman Turkish national identity formation while arguing convincingly against approaches that see both the markers of national identity, e.g. "Ottoman" and "Turk", as well as the policies of national identities, such as "Ottomanism" and "Islamism" as mutually exclusive categories.[30] Meeker's book, *A Nation of Empire: The Ottoman Legacy of Turkish Modernity*, examines the complex and intertwined relations of nations and empires, and emphasizes the strong elements of Ottoman legacy in the Turkish republic. In addition, Ülker discusses the concept of "Turkification" in the late Ottoman context, illustrating its composite and fluid nature, along with the geographical variations involved in Unionist identity policies, and examines it in relation to the ethnicization of religion following the Balkan Wars. Virginia Aksan's work examines the question of Ottoman legacy and the influence of the Ottoman past on post-Ottoman states, drawing attention to the complicated relationship between local communities and the imperial state. This theme of legacy is further explored by Yeşim Bayar, who looks at the influence of the Ottoman past on the Turkish republic, emphasizing the contradictions and tensions embodied in formulations of Ottoman Turkish national identity and showing the multifaceted, contingent, and processual nature of Ottoman-Turkish nation-building.

Particularly relevant for this study, however, is the attention scholars have directed on studying the empires and nations in new ways, while so doing challenging a number of notions hitherto dominating the field, such as placing empires and nations as opposites, or seeing nation-states as "modern" while depicting empires as "backward". Instead the continued interrelationship between empires, nations, and imperial nation-building

---

[29] Eissenstat, "Modernization, Imperial Nationalism, and the Ethnicization of Confessional Identity in the Late Ottoman Empire"; Eissenstat, "Metaphors of Race and Discourse of Nation"; Eissenstat, *Limits of Imagination*; Meeker, *A Nation of Empire: The Ottoman Legacy of Turkish Modernity*; Bayar, *Formation of the Turkish nation-state, 1920–1938;* Aksan, "Ottoman to Turk: Continuity and Change"; Ülker "Contextualising 'Turkification' nation-building in the late Ottoman Empire 1908–18."

[30] Eissenstat, "Modernization, Imperial Nationalism, and the Ethnicization of Confessional Identity in the Late Ottoman Empire", 448–449.

is highlighted.[31] In their recent edited work, S. Berger and A. I. Miller present the following argument:

> First, nations did not build empires - instead, nations emerged within empires and in the context of inter-imperial competition; secondly, nation-building cannot be understood without its imperial context - this is true for secessionist nation-building projects in imperial peripheries, but also for the nation-building processes in imperial cores; and thirdly, nation building and empire were very much entangled processes -nation-building in the core of empires was in fact one of the key instruments of empires to enhance and improve their competitiveness.[32]

While situating itself within this approach that focuses on imperial nationalism and nationalizing empires, this study further seeks to trace these developments into the nation-state framework, thus seeking to bring in new material and provide a better understanding of the relationship between the Ottoman Empire and the Turkish Republic. For instance, by shedding light on how transitions happened and how composite identities, carried over from empires, were redefined and adjusted according to new realities. While traditional scholarship was most interested in finding traces of ethnic nationalism or nation-state aspirations when studying nationalism in the Ottoman Turkish context, this study seeks to understand the multiple layers of meaning that could and did evolve in different directions. And from time to time different elements of these meanings came to prominence. Thus, when looked closer, even those traces often seen as prototypes of "Turkish nationalism" reveal in them highly multi-layered elements. Such an example is Yusuf Akçura's famous work, The Three Kinds of Policies, which is analysed here from a new perspective. By providing a different approach and interpretation, this study seeks to show that the positions were far from clear indeed. Akçura's composite identity, combining within himself the imperial state allegiance, religious affiliation, and ethnic identity all pointed in that direction. And he was not alone in such identity configuration, as will be shown. Hence, this study challenges the traditional depictions that claims the prevalence of secular ethnic nationalism in the Kemalist Republic. Instead, it argues that all three variations of Ottoman nationalism—Ottomanist, Islamist, and

---

[31] Kayalı, *Imperial Resilience*, 1–7.
[32] Berger & Miller, *Nationalizing Empires*, 30.

Turkist—developed during the late Ottoman period, coexisted in various forms and combinations, and continue to do so.

Thus, particularly important for the scope of this study is the concept of continuity, which encompasses the transmission of experiences, ideas, concepts, attitudes, and understandings within the ruling elite. These are reflected in parliamentary debates, the press, and memoirs. While it is acknowledged that there may be objections to focusing on the governing elites, it is important to note that nation-building in the Ottoman Empire and Turkey were primarily driven by the state and its elites.[33] This means that the book primarily examines the rhetoric and actions of political elites, analysing the agreements, disagreements, contradictions, and ambiguities in the formulations of the nation and national identity.

Another potential objection, tied to both the continuity perspective and the actors involved in the nation-building process examined in this study, concerns the limited attention given to the Arab provinces of the Empire. Admittedly, similar processes were unfolding within the Arab provinces, playing a crucial role in Ottoman nation-building efforts and significantly contributing to the development of the concept of Ottoman unity, particularly within the framework of Ottoman Muslim nationalism practised by both the Hamidian regime and the Young Turks. However, due to the study's analytical focus, Ottoman nationalism in transition from empire to republic, it primarily emphasizes the elements of continuity into the Kemalist republic during the crucial transitional period of 1908–1931. Therefore, in the post-WWI period, the study directs its attention to the developments in and around the resistance movement in Anatolia and Rumelia following the Ottoman defeat. While the movement, comprising a significant portion of the Ottoman military-bureaucratic leadership and local elites within its operational territory, continued to identify itself as "Ottoman" and referred to its state as the "Ottoman state" and "Sultanate-Caliphate", it opted to delimit itself to "Anatolia and Rumelia" (*Anadolu ve Rumeli*), excluding in the process the Arab provinces of the Ottoman Empire.

---

[33] Charles Tilly's concept of "state-led nationalism" and Rogers Brubaker's "nationalizing states" characterizes this type of state-led nation building attempts. See in this regard, Tilly, *Durable Inequality*, 175; Brubaker, *Nationalism Reframed*, 79–84.

The Source Material

I have relied on a wide variety of primary sources for this book: parliamentary minutes, archival data (the Prime Minister's Archive of the Republic [BCA] in Ankara, and the National Archives in London), newspapers, memoirs, and travellers' accounts. Using material from such a variety of sources enables exploration of the complex nature of the Ottoman-Turkish nation-building process and national identity construction from the perspectives of various participants and factions. Although the main actors of this study are politicians, it does not present a strictly political history of the time; rather, it offers an analysis reached through close reading of a range of relevant texts.

The proceedings of the Ottoman Assembly of Deputies (*Meclis-i Mebusan*) and the Grand National Assembly in Ankara constitute the principal primary source for this study. The parliamentary minutes—hitherto only subjected to systematic scholarly study by Ahmet Demirel's groundbreaking work (1994) on the opposition in the first Grand National Assembly in Ankara, thus limited to the period, 1920–23—offer an important platform in time and space. The successive assemblies with their altered composition, changing attitudes, and discursive formations, in close interaction with the rapidly transforming realities outside the parliamentary floor, renders parliament an important prism through which these discursive shifts can be analysed. Especially important in this regard are the ways in which processes of inclusion and exclusion took shape: how did the demarcations happen, whose voices were heard, and which concepts predominated? Where did these converge and where did they differ? How successful was parliament in negotiating a unity of purpose and belonging?

In order to explore the significant aspects and positions presented, certain speeches are juxtaposed with representations of these debates in the press, allowing us to follow public opinion on parliamentary debates and parliament's interactions with the public. Meanwhile, the rich collections of non-Ottoman primary material on the subject in the British Public Record Office are used to analyse parliamentary debates in the context of outer circumstances and realities outside parliament. These sources are supplemented, according to relevance, with a selected body of memoirs and travel narratives of contemporary foreign observers, and Ottoman autobiographical and literary works. As these contain accounts of a more personal character, they provide insight into how the issues of identity and belonging were experienced on a more personal level.

The Structure of the Book

Highlighting the processual aspects of Ottoman nationalism, this study follows a chronological structure, allowing for a deeper analysis of its development over time and the transformations of its associated themes and concepts within diverse contexts and events. The first chapter delves into the historical background that gave rise to Ottomanism as a nation-building endeavour designed to unify the diverse population elements of the empire under a shared Ottoman identity that transcended ethnic and religious differences. It examines how the ruling elites of the empire adapted their concepts and policies to align with evolving markers of political identity, whereby "Ottoman unity" was devised as a response to and in competition with existing nationalist ideological trends and movements within and outside the empire. This in turn led to a highly complex balancing act between broadening and narrowing the boundaries of the "Ottoman nation". These significant developments are traced back to two crucial periods: the Tanzimat (1839–1876) and the Hamidian era (1876–1908) respectively. Throughout this period, the Ottoman Empire underwent processes of modernization that resulted in changes to the imperial model of governance, the emergence of new elites and power dynamics, as well as conflicts and divisions. These transformations laid the foundation for a highly vibrant arena in which negotiations concerning identity and differences could take place.

Chapter 3 focuses on the theoretical aspects of nationalism in the Ottoman context in the prelude to the Young Turk Revolution, especially discussing the role of significance of ideology and theory, vis-à-vis practice and the pragmatism of the policymakers, in the development of Ottoman nationalism. To provide historical context, the chapter analyses a debate centred on Yusuf Akcura's influential work, "Three Kinds of Policy". Akcura, among several intellectuals who emigrated from Turkic regions of the Russian Empire, is widely recognized for his early contributions to Turkish nationalism. His formulation of identity policies presented to Ottoman policymakers will be discussed in relation to the responses from other Ottoman intellectuals. His perspective on national identity policy options, such as Ottomanism, Islamism, and Turkism contained a discussion of the identity policy options available to actors. In subsequent years, these options would be utilized based on the prevailing circumstances, but primarily due to their alignment with the instrumental or pursued political agenda rather than serving as an ideological foundation.

Chapter 4 deals with the Young Turk Revolution and its early phase, as Ottoman national identity, after initially becoming a focal point of reverence and celebration, soon was overshadowed by challenging events and issues brought about by the revolution. These included the (re)introduction of the constitution, elections, and parliament, but also the emergence of the army and the Young Turk officers as crucial factors in Ottoman politics. The chapter provides an analysis of the paradigmatic and systemic shift within the political system, examining how this transformation led to the emergence of new symbols and concepts related to Ottomanism, as well as the adaptation of pre-existing ones. Furthermore, it explores central themes such as experiences of pluralism and party politics while delving into the conceptualization and negotiation of issues related to national identity and unity. In this context, particular emphasis is placed on the rivalry between the governing party, the Committee of Union and Progress (CUP), and the liberal opposition, shedding light on their respective stances concerning Ottoman union.

Chapter 5 concerns the attempts by deputies to find solutions to central issues related to Ottoman unity and the loyalty of local populations, such as problems relating to language, education, schooling, taxation, maladministration, and popular discontent. Rather than opting directly for decentralization, these largely liberal deputies devised indirect strategies, which, if successful, would eventually result in greater autonomy for local governments. Importantly, these were solutions within the Ottoman imperial framework, thus marking parliament's promise as a negotiation platform, but also revealing its shortcomings. The potential for negotiation and compromise was brought to a sudden halt, however, by highly dramatic events that included the Balkan Wars, the CUP coup in 1913, and WWI. These events triggered strong reactions and heated public debates, channelled by the Unionist regime into mobilization of support for its intensified nationalistic vocabulary and antagonistic demarcations of Ottomanness—a development which culminated in the disasters of WWI, with ethnic cleansing, mass expulsion, and mass emigration changing the demographic face of Anatolia unrecognizably. This process was finalized during and after the Turkish War of Independence, leaving Anatolia almost entirely Muslim.

Chapter 6 deals with the Armistice period (1918–22) between the immediate aftermath of WWI and the end of the War of Independence, followed by the abolition of the Ottoman sultanate. With the congresses of Erzurum and Sivas, the last Ottoman parliament and the first Grand

National Assembly as focal points for analysis, the chapter identifies a discursive shift towards a new form of Ottoman nationalism containing a highly ethnicized understanding of Muslimness, while Ottomanness and Turkishness provided grounds for new interpretations and negotiation. The debates both in the last Ottoman parliament and the first GNA demonstrate that the understandings and definitions of the nation were characterized by a high degree of ambivalence. The last Ottoman parliament in particular witnessed some interesting discussions whose prevailing idea was that the Ottomans had to define and present themselves in Wilsonian national terms in order to obtain the right to existence in the eyes of the wider world, meaning the Great Powers of Europe.

The final chapter focuses on the early Kemalist republic and the ruling military-bureaucratic elite's efforts to yet again adapt to new political circumstances. As this was a period of transition, many issues and concepts related to national identity intersected, were reinterpreted, reconfigured, adopted, or discarded. More importantly, it is argued that the perceptions and expressions of national identity in the early Republic were not fundamentally detached from Ottoman nationalism. In other words, they were intricately connected to the many layers of Ottoman identity developed during the late Ottoman period within its imperial national configuration and context. In fact, state policies and rhetoric regarding national identity construction exhibited strong elements of continuity in content and methods, characterized by a high level of pragmatism and fluidity. Hence, although the "nation" finally changed its designation from "Ottoman" to "Turk", this was far from a clear-cut break hindering the two sides of a perceived barrier to communicate.

On the contrary, the very intensity of Kemalist deliberate efforts to emphasize a break between "Ottomanness" and "Turkishness" suggests other mechanisms at play. It is my argument therefore that the attempts to exterminate the names and signs of everything Ottoman, and to rewrite history and reshape collective memory, actually reflected the opposite of the general assumption in Turkish historiography that sees in these actions the final erasure of Ottomanness which had already lost its meaning. This preoccupation with erasure and forgetting itself constitutes a strong indication of the strength and resilience of Ottoman identity in collective memory and imagining, which, arguably, is why the Kemalists saw in it such a grave threat to the future of their regime. Furthermore, the very antagonistic paradigm of the Kemalist regime, depicting the Ottoman

Empire as the antithesis of the republic, was a principal factor in the adoption by alienated or dissatisfied groups of the idea and their gathering around idealized images of Ottomanness as a contrast to the republic.

This draws attention to questions of Ottoman legacy on national identity discourses and the unresolved problems in contemporary Turkey. While the society is still highly divided on issues related to the "nation", its characteristics, and group composition, the themes, practices, narratives, and rhetoric employed exhibit remarkable similarities with those witnessed during the late Ottoman and early republican periods. Especially significant in this context are the prevalent references found in public and official discourses that emphasize, with historical underpinnings, the critical importance of national "survival" (*beka*), preserving the state, preventing territorial loss, obtaining security against perceived external and internal enemies, and fostering national unity and solidarity. Another aspect of legacy, which had a profound effect on the early republic, and in fact continues to shape the political landscape of modern Turkey, concerns the political culture inherited from the Ottoman empire through its institutions and governing elites. The parallels between the Unionist and the Kemalist regimes, such as the persistent contradictions between ideals and practice within a political system functioning inside the framework of the constitution, parliament, and elections, but in fact practising authoritarian one-party rule—are discussed in reference to Unionist and Kemalist elitism, and the ways of defining and representing the "nation" as a political subject.

CHAPTER 2

Framing the Ottoman Nation

> In Europe scientific approach is replaced by patriotic zeal … but among us, by "homeland" our soldiers merely understand the areas within their native villages.[1]

> Each inhabitant of the protected imperial realms is considered a subject of The Sublime State and will be treated as a subject of The Sublime State. If a person is a subject of a foreign power, he is duly required to prove so.[2]

In the hope of a better understanding of the complexities of national identity formation in the late Ottoman Empire, we must first turn our attention to the lengthy and extensive processes of modernization sweeping through its state and society during the nineteenth century, which, due mostly to the hardships and turmoil encountered, has gained a reputation as the empire's longest and most difficult.[3] A deeper understanding of these processes of change and adaptation are not only vital for Ottoman history itself, but also essential for comprehending later developments in the post-Ottoman states. As such, the Ottoman experiences

---

[1] Ahmet Cevdet Paşa, *Ma'ruzat*, 114.
[2] The Ottoman law on nationality (*Tabiyeti osmaniyye kanunu*). *Düstur*, 1. Tertip, vol. I, 1289 [1873], 18.
[3] Ortaylı, *İmparatorluğun En Uzun Yüzyılı*.

may serve as a valuable case study for analysing the impact of modernity on a multiethnic empire, particularly in regards to unresolved issues related to political culture, national identity, minority rights, and societal unity.[4]

The Tanzimat (reforms/reorganization—1839–1876) and the Hamidian Era (1876–1908) constitute the immediate historical background to this study. During this period, the Ottomans witnessed crucial transformations within the political institutions, the economy, education, trade, industry, communications, ideas, science, and technology. Similar processes were taking place in other parts of Europe at the time, of course, with familiar patterns: sweeping socioeconomic changes, the dissolution of long-standing community bonds, efforts to establish new ones, the restructuring of political systems, reform movements, and revolutions. Nevertheless, due to its vast territorial expanse and remarkable diversity, the Ottoman Empire's internal dynamics, external relations, and geopolitical position endowed its experience of modernization and nation-building with distinctive features.

Given the empire's size and demographic diversity, particularly concerning ethnicity and religion, traditional Ottoman rule adhered to a recognizable imperial model, based on a decentralized system that connected different parts of the empire to the centre through local power brokers.[5] Representing the different religious and ethnic communities of the empire, the relationship thus forged between the centre and the provinces created an imperial system characterized by a "balance of coherence and diversity".[6] These communities were later organized around what came to be known as the *millet* system.[7] Although in current Turkish *millet* basically means "nation"—as in *Türk milleti* or the

---

[4] The fall and aftermath of empires has garnered significant attention in recent years, particularly with regards to the factors leading to the collapse of the Ottoman Empire and its outcomes. See in this regard: Brown, *Imperial legacy*; Motyl, *Imperial Ends*; Barkey, *After Empire*; Boyar, *Ottoman Turks and the Balkans*; Meeker, *A Nation of Empire*; Reynolds, *Shattering Empires*; Roshwald, *Ethnic Nationalism and the Fall of Empires*.

[5] Göçek, B*ourgeoisie*; Quataert, *The Ottoman Empire;* Keyder, *State and Class.*

[6] Barkey further notes: "Located at the center of where the West meets the East, the Ottomans gained their identity and forged a balance of coherence and diversity that remains a landmark in the modern world's search for precisely that balance", Barkey, *Empire of Difference*, 8.

[7] Aboona, *Assyrians, Kurds, and Ottomans*, 135–142.

"Turkish nation"—in the Ottoman context *millet* referred to a community of believers: one's nation was those with whom one shared the same religion.[8]

Under the *millet* system the different population elements were organized within the Ottoman imperial framework in categories like the *Rum* (i.e. "Roman") *millet* (the Ottoman designation for the empire's Greek Orthodox population), the Armenian *millet*, the Jewish *millet*,[9] and the Muslims, although not formally organized as such, in practice acted and was conceptualized as a *millet* (*millet-i Islam*).[10] Thus, in the eighteenth century-Ottoman world, being "Greek" or "Bulgarian" inside the *millet-i Rum* was a subcategory without major importance compared with the transnational identity signifier: being an orthodox and belonging to the orthodox *millet*'s organizational framework.[11] This system did not meet many difficulties until the impact of the French Revolution and its reverberations in the following decades, when the Ottoman government began facing serious challenges to its political, social, and economic fabric.[12]

The French Revolution and the effects of the Napoleonic wars thus sparked the rise of nationalism across Europe[13] and eventually found its way through different channels into the Ottoman Empire's European provinces in the early nineteenth century.[14] In terms of Gellner's four zones of nationalism in Europe, the Ottoman Balkans (*Rumeli* in Ottoman Turkish) were part of the third zone: the area, according to Gellner, where the new nationalist principles and the subsequent processes of state and nation-building resulted in the most fierce and violent conflicts of the four. This was not because the various communities were inherently violent or unable to coexist, but rather because they had long been intertwined and interdependent, making the eventual unravelling and separations all the more painful and violent.[15]

---

[8] Ahmad, *Young Turks*, 2–5.

[9] Braude & Lewis, *Christians and Jews in the Ottoman Empire*, 142–166.

[10] Karpat, *The Politicization of Islam*, 310–311 & 324–325.

[11] Davison, *Reform*, 12–19; Karpat, *Ottoman Population*, 46–55; Diamandouros, *Conceptions*, 164–169.

[12] Barkey, *After Empire*, 30–36; Davison, *Reform*, 23–36, 114-135.

[13] Hobsbawm, *The Age of Revolution*, 53–60, 115–121.

[14] Anderson, *Eastern Question*, 28–52.

[15] Gellner, *Encounters with Nationalism*, 29–30.

The Greek War of Independence (1821–32) marked a significant turning point in this regard, as it was the first example of an area of the Ottoman Empire separating itself from the main body, driven by a nationalist inspiration.[16] The fact that this movement for independence was produced by a nationalist revolutionary movement, *Philiki Etairia*, with links to other parts of the empire, demonstrated the scale of the problem and accelerated the Ottoman state elite's sense of alarm and realization of the need for change. To make matters worse for the Ottomans, Greek independence served as a source of inspiration for other nationalist movements within the empire, exacerbating the situation. In addition, Ottoman frustrations steadily grew due to repeated military defeats by the Habsburgs, resulting in the loss of territory and population, though the greatest threat was perceived to be the Russian Empire throughout the nineteenth century. Thus, the Ottomans entered the nineteenth century weakened internationally and domestically, unable to defend itself single-handedly against other European powers, and less able to rule effectively and mobilize people and money.[17] Constantly troubled by the influence of Great Powers and their various interests, known as the Eastern Question, the Ottoman state began its desperate search for solutions and adaptations.[18]

As part of the efforts to raise resources and armies more effectively, the Ottoman state initiated a process of centralization and reorganization, gradually eroding the traditional Ottoman models of rule, which in turn created serious problems for carrying out the project of reintegrating its populations.[19] What was lost was the centuries-old imperial power structure, with its complex system of negotiation and networks of local elites who usually enjoyed vast administrative autonomy vis-á-vis the central government, while remaining firmly linked to the centre by rights and obligations.[20] By dealing directly with the power-holders at the periphery, and at the same time accommodating local and regional differences by granting widespread autonomy to the provinces, the Ottoman

---

[16] Anderson, *Eastern Question*, 50–52.

[17] Zürcher, *Legacy*, 60–64.

[18] Anderson, *Eastern Question*.

[19] Quataert, *The Ottoman Empire*, 61–71; Barkey, *Empire of Difference*, 270–296; Zürcher, *Legacy*, 67–72.

[20] Barkey, *Empire of Difference*, 6–11.

state had created ties of mutual interest between the notables and the central government, making the centre indispensable as the only source of legitimacy and thereby securing the loyalty of its subject peoples.

With the centralization drive, which went hand-in-hand with modernization in communication, technology, and transport, the reach of the Ottoman state began to extend into areas that had previously been too remote and less accessible.[21] This however, caused local resistance in regions that had been virtually autonomous, like the nomad populations of Eastern Anatolia, and grew proportionately with the state's moves towards greater control and effective mobilization of resources, money, and people, often justified by references to a "civilizing" mission from the centre to the "backward" parts of the empire. In this regard, the Ottoman state policies were closely aligned with the developments happening in the rest of Europe at the time. Similar to processes of nation-building in Europe, the Ottoman state also implemented a wide range of policies aimed at reintegration of its populations, such as reforms related to identity, nationality, and citizenship, as well as adaptation of new symbols and "invented traditions".[22] This also entailed far-reaching implications for the perceptions and definitions regarding state-subject relations and framing a national belonging.

Previously, exhibiting the characteristics of empire, whereby the high culture of the centre demarcates the rulers from the ruled, the Ottoman imperial state had divided society into two categories: the tax-exempt *Osmanlı* (Ottoman) ruler caste, and the "rest" of the population, the taxpaying *reaya* (flock). The *Osmanlı* class were not overall concerned with the *reaya*, nor did its members feel the need to include them in the literate high culture of the elite or the channels of power that came with it. However, along with the growing dangers of separatist nationalism and a concomitant need for effective rule and better mobilization of resources came the development of a modern military and bureaucracy and increasing social and educational mobility resulting from the Tanzimat reforms. Consequently, the Ottoman state underwent what might be called a popular turn, on paper at least, resulting in the broadening of the definition of Ottomanness to go beyond the traditional meaning of *Osmanlı*. It was in this context; while the empire shaken

---

[21] Aboona, *Assyrians, Kurds, and Ottomans*, 155–161.

[22] Deringil, *Domains*, 32–34, 151–152.

by internal instability and a rebellion in Greece with both religious and national characteristics, Sultan Mahmud II (r. 1808–1839) introduced some of his famous reforms to symbolize the principle of "unity of elements" (*ittihad-ı anasır*), coined "Ottomanism" by later historiography.[23] "Unity" (*ittihad*) was to become one of the most enduring concepts of late Ottoman political vocabulary, and indeed survived as a fundamental theme of state policy in the Turkish republic as well.

To illustrate his reform mindedness and policies for change, however, the sultan turned to something very usual, clothing, which previous sultans in Ottoman history also had utilized to reemphasize legitimacy and authority especially in times of turmoil.[24] In this case, though, rather than highlighting piety and traditions, the sultan's new sartorial reforms were seen by large segments of Ottoman society, Muslim power groups in particular, as highly disruptive of established norms and structures.[25] A Muslim critic is quoted as having said regarding Mahmud II and his reforms, "infidel sultan, God will demand an accounting for your blasphemy. You are destroying Islam."[26] The most significant of these new sartorial symbols was the fez. Despite being an important part of Ottomans' clothing, headgear also played a significant role in Ottoman society, as a tool in displaying and regulating official, religious, and inter-community relations. Through the headgear social status and community affiliation were shown.[27] In short, it symbolized differences and structures of power, and thus a way of maintaining Muslim dominance in relation to non-Muslims.[28] A standardized headgear such as the fez was aimed to level some of the existing markers of difference and illustrate the newly framed inclusive Ottomanness, based on equality regardless of religion.[29]

Despite the initial opposition, however, the success of the fez as a major symbol of Ottomanness is best illustrated by its later fate, almost a century

---

[23] Mardin, *Religion, Society, and Modernity*, 128–129.

[24] Quataert, "Clothing Laws", 413.

[25] Davison, *Reform*, 31.

[26] Ibid.

[27] The type of headgear showing one's communal belonging and position in life also followed the person to the grave as tombstones would be engraved with the headgear of the deceased.

[28] It was not surprising therefore, that the same reforms were generally well received by the non-Muslim population. Quataert, "Clothing Laws", 414.

[29] Quataert, "Clothing Laws", 412–419; Berkes, *Development of Secularism*, 124–125.

after its introduction, when its use was abolished by Atatürk (1881–1938) in 1925 on the grounds that it was "unnational". In its stead was introduced the Western-style hat, with the goal of establishing the national and modern character of the new regime. While the hat and the fez came to symbolize a clash between the republic's "Turkishness" and its alleged antithesis, "Ottomanness", ironically Atatürk's sartorial reforms drew similar critiques as Mahmud II.

TANZIMAT REFORMERS AND NATION-BUILDING

The general line of national identity construction laid by Sultan Mahmud II was continued by his successors, Abdulmecid (r. 1839–61) and Abdulaziz (r. 1861–76), during the Tanzimat era, characterized by extensive reforms aimed at modernizing the empire. The most striking field of modernization during the Tanzimat (lit. "reorganization"), however, occurred within the core institutions of the state, the military, and the bureaucracy in particular, including the cadres staffing these institutions. Rather than relying on the army of provincial notables and the unruly Janissaries (eventually destroyed in 1826) for the defence of its territories, the Ottoman state began efforts to build a national army, which however would take many decades to complete. In the meantime, the Ottoman state, unable to defend itself successfully against its great power rivals by military means, reoriented its emphasis on diplomacy trusted to the care of the Ottoman central bureaucracy. One of the significant results of these efforts was the alliance forged between the Ottoman Empire, Britain, and France against Russia in the Crimean War (1853–56). Besides boosting the Ottoman self-image as an ally of great powers of Europe, the conditions and experiences during the Crimean War also reinforced the modernization drive in the empire, by providing a greater transfer of knowledge and technology.

Consequently, the central bureaucracy became the dominant state institution during the Tanzimat, leading to a shift of power from the palace to the office of the Grand Vizier, the Sublime Porte (*Bab-ı Ali*). State policies, including issues pertaining to Ottoman nation-building were thus decided by the bureaucratic cadres led by statesmen like Pashas Mustafa Reşit (1799–1857), Ali (1815–1871), Fuat (1815–1869), and Midhat (1822–1876). The Bureaucracy had already expanded considerably as a result of Mahmud's modernization policies, which continued during the Tanzimat, reinforced by improved education and the higher degree of rationalization and standardization in the conduct of governmental affairs.³⁰

The increasing importance and influence of the bureaucracy were also reflected in the Gülhane Reform Decree of 1839, in which the sultan's subjects, and thereby his bureaucrats, were guaranteed "security for life, honour, and possessions" (*emniyet-i can ve mahfuziyyet-i ırz-u-namus ve mal*). With their positions thus strengthened and secure vis-à-vis the sultan, coupled with the changing dynamics and restructuring within the state apparatus, involving a higher degree of formalization, specialization, and hierarchy, providing them with organizational cohesion and esprit de corps, the state elites' bureaucratic attitudes and self-perceptions gradually underwent a fundamental change.³¹ Instead of the traditional image as the slaves (*kul*) of the sultan, they now increasingly saw themselves as guardians of the state with a mission to save it.³² Indeed, saving the Ottoman state became the overriding theme of state elite thought in the late Ottoman period, and with it the prime motivation for achieving Ottoman national unity.³³

In this context, the nation-building endeavours of Ottoman political leaders have often been described as hopeless and futile attempts stemming from ignorance and "confusion" (*bocalama*).³⁴ Furthermore, claims have been made that these initiatives represented something artificial as "Ottomanness", which had no chance against nationalism—the most powerful ideological current of the age. Thus, Ottomanism is portrayed as a policy conceived as a reaction to nationalism, to hinder something rather than a proactive construction. In addition, because framed as a contrast to nationalism, with its irresistible force, the idea of Ottoman unity is automatically rendered stillborn.³⁵

Nevertheless, the Ottoman state's numerous undertakings since the early nineteenth century, explicitly stressing the need for moulding all the sultan's subjects into one Ottoman nation, are clear indications that

---

[30] Findley, *Bureaucratic Reform*, 140–147.

[31] Eissenstat, "Modernization, Imperial Nationalism, and the Ethnicization," 435.

[32] Zürcher, *Legacy*, 114.

[33] Sabahaddin, *Türkiye Nasıl Kurtarılabilir*; Davison, *Essays*, 116; Tunaya, *Hürriyetin İlanı*, 82–86.

[34] Berkes, *Development of Secularism*, 221–222.

[35] Kushner, *Turkish Nationalism*, 3–4.

Ottoman statesmen themselves were in fact trying to harbour positive potentials of nationalism, as well as targeting the dangers of alternative nationalist discourses.[36] Arguably, this was the reason they wanted to channelize it in the Ottomanist direction, in the belief that the best chance of success in the given circumstances would be to adapt existing categories of official identity to serve modern needs, thereby constructing an alternative nationalism.[37] The revised Ottoman national identity of the Tanzimat, made official policy by the Gülhane Decree (1839) and the Reform Edict (*Islahat Fermanı*) (1956),[38] aimed to be a secular, transnational, inclusive identity based on citizenship and equality for all regardless of religion or ethnicity.[39] Consequently, the Ottoman state elite sought to downplay the importance of ethnic national identity, viewing it as secondary to the overarching principle of Ottomanness. As such, in spirit, it was influenced by the patriotic nationalism of the French Revolution, rather than the romantic nationalism that emerged in early nineteenth century post-Napoleonic Germany.[40]

In the Reform Edict of 1856, promulgated in the aftermath of the Crimean War, the first formal acceptance and announcement of equality between Muslims and non-Muslims was formulated. The reforms entailed the participation of non-Muslims in provincial administration through mixed councils, the lifting of restrictions on conversions to other religions, the protection of freedom of religion and conscience, the abandonment of the poll tax, the inclusion of non-Muslims in the military, the opening of military and administrative schools to all, and the establishment of mixed courts.[41] Within the legal system a gradual process of secularization materialized, resulting in the introduction of new codes based on European ones, and at the same time creating a legal system, where Muslim religious law, the sharia, continued a parallel existence while losing ground vis-a-vis the secular laws and courts.

---

[36] Mardin, *Genesis*, 327–332, 389–395.

[37] Davison, *Essays*, 116–128.

[38] Inalcık, *Tanzimat*, 1–10.

[39] Poulton, *Top Hat*, 2–14.

[40] See in this regard Özkırımlı, *Theories of Nationalism*, 11–18.

[41] Findley, *Bureaucratic Reform*, 20–24, 178–182; Shaw, *Studies*, 213; Davison, *Reform*, 93–100.

This mode of thinking contained in itself both elements of old and new. On the one hand, it was quite new, as it aimed at building up an all-inclusive Ottoman national identity, regardless of religious affiliation. As homogenization on a national scale, this was a clear departure from old ways of maintaining, accommodating, and even cultivating difference, and ruling within a structure of organizational multi-religiosity. On the other hand, as pointed out by Deringil, it exhibited typical examples of imperial tendencies and had clear elements of old Ottoman experiences of transnational identity formations.[42] Before the nineteenth century, being a Greek Orthodox, Bulgarian, Arab, Serb, and Albanian had generally been regarded as irrelevant, these at the most being subcategories, while the main dividing line was whether one belonged to the religious superstructure or not.[43] When Tanzimat reformers signalled the coming into existence of the policy of Ottoman unity, on one level it merely represented another transnational identity, although much wider in scope.

As the Ottoman centre had in the past managed to incorporate elites belonging to different religions into Ottoman high culture, it became a question of whether this practice could be extended to the population as well, in a highly complex attempt to combine empire and nation-state features. With the elements of imperial rule, there was a political structure held together by an imperial elite and its high culture. Thus, rather than a national culture of a particular ethnic group, as was the usual case with nation-state developments in western Europe, the national integration of the Ottoman peoples was to be created on the basis of a secular metropolitan culture, resting in its turn on western universalistic modernity. In this framework, modernization *was* nationalization and the culture of secular nationalism was western modernity, a viewpoint that would influence generations of Ottomans, who then carried it into the Kemalist Republic.[44] To this were added concurrent nods to nation-building on the basis of common language, Ottoman Turkish (which itself was a hybrid construct), a patriotic vocabulary, and symbols of national unity. The latter included the issuance of national identity

---

[42] Deringil, *Domains*, 31–34.

[43] Davison, *Reform*, 112–116.

[44] It is noteworthy that, in post-Ottoman Turkey, a similar trend would become the fundamental state policy; Atatürk's nation building project was founded on two basic pillars: western modernity and the Turkish nation.

cards, the composition of a national anthem (by Giuseppe Donizetti),[45] and a national flag featuring a white crescent and star on a red background (used as the national flag of the Turkish Republic today).

An important question to be addressed, then, is whether this idea of Ottoman unity conceptualized increasingly in terms of an Ottoman nation (*millet*) was fundamentally an artificial entity, a defensive mechanism without any real content, in Hanioglu's words. Was it just a lofty idea devised by some concerned statesmen as an antidote to ethnic nationalism, without a soul or emotional appeal, with the sole purpose of saving the Ottoman state?[46] In this dominant take on Ottomanism, the Ottoman union only made sense when seen from the perspective of the Ottoman central state and its governing agents, while non-Muslims merely saw Ottomanness as an artificial identity, devised by Ottoman rulers to hinder their national independence movements.[47] As the argument goes, Ottomanism only ever obtained a degree of acceptance among the Muslim population elements of the empire and only until ideas of nationalism spread rapidly among these groups too. Interestingly this prevalent approach tends to regard Ottomanism as a discrete and well-defined entity, delimited from other forms of identity, when in fact the transnational citizenship-based idea of Ottoman union makes it hard to define and demarcate.

Especially difficult is the task of disentangling Ottoman identity from religious (Islamic) and ethnic (Turkish), which brings us to another crucial question, which is what exactly made Ottomanism a constructed artificiality, while rendering, say Turkish nationalism, as substantial. Both of these being constructed, just as other forms of nationalism, it seems more fruitful for a discussion and analysis to charter the very components and workings of this construct. What was its range, modes of operation, and effectiveness? It is especially important to assess the advantages and disadvantages of Ottomanism in terms of multicultural or transnational

---

[45] Deringil, "The Invention of Tradition", 9.

[46] Hanioglu, *Tunalı Hilmi Bey*, 107–144; Ahmad, *Young Turks*: Dündar, *Iskan Politikası*, 30–36.

[47] According to Hanioglu, "when a person once begins identifying himself as a Bulgarian, Serbian or Greek, he will not again show interest in this kind of higher categorization of identity" (Hanioglu, "Osmanlıcılık", 1390).

contexts. For instance, as an inclusive category, Ottomanism had, theoretically, the potential to meet with wider acceptance within the multiethnic makeup of the Ottoman population.

On the more disadvantage side, Ottomanism, especially in its Tanzimat formulations, the available options, compared to more ethnically exclusive formulations of nationalism, for constructing Ottoman identity reveal an absence, for instance, of an *other*. If claiming to be all-inclusive, which the Tanzimat's Ottoman nationalism did, how then could a counter-image to Ottoman national identity be conceived? Recognizing that every form of identity is constructed, in one way or other, by defining what it is in contrast to what it is not,[48] no single population element was a suitable candidate for such an image. Only foreign powers, such as Russia, provided an option against which to define and distinguish Ottoman from non-Ottoman as the self and other. However, the Ottoman state faced a significant limitation that restricted its ability to manoeuvre in this regard, seeing that the Empire's position of weakness compared to the other great powers of Europe made it difficult for them to use an anti-great-power sentiment as a tool to create national unity and identity. Additionally, the great powers were actively interfering in Ottoman internal affairs, claiming to protect selected Ottoman *millets* and creating patronage ties with them, often supporting particular nationalist agendas against the Ottoman state, in order to further their own interests and extend their sphere of influence.[49] This resulted in the Ottoman state facing competition within its own territory from foreign states in terms of national identity construction and gaining the loyalty of its own population.[50]

Another significant protest against the Tanzimat nation-building policies came from within the bureaucratic establishment itself, resulting in the so-called Young Ottoman opposition group of intellectuals.[51] According to the Young Ottomans, the Reform Edict of 1856 was announced under the pressure of European states, as a document not of solidarity, but of privileges to the non-Muslims in order to create for them a more advantageous position vis-a-vis Muslims. While clearly

---

[48] Derrida, *Difference*, 159–161.

[49] Russia for example declared itself the patron of Ottoman Orthodox Christians, while the French were the protectors of the Catholic *millet*, and the British the Protestant respectively. Davison, *Reform*, 114–123.

[50] Makdisi, *Sectarianism*, 84–86.

[51] Mardin, *Genesis*, 44–56, 78–80.

emphasizing their Muslim identity and Islamic point of view, the Young Ottomans, at the same time highlighted Ottoman unity based on an inclusive citizenship. They demanded the end of the authoritarian rule of the central bureaucracy and the establishment of a constitutional system of government. Namık Kemal (1840–1888) for instance believed that constitutional rule would strengthen Ottoman national identity. Also, widely known as an early figurehead of Ottoman patriotic nationalism, he presented the Ottoman territories as a united "homeland" (*vatan*)—a readjusted term thus entering the political vocabulary as another expression of the Ottomanist ideal.[52] This homeland, Namık Kemal imagined, was built upon the solidarity between citizens sharing equal rights and duties, united as Ottomans under a just, representative, constitutional government.

THE CONSTITUTION AND THE OTTOMAN CITIZEN

The climax of the Tanzimat, vis-à-vis Ottomanism, was arguably the proclamation of the Ottoman Constitution in 1876 and its definition of citizenship, which reflected the institutionalization of secular Ottoman nationalism built up during the reform period. The precursor to this was the Ottoman citizenship law of 1869, which defined Ottoman citizenship to include "every individual residing in the imperial Ottoman domains".[53] The definition was so inclusive, in fact, that individuals would be regarded as Ottoman citizens/subjects until proven otherwise, meaning that if someone wished to claim foreign citizenship, they had to provide supporting documents. Expanding upon this definition, the Ottoman constitution declared that "All citizens of the Ottoman state are collectively called Ottomans, irrespective of their religion and sect".[54]

---

[52] Namık Kemal, *Vatan Yahut Silistre*.

[53] *Düstur*, 1. Tertip. (1289 [1873]). 16–18. Article 9 reads: "Every individual residing in the imperial Ottoman domains of the sultan is considered a citizen of the Ottoman state and is treated as such. If the person holds foreign citizenship, it is obligatory for them to prove their citizenship according to proper procedures." (*Memalik-i mahrusa-i padişahide ikamet eden her bir şahıs tabiiyet-i devleti aliyeden ma'dud olub hakkında Devlet-i Aliye tabii muamelesi icra olunur. Eğer kendisi tabiiyet-i ecnebiyeden ise tabiiyetini usulen isbat etmesi lazım gelir*).

[54] *Devleti Osmaniye tabiyetinde bulunan efradın cümlesine herhangi din ve mezhepten olur ise olsun bilâ istisna Osmanlı tabir olunur*. *Düstur*, 1. Tertip, vol. IV, 7 Zilhicce 1293 (23 December 1876), 4–5.

Inspired by the constitutions of other contemporary European states,[55] the Ottoman constitution, included similar provisions emphasizing the rights and duties of its citizens. For instance, it asserted the equality of all Ottomans before the law, ensuring personal liberties (Article 10), property rights (Article 21 & 24), freedom of education, work, and residency (Articles 15, 19, and 22), and freedom of religion (Article 11).[56]

Nevertheless, the Ottoman example poses interesting differences compared to other parts of Europe, especially regarding its particular circumstances that, in turn, influenced its categories for citizenship and common political identity. The relative weakness of the empire against its rival states, the power of push and pull effects, and its unstable territorial integrity all contributed to this. Although the constitutional movement, as in other places in Europe, also aimed at constraining the powers of the monarch, in the Ottoman context the constitution was closely linked to identity politics and nation-building in general, and the idea of Ottoman unity in particular.[57] Thus the question of representation, which became a major factor behind the constitutional movements in many parts of Europe, was overshadowed by the primary goal of Ottoman statesmen and intellectuals to counteract separatist nationalism by uniting the Ottomans around a constitution based on the principle of equality and solidarity.[58] Thus, rather than being a result of middle-class driven struggles for power and political influence, legitimized through principles of political representation and institutionalized through a constitution, elections, and parliament, the Ottoman case puts before us the idea of a constitution and parliament as instruments and symbols of national unity and equality among the Ottoman peoples. As such, the ideas of constitution and parliament were inextricably linked to secular Ottoman nationalism, assigning to the parliament a unifying mission.

---

[55] While Tanör cites Belgium, Poland, Prussia, and France as sources of inspiration for the Ottoman constitution (Tanör, *Anayasal Gelismeleri*, 133), Berkes mentions the Belgian, French, and imperial German constitutions (Berkes, *Development of Secularism*, 242). However, Berkes adds that despite the translation of the 1875 constitution of the French Republic, it was later rejected as a model since it did not align well with the Ottoman monarchy (ibid, 243).

[56] *Düstur*, 1. Tertip, vol. IV, 5–6; see also Shaw & Shaw, *History*, vol. I, 174–178.

[57] Sohrabi, *Revolution*, 61.

[58] Ibid., 39–45.

Constitutional ideals, however, were also met with concern in Ottoman governing circles. It was widely discussed by Ottoman intellectuals and statesmen, especially from the second half of the 1860s, whether a broad representative government would strengthen the sense of collective identity and unity of purpose—thus serving to prevent nationalism and separatism—or, rather, increase the influence and freedom of nationalist movements, enabling them to disseminate separatist ideas under more favourable terms.[59] The parliament had the potential to interconnect and unify Ottoman peoples through their local representatives, but the broadening of political rights and freedoms that lay at the heart of constitutional and representative government could also broaden division. The presence of this dilemma was seemingly the reason why Tanzimat reformers like Fuat Pasha and Ali Pasha combatted the constitutional movement, arguing that although the constitution and parliament were desirable things, per se, the conditions of the empire were not suitable for them and its population not ready.[60]

When the Ottoman Assembly of Deputies (*Meclis-i Mebusan*) finally opened on 19 March 1877, the concerns of the Tanzimat leaders would be put to the test.[61] Parliamentary records illustrate that Ottomanness as a general marker of identity did not cause disagreement; on the contrary, the members of the Assembly of Deputies (*Meclis-i Mebusan*, the second chamber of the Ottoman parliament) repeatedly underlined its importance. As is shown by the following debate from the parliamentary floor, a process of intense negotiations occurred on the meaning and preconditions of Ottoman unity and Ottomanness, its relation to other identities, ethnic and religious in particular, and how to align these subcategories of identity with Ottomanness. The immediate context of the debate was the Ottoman provincial law and its provisions regarding the religious communal composition of local administrative councils, meaning whether representation based on Muslim–non-Muslim divide should be maintained or lifted. In the latter case, the question arose how a fair and equal representation on the local and national level could be secured for all Ottomans regardless of religion and ethnicity:

---

[59] Ahmet Cevdet Paşa, *Maruzat*.
[60] Davison, *Reform*, 88.
[61] Us, *Meclisi Mebusan*, 4–6.

Solidi Efendi: During the debates on the parliamentary election law, it was acknowledged how harmful the division of Ottomans into two parties, Muslims and non-Muslims, would be to the true and essential interests of our sacred homeland, in a time when it is in dire need of unity. The members of parliament, who initially did not see any harm in this division, have come to discover the damaging effects thereof after careful examination and investigation, as is evident by the subsequent speeches delivered.

The division of Ottomans into two parties in the provincial law was seen by the European press, which means the European public, as evidence that we have still not rid ourselves of religious fanaticism [*taassubat-ı diniyye*], and that we are unable to fully implement the constitution, that the goal of unity cannot materialize. In addition, the local press and other written sources have shown that the term "non-Muslim" [*gayr-i müslim*] has had a negative impact on great many of Ottomans. In the present era of justice, it is evident that such ill-considered and hated designations, like the "fidelis" and "infidelis" division of the Spaniards in previous times, do not suit the glory of the country and the people and our nation's sense of humanity and ancient moral virtues.

Accepting a division based on the argument that local language proficiency is necessary in provincial councils, where local matters are discussed, would mean to prioritize personal interests over public interests and harm the nation's true and essential interests. Language proficiency is not a concern, as even in regions where Turkish is not generally spoken, different groups, especially prominent people, are educated in the language. Besides, in most regions Turkish constitutes the common language. *Mufti*s and religious leaders will also be present in the councils, so there are no obstacles in regards to religious affairs. Therefore, to show both friend and foe that our sacred homeland stands united on the pillars of freedom and justice under His Majesty the Sultan, and also to prevent causes for excuses or complaints, we propose removing the Muslim-non-Muslim divide from the provincial law to allow for free elections.

Yenişehirli zade Ahmed Efendi (İzmir): Let the Ottomans be subdivided into categories, there is no harm in that. The term "Ottoman" is not a designation of a religious community. All Ottoman citizens are as one. If someone goes to a foreign country, and is asked where he is from, he says 'I am from the Ottoman soil' [*Osmanlı toprağındanım*]. The Ottoman constitution confirms and consolidates the unity of the Ottomans. The mention of 'Muslim' and 'Christian' in earlier election was because it was before the constitution, whereas now there is no need for that.

Simonaki Bey (Konya): I do not want to say Muslim or non-Muslim. We are all Ottomans; however, the people think that the term 'Ottoman' is a name exclusively for Muslims. Otherwise, I also do not accept the separation of Muslim and non-Muslim.

The president [of the Assembly of Deputies]: I see there is a consensus between all the members of the Assembly on this issue. If it is a concern that the term 'Ottoman' cannot be understood in some places, then a clear instruction should be written so that the situation can be explained to everyone.[62]

This debate presents a remarkable example of the ways to reframe the "Ottoman" as a national identity under the process of negotiation and reconstruction.[63] While so doing, it illustrates the multidimensional aspects of Ottomanism, including the perceptions of old and new forms of identity, the importance attributed to European norms as a point of reference, and not least the framing of religious and ethnolinguistic group belonging in relation to Ottomanness as a multiethnic national identity. The emphasis on Ottoman Turkish as a common ground, and the reference to the perception of the local population and the need for spreading the precise meaning of Ottomanness to "everyone", as a state-sponsored instruction, is telling in that regard. Unfortunately, the first Ottoman parliament, which during its brief existence delivered a vibrant and enthusiastic performance, could not see the fruition of its work, as war and the ensuing political turmoil brought about an untimely end to the parliamentary experimentations with national identity construction and negotiations of difference.

ABDULHAMID II AND OTTOMAN MUSLIM NATIONALISM

Both constitution and parliament were born amidst war with Russia in 1877–78, with disastrous results for the Ottoman Empire, and traumatic effects on Ottoman collective memory.[64] Besides the vast territorial losses in Ottoman Europe, or *Rumeli* (Rumelia), the war resulted in the

---

[62] Us, *Meclis-i Mebusan* (15 May 1877), 255.

[63] On the debates concerning how to create an inclusive Ottoman identity while retaining the local, religious, and geographical identities, see also Us, *Meclis-i Mebusan*, 84–86.

[64] McCarthy, *Death and Exile*, 109–116.

mass migration of the Muslim population subjected to heavy massacres into remaining parts of the empire, especially hitting hard the capital with destitute refugees, and altering the demographic composition of Anatolia.[65] The ensuing turmoil had a lasting effect on political life as well. Using the war as a pretext, Abdulhamid II took a decisive step by suspending the constitution and dissolving parliament. While marking the beginning of Abdulhamid II's autocratic rule, the suspension of the constitution had a highly damaging effect on the image of his regime both in his own time and later. In traditional historiography, the Hamidian era was depicted as a period of Islamic conservatism and reaction against the modernization of the Tanzimat.[66]

However, three decades of in-depth studies in the field have prompted a significant revision of this narrative, suggesting that the period was a continuation of the modernization processes initiated by the Tanzimat.[67] This is evident in the substantial economic development taking place, particularly within the coastal urban centres throughout the empire, where advances in trade, transportation, technology, mechanization, communication, and education converged to shape a thriving Ottoman middle class and its associated cosmopolitan public space.[68] In this cosmopolitan setting, diverse ideas and conditions related to a new Ottoman citizen could be imagined and discussed. These encounters left an enduring mark on a rich and diverse literary landscape, including novels, short stories, and plays, as well as a vibrant press, which served as a widely utilized public platform connecting various socioeconomic groups and population elements, both Muslim and non-Muslim alike.[69]

Despite the strict censorship imposed during the Hamidian era, the abundance of newspapers and journals in circulation suggests that Ottoman society had no difficulty engaging in public discourse. While political discussions and opposition were strictly forbidden, many issues could still be addressed through implicit and creative means, such as

---

[65] Karpat, *Ottoman Population*, 75.

[66] Berkes, *Secularism*; Tunaya, *Islamcılık Cereyanı*.

[67] See esp. Deringil, *Domains*; Fortna, *Imperial Classroom*; Hanioglu, *Preparation*; Göcek, *Bourgeoisie*; Keyder, *State and Class*; Quataert, *Ottoman Empire*; Sohrabi, *Revolution*.

[68] Quataert, *Ottoman Empire*, 180–185.

[69] Emrence, *Remapping the Ottoman*, 43–45.

storytelling of past societies that were destroyed by corruption, injustice, and tyranny. The use of a long list of words like "freedom", "equality", "republic", "reform", "despotism", "constitution", "parliament", and "revolution" was banned, but to read and write about conditions leading to these political processes in countries outside the Ottoman Empire was not.[70] Additionally, many books and articles, obviously not considered a political threat by the sultan, on subjects such as science, culture, philosophy, language, and gender roles were widely discussed among the Ottoman public.

As demonstrated by Deringil, the Hamidian regime reflected the practices of contemporary European states, utilized similar tools of governance available, and encountered comparable challenges.[71] Like other monarchies of the time, Abdulhamid's regime also struggled with maintaining legitimacy and integrating society amidst rapid change, and sought to rebuild its legitimacy with new symbols, traditions, and methods. However, the Ottoman Empire's situation was particularly precarious both domestically and internationally. In the remaining parts of Ottoman Europe, particularly Macedonia, separatist movements persisted and posed difficulties for the empire. The intervention of great powers in different regions, combined with the growing European economic control and interests in the Ottoman Middle East and the Persian Gulf, increased the pressure and threatened territorial losses.[72] This left the Ottoman Empire of Abdulhamid II exposed and in a position of relative weakness, causing a desperate need for cohesion and a better self-image in the eyes of its own population.

It was in this context, amidst radical political, demographic, and territorial change, Ottoman state nationalism was reframed, often described as a transition from Tanzimat's (Pan-)Ottomanism to Abdulhamid's (Pan-)Islamism. As pointed out by Selim Deringil, however, it was essentially an attempt by Abdulhamid II to adapt state policy and ideology to the evolving circumstances and challenges facing the empire. The most significant change in this regard was arguably the loss of a large part of the empire's European provinces and, consequently, a substantial portion of its non-Muslim population, occurring at the very beginning of the sultan's

---

[70] Topuz, *Basın Tarihi*, 56–57; Koloğlu, *Türkiye'de Basın*, 43–53.

[71] Deringil, "The Invention of Tradition", 3–6.

[72] Kayalı, *Arabs and Young Turks*, 31–33; Deringil, *Domains*, 57–63.

accession to the throne in 1876. This alteration changed the demographic composition of the Ottoman population, making it proportionally more Muslim than ever before in its history.[73] Unsurprisingly, it also had a profound impact on state policies and discourses on national identity, entailing a shift towards a special appeal to and emphasis on the Muslim majority to secure their loyalty and reconstruct state legitimacy.

This reframing, however, did not imply the replacement of Ottomanism with Islamism as mutually exclusive categories. Rather, as discussed by H. Eissenstat, it entailed readjustments and redefinitions of interconnected categories within the same conceptual and policy framework.[74] Hence, despite the adjustments in which the Muslim aspect gained prominence, Ottomanness retained its position as the general marker of identity within the Hamidian nation-building framework, and the construction of Ottoman unity remained a central element of state policy. The Islamic-oriented variations of Ottoman nationalism persisted as well, most notably manifesting itself during the National Struggle (1918–22) and surviving in various forms into the Turkish Republic.

The opposition to Abdulhamid's rule, the Young Turk movement, which was composed of different segments of Ottoman society, Muslim and non-Muslim alike, on the other hand, highlighted different aspects of Ottomanness, both as an idea of Ottoman national unity, in this case with a more secular and civic outlook, and as a political program centred on constitutional parliamentary government. This demonstrates the highly fluid and flexible nature of the concept *Osmanlı* (Ottoman), which was able to accommodate many layers of identity, and transcend religious and political divides within Ottoman society. As the next chapter will discuss, towards the end of the Hamidian era, new elements were added to the concept, among these the term "Turk".

---

[73] Deringil, *Domains*, 57–60.

[74] Eissenstat, "Modernization, Imperial Nationalism, and the Ethnicization", 451.

CHAPTER 3

Ottomanism Between Ideology and *Realpolitik*

> Ottomanism's community was nothing more than an imaginary construct. The ideal of Turkism eliminated this imaginary community construct. In its place, it brought out the real and true community of Turks.[1]

This chapter deals with Ottomanism in the prelude to the constitutional revolution and the formative phase of the Young Turk regime, when the movement's opposition still primarily consisted of formulating and disseminating ideas through the press and other literary works. The main focus of this chapter is on the diverse conceptual and theoretical understandings of Ottomanness, particularly in relation to alternative notions of nation, as presented in the writings of leading Young Turk intellectuals at the time. Through an exploration of the conceptual and theoretical frameworks generated by these actors, the primary aim is to illustrate the range of interpretations and choices initially open to the new political elites. This approach in turn highlights the role of contingency, plurality, and ambivalence in the processes of conceptual restructuring, and how existing arrangements of meaning undergo modification and redefinition in response to new circumstances and events.

In this context, Ottomanness (*Osmanlılık*) serves as a multifaceted marker of identity, embodying the idea of Ottoman national unity. It is

---

[1] Tekin Alp, *Türkleştirme*, 62.

© The Author(s), under exclusive license to Springer Nature Switzerland AG 2024
A. Simsek, *Ottoman Nationalism in Transition from Empire to Republic, 1908–1931*, Modernity, Memory and Identity in South-East Europe, https://doi.org/10.1007/978-3-031-56928-9_3

noteworthy that despite the substantial efforts invested by intellectuals and political actors in constructing such national unity, these endeavours were later dismissed and criticized as insincere and artificial. In contrast, this approach prioritized the importance of ethnic nationalisms, such as the "Turkish", consequently rendering Ottomanism a dead letter, lacking relevance or impact. This is certainly the case in mainstream Turkish historiography, moulded in considerable degree by a statist Turkish nationalist perspective. Hence, according to the classic view, outlined by authors like Mehmet Ali Ayni and Tarık Zafer Tunaya, the policy of Ottoman national unity died when Sultan Abdulhamid II dissolved the parliament in 1878 and suspended the constitution, thereby putting an end to the Tanzimat.[2] At the same time, non-Muslims were clearly demonstrating their unwillingness to live under the Ottoman political roof.[3] This was the sad truth, Ayni said, which the Young Turk revolutionaries had realized before becoming Turkists as a remedy. However, they were unable to reveal their true, Turkish nationalist inclinations, which is why, he argued, the identity policies of the unionist regime could only be hesitant and ambiguous. Nonetheless, however tentatively, with the coming to power of the Unionists the Ottoman Turks had set foot on the path to the Turkish nation-state.[4]

A highly influential historian of the Turkish Republic, Tarık Zafer Tunaya, supported and extended Ayni's line of reasoning. According to him, all the elements except the "Turks" had transformed themselves into "romantic" (*romantik*) nations by the time of the constitutional revolution—meaning they had become conscious of their national culture and character—and all wanted either autonomy or complete independence in order to become nation-states.[5] In this chaotic situation, the Turks were the only people left out, deprived, and suffering due to their inability to become a nation. However, Tunaya continued, the Young Turk leaders had seen the light. They knew that the right course of action lay in Turkish nationalism, although the circumstances demanded they hide their real intentions. Therefore, for a short period, they went along with

---

[2] Ayni, *Milliyetçilik*; Tunaya, *Medeniyetin Bekleme Odasında.*

[3] Ayni, *Milliyetçilik*, 293–321.

[4] Ibid, 321.

[5] Tunaya, *Siyasi Partiler*, 375; Ayni, *Milliyetçilik*; Tunaya, "Romantik milletler" in *Vatan*, 10 June 1949.

the more or less false notion of the unity of all Ottoman peoples, until the time was ripe for full-blown Turkish nationalism to be publicly articulated. Therefore, the argument goes, the Young Turk period constituted a mere prelude, a "laboratory of the Republic".[6]

This sums up the classic Turkish view, which today represents a well-established narrative permeating historiography both within and outside Turkey; however, it is highly biased in favour of the logic of Turkish nationalism and coloured by the republican nation-state environment. The primary foci of attention in the narrative are conflict, national birth, and "breaking free" from Ottoman rule. Consequently, all the peoples of the Ottoman domains are classified as nationalists wanting to shed the yoke of Ottoman rule. They are seen as "romantic" nations, influenced by strong nationalist sentiments, that wanted autonomy or total independence. All save the "Turks" had already completed, or were about to complete, processes of cultural and traditional nationalization, self-interested struggles that raged under the blanket (*örtü*) of empire. Although, according to Tunaya, the Turks were the central element of the Ottoman population and so deserved a predominant place, they were socially and economically "slaves of those who were their subjects politically".[7] Turks were bureaucrats and peasants, so they were the "real" producers. They were nevertheless pushed, Tunaya argued, into the role of consumer, a passive and submissive position, and not allowed to enjoy the social and economic benefits to which they were entitled as producers.

As is normally the case within the traditional narrative outlined above, however, it is far from clear who exactly the "Turks" comprised in this case. According to Tunaya, "Turks" constituted a mass of people who, in some implicit way, formed a unit, while divided on the micro-level and in desperate need of national ideals. According to this, somewhat conflicting, reasoning—although it was quite in line with traditional nationalist discourses, its perennialist version in particular—the Turkish nation was there, and yet was not. Thus, Tunaya claimed, the Turks existed as a people, but were unaware of their "Turkish" identity; their only salvation, he said, rested on raising their national consciousness in order to unite them into a totality (*bir bütün*) as "nation". With that

---

[6] Tunaya, *Medeniyetin Bekleme Odasında;* Tunaya, *Siyasal Partiler, I, 19.*

[7] Tunaya, "Romantik milletler" in *Vatan,* 10 June 1949.

goal in mind, Tunaya pointed out, it was necessary not to limit the nation-building efforts to the political field focused solely on the state level, but also to move beyond it, to bring about nothing less than a wholesale social and economic revolution in tune with the requirements of the modern age.[8]

Exploring this perspective further within Ottoman history, Tunaya stressed socioeconomic aspects of developments towards nationalism. The main cause of the "national" conflict in the Ottoman Empire, Tunaya claimed, was a class struggle based on economic and social group interests, although it took the appearance of an ethnoreligious conflict. On the one side, Tunaya situated the "Turks", which in this case obviously meant "Muslim", socioeconomically characterized as bureaucrats and peasants, while on the other, we find the propertied classes of society, non-Muslims, occupied with trade and industry. In possession of money and status, the latter turn the "Turks" into slaves, economically and socially.

The hegemonic aspect of nationalism, as a relation of power and political dominance between groups in society was taken up by another early writer on nationalism in the Ottoman Empire and Turkey. Developing it into a grand narrative explaining Turkish nationalism, Mehmet Ali Ayni, split up the Ottoman population into two main groups, the "dominant nation" (*hakim millet*), composed of Turks, Arabs, Albanians, Kurds, Bosnians, Circassians, Abkhasians, Georgians, Daghestanis, Chechens, and Laz—in short, the Muslim population.[9] The second category, non-Muslims, he defined as the "subjugated nations" (*mahkum milletler*), interestingly in the plural (*milletler*) while the Muslims were referenced in the singular (*millet*).[10] In this second group, he included Rums, Armenians, Bulgarians, Serbians, Montenegrins, Croats, Jews, Nestorians, Chaldeans, Assyrians, and Vlachs. In this narrative, Ayni explained how the "Turks" on the verge of losing everything, finally managed to restore their state, dominance, and nationhood.

This line of reasoning and its terminology was to a large extent coloured by the writings of some of the Young Turk ideologues themselves, such as Ziya Gökalp (1876–1924), Ahmet Ağaoğlu (1869–1939),

---

[8] Tunaya, *Siyasi Partiler*, 376.

[9] Ayni, *Milliyetçilik*, 223–321.

[10] Ayni, *Milliyetçilik*, 293. This implicit articulation of Muslim unity is particularly interesting seeing that Ayni's work is written from a Turkish nationalist perspective during the Kemalist period.

Tekin Alp (born Moiz Cohen, 1883–1961), and Yusuf Akçura (1876–1935). Belonging to the group of intellectuals of Turkic origin who emigrated to the Ottoman Empire from Russia, Akçura is of particular interest here. Not only because of his early literary and theoretical contributions in relation to nationalism in the Ottoman Empire but also because of the link he, among others,[11] represented between the early stages of Turkish nationalism and Turkism in the Russian Empire, often written with the suffix pan—to convey its envisioned Turkish unity across Ottoman and Russian borders. This encounter in turn brought about Akçura's characteristic attempt to forge a workable conceptual rearrangement of existing general markers of identity within the Ottoman Empire.

This attempt found its most famous expression in Akçura's essay, *Üç Tarz-ı Siyaset*. (Three Kinds of Policy), printed in Cairo in the Ottoman newspaper, *Türk*. Although only later rising to fame as one of the foundational texts of Turkish nationalism, initially *Three Kinds of Policy* did not receive much attention or praise at the time of its publication in 1904.[12] On the contrary, as will be discussed below, it was often criticized and dismissed by Ottoman intellectuals and politicians alike. Its importance was gradually recognized, particularly after the founding of the Turkish Republic. Subsequently, however, Akçura's way of framing the national question in the Ottoman context and his terminology played a major role in shaping the historiography of the late Ottoman period. Adopting Akçura's tripartite template, historians have traditionally viewed the origins and evolution of Turkish nationalism as a one-way progression of mutually exclusive "three kinds of policy", from Ottomanism, through Islamism to Turkism,[13] historically attributed to the Tanzimat, the reign of Abdulhamid II, and the Young Turks respectively.[14] This notion, however, has attracted increased criticism by recent scholarship, highlighting the multifaceted nature of the development of Turkish nationalism, and pointing out that the various options available to the

---

[11] Other prominent intellectuals belonging to this group were Hüseyinzade Ali Turan (1864–1941) who, like Ahmed Ağaoğlu, was from Azerbaijan, and Ismail Gasprinski (known to the Ottomans as Ismail Gaspıralı) (1851–1914) from Crimea.

[12] Zurcher, *Unionist Factor*, 126; Lewis, *Emergence*, 348.

[13] For a discussion of Akçura's concept of Turkism, see Georgeon, *Akçura*, 24–30 and Lewis, *Emergence*, 326–327.

[14] Akçura, *Üç Tarz-ı Siyaset*, 19.

policymakers, including Ottomanism, Islamism and Turkism, were not mutually exclusive categories.[15]

In the aftermath of the constitutional revolution, Akçura took part in founding and publishing influential journals like *Türk Yurdu* (Turkish Homeland) and *Halka Doğru* (To the People). What is less known about Akçura is his role in the nationalist turn of the 1930s in Kemalist Turkey, reminding us that the flow of life stories continued even though the so-called Young Turk period ended. In the Kemalist republican context, he served as one of the chief architects of the Turkish History Thesis (*Türk Tarih Tezi*), which put forth the claim that the major civilizations of the world, including the "Western", had an ancient source, Turkish civilization.[16] A year later, this "thesis" was augmented by the Sun Language Theory (*Güneş Dil Teorisi*),[17] which stated that this ancient source linguistically belonged to the Turkic family of languages, likewise making Turkish the mother of all languages.

Although the Turkish nationalist Akçura of the 1930s sounded quite sure about his Turkish nationalism, the Akçura of 1904 was not, despite *Üç Tarz-ı Siyaset*'s generally being seen as the principal work of early Turkish nationalism. A careful reading reveals the experimental nature of this text. Instead of offering a clear-cut definition of an ideology, what we see is rather an attempt to frame the different kinds of nationalism policies accessible to the Ottomans at the turn of the century. As it was published just a few years prior to the constitutional revolution, Akçura's essay, as well as the debate it generated, constituted an important reflection of the perceptions and visions of the Ottoman political elites regarding nationalism in general, and Ottoman nationalism in particular.

Although Akçura's essay has been read primarily for his views on and aspirations *for* Turkish nationalism, what is particularly of interest for this study is his argument *against* Ottomanism. Rather than drawing a picture of Turkish nationalism, which Akçura, writing in 1904, admitted was still a very new phenomenon, weak in emotional appeal and vague in content, his attempt was directed against the most common identity policies in existence in the Ottoman Empire thus far. Most of his arguments had the aim of explaining why the Ottoman state should

---

[15] Eissenstat, "Modernization, Imperial Nationalism, and the Ethnicization", 437.
[16] Türk Tarih Kongresi, *Birinci Türk Tarih Kongresi*.
[17] Türk Dili Kurultayı, *Birinci Türk Dili Kurultayı*.

pursue neither a policy of Ottoman national unity nor Pan-Islamism as the basis of political legitimacy and nation-building. Refuting the two main options, Akçura claimed that the Ottoman statesmen would be left with the untried alternative of Turkish nationalism based on race and ethnicity.[18] He wrote:

> For which community's interests should we strive? This question cannot be answered logically. In fact, why should we work for the benefit of Turks or Muslims, and not for example, for the benefit of Slavs or the Orthodox? Especially considering that the benefit of one community is often obtained at the expense of another, on what reasonable basis can we justify causing harm to another part of humanity?
>
> This question can only be answered by our natural inclination, in other words, by our emotions, which our minds have not yet managed to understand or justify. I am an Ottoman Muslim Turk. Therefore, I want to serve the interests of the Ottoman state, of Islam, and of all Turks. But are the interests of these three communities, which are based on political, religious, and ethnic grounds, mutual? Does the strengthening of one community lead to the strengthening of the others?
>
> The interest of the Ottoman state is not contrary to the interests of all Muslims and Turks. Because the Muslims and Turks who are its subjects also become stronger with its strengthening, and other Muslims and Turks also find a strong support thereby.
>
> However, the interests of Islam do not completely align with the interests of the Ottoman state and that of Turks. This is because the strengthening of Islam would ultimately lead to the loss of a portion of the Ottoman subjects (the non-Muslims) and consequently entail the disappearance of a part of the Ottoman state's current society. It would also cause division between Muslim and non-Muslim Turks, leading to their weakening.
>
> As for the interests of the Turks (*Türklük*), they also do not entirely correspond to the interests of either the Ottoman state or Islam. For they [the interests of the Turks] weaken the Islamic community by dividing it into Turkish and non-Turkish parts, and as a result, sow discord among the Muslim Ottoman subjects, leading to the weakening of the Ottoman state.[19]

---

[18] Muallim Naci. (1308 [1891]). *Lügat-ı Naci*. İstanbul.
[19] Akçura, *Üç Tarz-ı Siyaset*, 26.

Overall, Akçura exhibited remarkable insight into the history of nationalism in Europe throughout the nineteenth century. He claimed that the Ottoman Empire intended to build a nation along American and French lines, but this project was doomed to fail, therefore it would be forced to follow the German example.[20] According to Akçura, the idea of creating an Ottoman nation was already dead at the hands of Abdulhamid II and was never to be revived again.[21] He further claimed that civic nationality after the French model was impossible to realize in the "East" (*Şark*), because of irreconcilable interests and ancient hostilities. Akçura then presented a striking observation on the Islamic nationalism of Abdulhamid II. He saw it as a departure from the civic model of Ottomanism because of its failure to create unity between the population elements, while the turn in Abdulhamid's identity policy was an indication of a move towards ethnic nationalism. This would be based on religion, in line with the motto "religion and the nation are one" (*din ve millet birdir*), in order to create one single nation (*millet*), thus "giving the word *millet* the same meaning as in recent times".[22]

Although Akçura presented rational arguments for the abandonment of Ottomanism as policy, he nevertheless was not able to refrain from showing a close affinity with Ottomanness, which may be seen as an interesting example of the ambiguity permeating the discourses of the Ottoman intellectuals at the time. His composite identity further pointed to the Ottoman elites' multi-vocal identities under the hybrid of Ottomanness. Remarkably, then, while he rejected Ottoman nationalism and Pan-Islamism as a single polity, in favour of Turkism, Akçura seemingly found no contradictions in reconciling on the personal level religious, ethnic, and civic identity. In so doing, while still rejecting Ottomanism, he was actually suggesting that Ottoman national unity could work if configured in another way. Indeed, conceptual and theoretical reasoning aside (which led him to conclude that ethnic Turkish nationalism would be the right path to follow), his framing of identity on a personal level suggests he was not yet ready to let go of "Ottomanness" (*Osmanlılık*).

---

[20] Ibid, 19.
[21] Ibid, 21.
[22] Ibid, 21.

Thus, for Akçura, Turks could still remain Ottomans as well as Turkish nationalists simply by co-opting the Ottoman state; what was left was reconciling Islam's place in society into this overall structure. In Akçura's view, the strongly Islamic identity of Turks would solve this problem. He believed that as the raw material to be moulded into a Turkish nation, Turks would naturally endorse both Islamism and Turkism simultaneously. Therefore, Akçura argued, Turkists had no grounds to dismiss Islam, as Islamism could work practically in conjunction with Turkism to garner support for the ideology. In this configuration, Islam was to be the vessel to promote Turkism. The ambiguity is clear, however, when there is a shift from the theoretical thinking about nationalism to the practical and personal level. Unfortunately, Akçura did not provide a clear definition of his concept of "Turk" and "Turkishness", and what it meant in the minds and vocabulary of the new generation of Young Turks, other than his overall suggestion that it comprised "Turks" in and outside the Ottoman Empire. To whom exactly the term "Turks" referred would indeed often cause heated public debates in the following decades witnessing some highly dramatic changes within the perceptions and constructions of "us" and "them".

In order to explain the uselessness of Ottomanism, Akçura began by defining his understanding of the concept. The central goal of Ottomanism, he said, was to create a composite Ottoman nation, based upon liberty and legal equality, by bringing together various religious and ethnic groups. In this arrangement, the people would be united only by the ideas of homeland (*vatan*) and nation (*millet*). As a result, the conflicts caused by religious and ethnic differences would cease, and the different population elements would be fused into a unity.

In this manner, Akçura said, the Ottoman Turks, as the founders of the Ottoman state, would be satisfied with the spiritual gain of associating their homeland and nation with "Osman", the name of the first Ottoman sultan. Their motives for approving this rather disadvantageous position would be to put an end to further partitioning of the empire built by their ancestors.[23] The Turks might, however, be forced to relinquish even the acknowledgement of their past as the name "Ottoman" could be considered a symbol of oppression by those who were formerly conquered. Consequently, in a free society where the latter constituted

---

[23] Ibid, 26.

the majority, the name "Ottoman" might be abolished if the population wished to do so. Although the Ottoman Turks could maintain their dominance for a short period due to their past positions of power, Akçura argued, that being relegated to a secondary position could result in stagnation and weakness, similar to what occurs in nature. The inevitable end result of all this, Akçura claimed, would be the Ottoman Turks' losing their political dominance.

Next Akçura addressed one of the main concerns occupying the Ottoman ruling elite, that is, how to save the state. Would an Ottoman nation strengthen or weaken the state? Akçura noted that the Turkish and Muslim communities would experience a decline in power, but the Ottoman state could become more powerful if its people were united in an organized and cohesive manner, instead of constantly being in conflict and chaos. Yet the basic problem remained, Akçura wrote, of whether different ethnic and religious groups, who had hitherto been in conflict with each other, could come together and cooperate willingly.[24] He then went on to list several reasons why Ottomanism would never work. Above all, he said, hardly anyone wanted Ottoman national unity to succeed, including Muslims, non-Muslims, the great powers, and the Balkan states.

According to Akçura Muslims, especially the Ottoman Turks, had no desire to reconcile with non-Muslims, as doing so would mean forfeiting their 600-year reign and being reduced to the same status as the *reaya*, whom they had always seen as subjugated people. In practical terms, this would mean that the *reaya* would gain entry into the government and military, taking over roles that the Muslims had previously held exclusively. As a result, they would lose their grip on positions they deemed honourable and be compelled to enter into unfamiliar fields like trade and industry, which they had previously looked down upon.[25]

Furthermore, Akçura argued, that Muslims were not interested in the success of Ottoman national unity, as Islam did not recognize the full legal equality of Muslims and non-Muslims. According to Islamic law, non-Muslims, categorized as *zimmis*, were always considered inferior. Additionally, Islam, being a religion rooted in the supernatural realm and based on absolute truths, would not accept complete freedom of thought and conscience solely for the purpose of human happiness.

[24] Ibid, 27–28.
[25] Ibid, 28.

Non-Muslims did not want it to succeed either, Akçura stated, because they had had their own independence, their own governments, and their own pasts, which were now being celebrated due to their emergent national consciousness. One of the features of this consciousness was the predominant image of Muslims, especially Turks, as culpable for ending the independence of non-Muslim *millet*s and destroying their governments. They felt that they had endured injustice, contempt, inequality, and misery under Ottoman rule.[26]

Further, Akçura noted, in the nineteenth century non-Muslims had become more aware of their history, rights, and national identity, while the Ottomans, their superiors, became weaker. Additionally, the conditions had now shifted; albeit unwillingly and hesitantly, their weakened masters were showing them signs of brotherhood, wanting to share sovereignty and establish equality. The people in question saw the true motive behind this new policy, however, recognizing that it was a result of European great power pressure. Akçura claimed that, although the Christian population had a material interest in remaining under Ottoman rule, in terms of emotional attachment they did not want this kind of unity and coexistence (*imtizac*), as they would not be willing to blend with people that had previously put an end to their independence through conquest.[27]

Moving his discussion further afield, Akçura added that Russia and the Balkan states did not want Ottoman national unity to succeed either. Russia, which Akçura pointed out as "the greatest enemy of the Ottomans", wanted to get possession of the Straits and Istanbul, Anatolia, the Balkans, the Holy Lands and Iraq, thereby realizing its goal of political, economic, national and religious dominance.[28] As it was in Russia's interest to keep the Ottomans weakened and divided, it would not allow the creation of an Ottoman nation. Furthermore, the potential impact of irredentism on relatively young states like Serbia and Greece would make them hostile to the creation of an Ottoman nation. They would want to continue to increase their populations under Ottoman rule, an aim that would be attainable only if Ottoman communities remained divided.

---

[26] Ibid, 28–29.
[27] Ibid, 29.
[28] Ibid, 29.

Finally, Akçura observed, that the European powers would also be opposed to the success of Ottoman national unity because the European public opinion was still influenced by the historic religious conflict between Christianity and Islam with roots in the crusades. The Europeans aimed to liberate Christians from the "Muslim yoke" and rid Europe and Christian lands of the Muslims, thus rescuing European nations, whom they deemed capable of progress, from the "semi-barbaric, oppressive Turanians" who were always engaged in conflict and war.[29]

Therefore, Akçura concluded, that the idea of an Ottoman nation was nothing but an impossible endeavour conceived and implemented by a small group of individuals in the Ottoman government, against the wishes of the various population elements. Moreover, even if these political leaders were highly skilled, they would not be able to overcome so many obstacles, and to try to do so would be "futile" (*beyhude*).[30]

The Response: Ali Kemal and the Liberal Critique

While still in the imperial Ottoman setting, Akçura's essay did not have significant appeal among Ottoman political elites and intellectuals alike. Furthermore, his ideas on (Pan-) Turkish unity faced criticism as being non-Ottoman and too idealistic. Before long, the responses in the press grew into a heated debate on identity, nationalism, and the future of the Ottoman Empire.[31] The polemic between Yusuf Akçura, Ali Kemal and Ahmet Ferit are of particular interest here.[32] Ali Kemal (1869–1922)[33] was a famous journalist, author, and politician, as well as a leading member of the liberal faction of the Young Turk movement. He published his comments on Akçura's essay in an article in *Türk* with the heading "Our Response" (*Cevabımız*). Ali Kemal's interpretation of Ottoman nationalism was generally in line with that of Prince Sabahaddin, and thus also with the party programs of the Ottoman Freedom Party

---

[29] Ibid, 30.

[30] Ibid, 31.

[31] Georgeon, *Akçura*, 12–15, 24–27, 52–59.

[32] All three, Yusuf Akçura, Ali Kemal and Ahmet Ferit, became members of the Ottoman Parliament, the Assembly of Deputies (*Meclis-i Mebusan*) following the constitutional revolution in 1908.

[33] "Ali Kemal", *Atatürk Ansiklopedisi*, https://ataturkansiklopedisi.gov.tr/bilgi/ali-kemal-1869-1922/.

(*Osmanlı Ahrar Fırkası*)[34] and the Liberal Alliance Party (*Hürriyet ve Itilaf Fırkası*),[35] which subsequently served as the main opposition to the CUP in the second constitutional period.

In Ali Kemal's view, the idea of Ottoman national unity was political in nature, and not cultural. He claimed that the Tanzimat sultans, viziers, and reformers had never intended to sponsor Ottoman unification on a cultural basis. To him, Ottomanness, Muslimness, and Turkishness constituted a trinity, not possible to separate from one another. Rather than trying to force Bulgarians, *Rum*s, Serbs, Armenians, Vlachs, Maronites, and Chaldeans into "the character of an Ottoman nation", the right way forward was to:

> reform the Ottoman methods of rule in a moderate way according to the modern ideas of Europe in order to make beneficial use of the political developments of our age in an effort to obtain the allegiance of all these peoples to our state.

According to Ali Kemal, Pan-Islamism was just an empty ideal, while Pan-Turkism was a plain "monstrosity". "The important thing", he wrote, "is to continue on the path of civilization, work to this end, and above all to make the Ottoman government modern and just". Rather than promoting Turkish unity, it would be better to strive for advancement on the individual level. In this way, he claimed, "the civilized world will be forced to regard us as people of Europe and accept us into the community of nations".

AHMET FERIT'S REALISM

Another important reply to Akçura came from Ahmet Ferit (Tek) (1878–1971),[36] who also belonged to the Young Turk movement. It is interesting to note that Ahmet Ferit served as MP in the Ottoman Parliament, the first Grand National Assembly in Ankara and the second, which

---

[34] For more information on the Ottoman Freedom Party (founded 14 September 1908), including a reprint of its program, see Tunaya, *Siyasi Partiler*, 239–254.

[35] For the Liberal Alliance Party (founded 21 November 1911) and related documents, see Tunaya, *Siyasi Partiler*, 315–344.

[36] "Ahmet Ferit Tek", *Atatürk Ansiklopedisi*, https://ataturkansiklopedisi.gov.tr/bilgi/ahmet-ferit-tek-1878-1971/.

proclaimed Turkey a republic, becoming its first Minister of the Interior. He was accused and criticized in 1924, by members of the second parliament (1923–27), for having been too accommodating towards Armenians wanting to return to Turkey after the War of Independence, accusations he firmly denied.[37]

In his response, Ahmet Ferit began with an evaluation of Islam as the basis of Ottoman national unity.[38] In his opinion, the most efficient means of creating unity and legitimacy was through the use of Islam due to the "semi-civilized state of the people" (*millet yarı medeni olduğu için*). Islam, he continued, was a powerful factor when mobilizing people and gaining support from Muslim intellectuals; however, it was impossible to implement politically. Furthermore, in matters of modern politics, the notion of nationhood (*milliyet*) was superior to religious convictions, so future nationalism would probably require the replacement of the religious basis for politics (*dini siyaset*) with secular legitimization. Then he clarified that by "nationalism" he was not referring to ethnic Turkish nationalism, but a secular Ottoman nationalism, because the idea of a union of Turks was currently nothing but a dream, but could be a realistic option for the future, "provided modern civilization advances in the path of humanism".[39] Although he did not see any positive use for Turkish nationalism for the time being—putting the needs and interests of the Ottoman state to the fore—he greatly appreciated the positive gains the political use of Islam might offer the Ottoman state:

> It does not mean that the Ottoman state should not make use of the power of Islam to strengthen its political existence. In fact, the moral and spiritual bonds provided by Islam could be diffused among the population through a variety of means by the state, which would be highly beneficial. Therefore, the Ottoman government should deem important the policy of Islamism and Islamic union.

In conclusion, Ahmet Ferit stated that the idea of Ottomanism was the most vital for the Ottoman government to date. It was also the most essential of the three policies and the most applicable. The other two could, at best, be supportive elements in the struggle for survival,

---

[37] TBMM ZC, D: 2, Cilt 8, 20 April 1924, 647–652.
[38] Akçura, *Üç Tarz-ı Siyaset*, 45–55.
[39] Ibid, 54.

while the policy of Ottomanism was its most powerful armour, greatest defensive weapon, and most appropriate goal. He wrote:

> The author of the Three Kinds of Policy has been led to make wrong judgments in this regard because he is preoccupied with logical and philosophical certainties, rather than focusing on facts and the physical reality. Logical reasoning tends to make positive and final judgments. But life, thus the utterly complex societal life, sometimes, or not just sometimes but most of the time, will defy these judgments.[40]

Later Ahmet Ferit recounted what these harsh Ottoman realities entailed, what could be done about them and, maybe more importantly, what could not:

> Yes, most probably the Ottoman state will not be able to defend all its territories and its subject peoples, not provide absolute unity among its citizens, and will not succeed in moulding them into Turks. So what? No harm in that. Whatever happens there is a people in existence right now, strong and vital with life. It is for the sake of this people, the Ottoman domains must be protected. And this people is the Ottoman nation. What we can do is to try to defend and represent what we have, and devote all our minds to the good of the Ottoman polity [*osmanlı siyaseti*]: those we succeed in keeping will remain with us, what does not remain will be gone. We will call it fate [*kader*] or the necessities of the laws of nature. We will lose nothing more than what we surely are to lose. But if we are to succeed we can only do that by following this path. ... Our state's primary goal must be that of the Tanzimat, the Reform Edicts and the Constitution; that is the policy of Ottoman national unity. This is the true protection for our national existence.[41]

With his long answer to Akçura, Ahmet Ferit was not only defending Ottoman nationalism but also illustrating his fundamentally different point of departure. It is at this juncture that the difference of opinion between Russian emigre intellectuals and Ottoman political thinkers becomes most clear, highlighted by the most striking aspect of Ahmet Ferit's approach, his pragmatism and realism, which in the coming years would become the predominant characteristic of Unionist policy and

---

[40] Ibid.
[41] Ibid, 55.

rhetoric. It is on this basis that he accused Akçura of letting himself be blinded by theoretical reasoning, thereby becoming unable to see the complex realities of Ottoman society, which would elude every attempt to capture the content and dynamics of Ottoman identity in logical, clear-cut definitions.

A notable aspect of Ahmet Ferit's realism was his relative equanimity regarding the loss of Ottoman territory, which differed sharply from the more idealist attitudes of Ottoman intellectuals such as Namık Kemal (1840–1888), known as the propagator of the ideas of *vatan* (homeland) and *hürriyet* (freedom) in Ottoman thought. In his famous work, "Vatan Yahut Silistre" (Homeland or Silistra), originally written and performed as a play containing strong elements of Ottoman Muslim nationalism, Namık Kemal dealt with the delicate question of whether one part of the empire, in this case, the besieged town of Silistra in today's northern Bulgaria, was to be regarded as an indivisible part of the homeland or just as some territory under Ottoman rule. If the first, then Silistra had to be defended to the last man; if the second, it was an issue of politics and diplomacy, thus merely a question of revising the borders. The answer was self-evident according to Namık Kemal.

To Ahmet Ferit, however, realities rather than ideals and intellectual thinking would shape the future trajectory of the Ottoman Empire and thus the prevalent configurations of national identity. This perspective emphasized that the thoughts and actions of Ottoman policymakers would be moulded by concrete circumstances rather than by ideology and philosophical reasoning. This insight proved crucial in understanding the perceptions and policies of the Young Turk elite who came to power following the constitutional revolution.

The response of Ottoman intellectuals to Akçura's essay also highlighted significant differences arising from a diverse range of interests, perspectives, and political positions among the individuals involved. One of them was the notable divergence between emigre intellectuals such as Akçura, who envisioned a sense of national unity extending beyond Ottoman borders into the Russian Empire, and intellectuals whose places of origin were within the Ottoman Empire itself and who seemed to prioritize the regional and local circumstances of the Ottoman Empire. The latter group differed widely within themselves, however, as exemplified by the viewpoints of Ali Kemal and Ahmet Ferit, among others. Ali Kemal, for instance, was an Istanbul-born intellectual affiliated with the liberal camp, who advocated for socioeconomic and administrative development as a means to achieve Ottoman unity and societal reintegration. He actively supported reforms that aimed to enhance local conditions and establish decentralized rule. Ahmet Ferit, on the other hand, also born in Istanbul and hailing from a long line of bureaucratic family background, was a member of the CUP and seemed above all to be preoccupied with the preservation of the Ottoman state. Unsurprisingly, these distinct perspectives led to highly varied conceptualizations of Ottoman national identity.

Nevertheless, among the Ottoman state elites, Ahmet Ferit's views predominated. Preservation of the Ottoman state constituted the main focus, their discourses on Ottomanism revolved around this basic theme, and the attempts to find remedies for the Empire's troubles. In a demographic makeup such as the Ottoman characterized by a high level of ethnic and religious diversity, the risk of separatism constituted a major concern. For the same reason, the prospects of an official nationalism based on a single ethnic group seemed a less suitable venue for the construction of Ottoman unity. Hence, Ottoman political leaders and intellectuals, who might qualify as "Turkish" members of Akçura's envisioned a community of "Turks", were obviously more concerned with preserving the Ottoman state than creating an alternative to it. From that perspective at least, Akçura's Turkism at the time of the publication of his essay in 1904 seemed the least realistic and viable of the "three kinds of policy". It was hardly surprising therefore, that Ottomanism, in its various forms, came to constitute the cornerstone of the new regime's identity policy in the aftermath of the Young Turk revolution. Under the given circumstances and needs, Ottomanism was adopted as the most viable option, contrary to Akcura's advice.

At this crucial point, the fluid nature of Ottoman nationalism demonstrated both its strengths and weaknesses. Its weaknesses became apparent when attempting to expand the scope of the "nation" to align with the vast Ottoman imperial structure. This would have required an identity configuration inclusive enough to accommodate the various ethnic, cultural, and religious groups, while at the same time distinctive enough to demarcate sameness and, consequently, difference. In short, to construct a "them" and "us" within an imperial structure or, put differently, an "imperial nation".⁴² Attempts by the Ottoman state elite to nationalize the empire's various populations could therefore hardly ever be introduced on clear ethno-national lines. Even if the Ottoman centre wanted to homogenize the population based on culture, it would be highly difficult to translate into an ethno-nationalist policy, as the imperial state culture was itself not bound to any one ethnic element.

Its strength, on the other hand, lay in its highly flexible and adaptable nature well suited for the circumstances at hand, which in turn highlights one of the significant shortcomings of Akçura's framing of Ottomanism as a fixed and exclusive category. In his opinion there was only one "Ottomanism", when in fact Ottoman identity was above all characterized by its fluid boundaries and dynamic content, qualities clearly demonstrated by Akçura's own self-definition as Ottoman, Muslim, and Turk, all in one breath. These combinations could be extended even further, as "Ottomanness" was inclusive enough to serve as an overall identity marker for the Ottoman population elements at large. It is telling in that regard that while the term gained wide acceptance among Muslims and non-Muslims alike, the term "Turk" was generally rejected for the role. Virtually any subject of the Ottoman sultan could call himself an Ottoman, without thereby having to subscribe to any particular ethnicity or religion.

Pavli Karolidi Efendi, MP for Izmir, identifying himself as an "Ottoman, Christian, and *Rum*" only a few years later, illustrated this point most clearly, while his emphasis on and characterization of the composite nature of Ottoman identity showed that this indeed was a common theme not restricted to "Ottoman Muslim Turks" like Akçura. In his speech in parliament, Karolidi Efendi declared: "We are both *Rum*, Christian and Ottoman. If I was not a true *Rum*, I could not have been a true Ottoman. (...) If I were to say 'I am only Ottoman', I would be betraying both my *Rum*ness and Ottomanness".⁴³ Thus, according to Karolidi Efendi these modes of identity were not only possible to reconcile, but also closely linked and interdependent. On the other hand, noted

---

⁴² For a discussion of "imperial nation" and "imperial nationalism", see Berger & Miller, *Nationalizing Empires*, 4–30; for a usage of the concept in the Ottoman context, see also Çevik, "Ottomanism and Varieties of Official Nationalism," 59–64; and Eissenstat, "Modernization, Imperial Nationalism, and the Ethnicization.".

⁴³ MM ZC, D: 1, S: 1, Cilt 5, 7 Temmuz 1325 (20 July 1909), 453.

Karolidi Efendi, trying to disentangle them would pose the real challenge. The significance of his claim asserted itself most dramatically during and after WWI, when the "unmixing of peoples" became a major concern of the new regimes at the end of the empire.[44] The magnitude of difficulties faced in that regard in turn brings us back to Pavli Karolidi's argument on the prevalence of composite identities in the Ottoman context.

---

[44] Hirschon, *Crossing the Aegean*, 3–7.

CHAPTER 4

Revolution and Disillusion

Following the Constitutional Revolution every Ottoman now has declared his solidarity in duty, taxes, and rightful demands of the homeland.[1]

In this way we will have saved this state and it will exist for ever.[2]

The Young Turk Revolution of 1908 and the ensuing CUP regime constitute a crucial shift in the political history of the Ottoman Empire and Turkey. Its immediate result, the reinstatement of *Kanun-i Esasi* (the Ottoman constitution of 1876), and the reconvening of parliament, prorogued by Abdulhamid in 1878, allowed the new Young Turk elites to make legitimate claims to power as speakers for "the people" and the "national will". To mark the event, the date of the revolution, 10 July (23 July according to the Gregorian calendar) was declared the main national holiday, celebrated by the Kemalist republic as well until 1935. Furnished with a set of high ideals and symbols of "Ottomanness" and a liberal rhetoric the declared purpose of the revolution had been to revive the short-lived constitutional regime of 1876–78, but more concretely it aimed to put an end to Abdulhamid's more than 30 years of authoritarian rule. The prelude to the revolution was characterized by a state of chaos,

---

[1] Yorgi Honeus Efendi, MM ZC, D: 1, S: 1, Cilt 5, 13 Haziran 1325 (26 June 1909), 5.

[2] Pançedoref Efendi, MM ZC, D: 1, S: 1, Cilt 5, 13 Haziran 1325 (26 June 1909), 6.

however. Indeed, the vastness and complexity of the Ottoman domains make it hard to grasp the effects and implications of this peculiar incident that was called the Great Revolution (*Inkilab-ı Kebir*).[3]

After almost 20 years of Young Turk opposition, conducted mostly from abroad through writings in the press and intellectual discussions on various platforms, the actual impetus to overthrow the sultan came from military officers stationed in Salonica (Thessaloniki). The primary reason given is the widespread discontent among the Ottoman officers over the Macedonian question, which had become the focus of Great Power politics after 1878. Following the treaties of San Stefano and Berlin, Macedonia, taken to be the "unredeemed" part of "Greater Bulgaria", had gradually become the object of a fierce dispute in and outside the Ottoman Empire,[4] with strong push/pull effects coming from surrounding Balkan states like Bulgaria, Greece, and Serbia.[5] It was a violent process deeply unsettling age-old community relations and socioeconomic structures in the region.[6]

The spark for the Young Turk revolution came in the form of a meeting in Reval on 9–10 June 1908, between Tsar Nicholas II and King Edward VII, where Russia and Great Britain reached an agreement on autonomy for the three Ottoman provinces of Salonica, Kosovo, and Manastır, under foreign supervision.[7] The backdrop of this meeting was the tumultuous state of affairs in Macedonia going back to the Ilinden uprising in 1903 led by IMRO[8] in an attempt to secure autonomy for Macedonia, similar to that of Lebanon, Crete, Bulgaria, and Eastern Rumelia, by persuading European powers to intervene.[9] The latter refused to do so, these efforts were unsuccessful and the uprising was violently crushed by

---

[3] It has been intensely debated whether it really constituted a revolution, or was rather a coup d'état. See Zürcher, *Legacy*, 26–31, and Kansu, *1908 Devrimi*, 1–17 & 30–34, for further details.

[4] Both the archival accounts and memoirs still talk about relative peace and security well into the 1880s, which began to change for the worse as the turn of the century approached. For an account see Fazlı Necip, *Rumeli'yi Neden Kaybettik*.

[5] Ünal, "Ottoman Policy", 137–140; Yosmaoğlu, *Blood Ties*, 21–23.

[6] Yosmaoğlu, *Blood Ties*, 164–166, 205–208, 290–292.

[7] For a comprehensive historiographical discussion about the Macedonian question and its effects on the Young Turk Revolution, see Zürcher, *Legacy*, 26–40.

[8] Internal Macedonian Revolutionary Organization, established in Salonica in 1893.

[9] Yosmaoğlu, "Counting Bodies, Shaping Souls", 59–62.

Ottoman forces.[10] This, however, prompted a reaction from Franz Joseph of Austria-Hungary and Tsar Nicholas II of Russia, who in a meeting in Murzsteg agreed on new reforms for Macedonia. These involved the restructuring of the gendarmerie, by placing it under the command of a foreign general assisted by a team of foreign officers assigned to five administrative districts.[11]

These measures, while further weakening the central government's authority in the province, did not provide the intended stability and effective administration, however. Once again, in 1905, the European powers forced the Ottoman government to accept foreign intervention, by allowing the establishment of an international commission to oversee financial matters in Macedonia. Such interventions were viewed by many Ottomans in the region as plans for dividing Macedonia, often leading to public frustrations demanding action from the Ottoman government, which ultimately did not materialize.[12]

The frustrations found a response among the Ottoman officers within the Third Army stationed in Macedonia. During the summer of 1908, these young officers were referred to as "Unionist" (*ittihatçı*), a name derived from their organization, Committee of Union and Progress (*Ittihat ve Terakki Cemiyeti*),[13] had planned to take action against the policies of the sultan.[14] However, unforeseen circumstances and events, such as the Reval meeting, escalated their dissatisfaction into a full-fledged rebellion, initiated by senior captain Niyazi Bey by raiding an army depot in his hometown, *Resne* (Resen) on 3 July and leading a few hundred men to the mountains of Macedonia.[15] He was soon thereafter joined

---

[10] Knight, *Awakening*, 78; Gawrych, *The Crescent and the Eagle*, 135.

[11] Tokay, *Makedonya Sorunu*, 120.

[12] Dündar, *Modern Türkiye'nin Sifresi*, 54–55.

[13] For more on the Young Turk Revolution see esp. Ahmad, *The Young Turks*; Hanioglu, *Preparation*; Ramsaur, *Young Turks*; Kuran, *Inkilap*; Aksin, *Jön Türkler*; Kansu, *Revolution*; Gawrych, *The* Sohrabi, *Revolution*. Gawrych, *The Crescent and the Eagle*; Sohrabi, *Revolution*.

[14] FO371/544/24038, Barclay to Grey, 7 July 1908; FO371/544/24315, Barclay to Grey, 9 July 1908; FO371/544/24797, Barclay to Grey, 17 July 1908.

[15] Kansu, *1908 Devrimi*, 122. For more on this earliest phase of events leading to the Young Turk Revolution, see Ahmed Niyazi, *Hatirat-i Niyazi Yahud Tarihçe-i Inkilab-i Kebir-i Osmani'den Bir Sahife*. This is the most important memoir of its kind, produced by Niyazi of Resne (in the province of Manastir), who was hailed as the hero of the revolution and its initiator. Completed in September 1908 (1324), only two months after

by other Unionist officers, including Enver Bey, and in a short time, they were able to gain support among the local populations for the rebellion.[16]

In the early stages, the officers communicated their grievances to the sultan via telegrams, with their complaints primarily centring on favouritism within the military, which had detrimental effects on promotions and salary payments for many young officers.[17] This was a common source of discontent in the Ottoman army, despite military personnel being considerably better off in this regard compared to other state employees. The ensuing low morale resulted in frequent desertions among troops, posing significant challenges for the military engaged in combating widespread separatist guerrilla bands in the field.

The situation of the Second Army at Edirne was somewhat different, which perhaps explains why it was the Third Army rather than the Second to become the hotbed of political agitation, beyond the obvious one that the Third Army was being stationed in one of the most troubled regions of the empire. Barclay, an official of the British Embassy in Istanbul, writes that the rank and file of the Second Army were "fairly contented, but an exception must be made in the case of those whose time has expired and who are awaiting discharge".[18] There was, however, widespread sympathy for the rebelling officers within both armies. According to Major Samson, the British Consul at Edirne, political matters were being discussed more openly by officers in public places than had been the case three months earlier, and he was assured that a very large number of them were favourably disposed towards the rebelling Young Turk officers.[19]

---

the revolution, the memoir was published the same year. Another important memoir is Ahmed Refik's *Inkilab-ı Azim* (1324/1908).

[16] FO371/545/27643, Lowther to Grey, 4 August 1908; Kansu, *1908 Devrimi*, 123–125.

[17] The officers were particularly dissatisfied with the unfair promotion of those who had risen from the ranks, the *alaylı*, as opposed to those educated in the military academy, the *mektepli*. By July 15, a significant number of promotions had taken place, leading to some improvement in morale. However, many others continued to demand promotion. Interestingly, the *alaylı* officers were also discontented. Considerable resentment existed because, as a rule, they were not allowed to perform the duties of their rank in the field exercises. Instead, these duties were assigned to "educated" officers, who, in many cases, were younger. FO371/544/25648, Barclay to Grey, 20 July 1908. See also Kansu, *1908 Devrimi*, 111–114.

[18] FO371/544/25648, Barclay to Grey, 20 July 1908.

[19] FO371/544/25648, inclosure 1 in no 1, Samson to Barclay, 15 July 1908.

The uprising soon organized itself in militia bands and mobilized volunteers from villages they roamed in small groups. When they visited Christian villages, they were keen on treating the inhabitants well, promising them protection, and in many cases paying in full for the supplies they took.[20] However, there were also complaints and considerable scepticism on the part of the villagers. It did not go unnoticed, for instance, that those making the charm offensive included the very same Ohrid notables who shortly before had been the leaders fighting Bulgarian and Greek bands, and were known for keeping "the villagers in a state of terror".[21] Nonetheless, the attempts of the CUP officers to recruit local supporters among Muslim and Christian alike, as well as notables and villagers, military and civil, etc., indicated their willingness to include a wide range of people, ideas, and interests, which would find another expression during the War of Independence in 1919–22, when the military-bureaucratic leaders of the resistance movement were forced to include local forces in their fight against the central government in Istanbul. Similar to the resistance leaders, the Unionists especially welcomed local notables, a course of action also practised when consolidating their regimes.[22]

Thus, from the early stages of the revolution, the CUP sought legitimacy and justification for their actions in popular backing, propagating the image as a revolutionary movement supported by all the peoples and groups of Rumelia. It was their first open attempt to unify all "Ottomans" under one banner, that of "liberty" and "constitution". To some extent, this image found substance in the general dissatisfaction built up through the long years of Hamidian rule. An appeal was also made to the Great Powers to gain, if not their direct support, at least their tacit approval. Heathcote, the British Consul in Manastir, transmitted a written declaration to the Foreign Office issued by the CUP, that formulated the

---

[20] Niyazi, *Hatırat*; Temo, *Ittihad Ve Terakki*.

[21] FO371/544/25649, Barclay to Grey, 20 July 1908.

[22] As Consul Heathcote wrote, however, this was not without risks as, on the one hand, CUP members were outwardly expending considerable effort on avoiding any action against the Christian population in Macedonia while, on the other, they were evidently trying to draw recruits from all classes of people, whom it was far from certain if they would be able to control when let loose. FO371/25649, inclosure 2 in no 1, Heathcote to Barclay, 13 July 1908.

purpose and goals of the "Ottoman Committee of Union and Progress", summarized by Heathcote as follows:

1. The objective of the Committee is to secure the application of the Constitution of 1876 (1292). The present bad situation of the Empire is wholly due to the existing regime of despotism, favoritism, and corruption. Let Europe recognize that improvement can only be attained by substituting for this a constitutional regime. The Great Powers can show their good-will towards the peoples of Turkey, by earnestly urging His Majesty the Sultan to yield to the legitimate demands of his subjects, who are loyal, though in revolt against the shameful situation of their country.
2. The Committee solemnly declares that it is not hostile to the non-Moslems, but that constitutionalism implies security for the life, honor, and property of all alike.
3. If the Committee sometimes employs "energetic methods", it is only in extreme cases against the enemies of liberty.
4. We avoid useless bloodshed, of which too much has been caused by the government. It may even be feared that the Government will this time again provoke a massacre between Moslems and non-Moslems, to throw the blame on our party.
5. The fighting corps will not attack the villages, but will defend them from the incursions of bands from without, and will preach good will and fraternity.
6. To prove once more the unscrupulousness of the Government, it is sufficient to quote the following recent incident: Semsi Pasha, in order to bring his personal guard of Basibozuks, had represented the Resna affair to them as a Serbian insurrection. Is not the employment of these lawless plunderers a contempt of the friendly advice constantly given by the Great Powers?[23]

---

[23] The British consul, Heathcote, told the Foreign Office that the CUP had begun handing out proclamations to the representatives of the Great Powers. On one such an occasion Heathcote was visited by a civilian "of some standing", who expressed "anxiety lest the strength of the party should be underrated, and its aims misunderstood in Europe, foreseeing that in both these senses misrepresentation might be used against them by their opponents". According to Heathcote, this "civilian" then handed him a paper bearing the seal "Comité d'Union et de Progrés Ottoman". FO371/544/25649, inclosure 2 in no. 1, Heathcote to Barclay, 13 July 1908.

Although the Young Turk Revolution has been referred to as "bloodless",[24] it in fact claimed several victims, as the CUP launched a series of assassinations against high-profile figures, including Şemsi Pasha, who had been instructed to quell the rebellion, Sadık Pasha, the sultan's A.D.C., and Osman Hidayet Pasha, the commander of the Manastır garrison, who was shot while announcing an imperial edict.[25] More significantly, not only did the government appear unable to prevent the violence perpetrated by the CUP, but it also seemed to have lost control of its armed forces, illustrated most strikingly by the unwillingness of the Macedonian troops to suppress the rebellion. This was especially evident among the officers of the Third Army stationed in Manastır showing clear signs of sympathy for the rebelling officers. From their unrest would soon spread to Salonica, making these two major cities of Ottoman Macedonia, not only home to the Third Army but also the two main branches of the CUP, the epicentre of events.

Subsequent defections from the army demonstrated that a growing number of Unionists were willing to participate in the movement.[26] Shortly before the reinstatement of the new constitution, Hilmi Pasha, the inspector general of Rumelia, wrote to the sultan, expressing the seriousness of the situation and stating that most of the officers in the Third Army were loyal to the CUP.[27] The sultan in a last desperate attempt dispatched additional troops from Anatolia, but to no avail, as they also refused to engage the rebel forces, which suggests that the activities of the CUP were not held to be illegitimate in military circles, with Macedonian and Anatolian officers passively supporting its cause.[28] The CUP then decided to proclaim the constitution on 23 July in various cities in Macedonia, such as Manastır, Üsküp, and Seres, hoping that it would inspire

---

[24] FO371/545/29286, Lowther to Grey, 16 August 1908. See also Der Matossian, "From Bloodless Revolution."

[25] FO371/544/25086, Barclay to Grey, 15 July 1908; FO371/544/26958, Barclay to Grey, 28 July 1908.

[26] FO371/544/25649, inclosure 2 in no 1, Heathcote to Barclay, 13 July 1908.

[27] FO371/544/25303, Barclay to Grey, 16 July 1908.

[28] FO371/544//25514, Barclay to Grey, 22 July 1908.

similar action throughout the empire.[29] They also sent a series of ultimatums to the sultan, who finally gave in. On the same day, an imperial decree was issued restoring the Ottoman constitution of 1876.

The Reception

On the first day of the proclamation of the constitution, Istanbul was quiet. It seemed that the capital's population was hesitant about rushing into the streets to celebrate, which must be seen in the context of decades of espionage and political oppression. Such an act of support could result in unpredictable government reactions. Therefore, Ahmet Emin Yalman notes in his memoires, the initial popular response consisted merely of shouting "Long live the Sultan" to the military detachments passing through the streets.[30] The safest way to express enjoyment of the new constitution seemed to be to offer gratitude to the sultan. In contrast, in Salonica, close to the epicentre of the revolution, officers and civilian CUP members made great efforts to inform people of what was going on. They delivered speeches to crowds from government buildings and hotel balconies, in favour of "liberty" (*hürriyet*) and representative government. It was only two days later, on the 25th, that people seemed to feel secure enough to generate expressions of enthusiasm for the event. Halide Edip describes the general atmosphere:

> The first two months of the constitutional regime belong to lyric art rather than to critical history. The collective emotion was so strong, the rejoicing over the principles of liberty, equality, and justice so intense, that no one in Turkey who has lived through those moments can ever think of them without being profoundly stirred. It was the delirium of the French Revolution without its bloodshed. People kissed and embraced each other instead of tearing out each other's throats. Never before or since in Ottoman history have all the "elements" believed in the same ideal and loved the same country.[31]

Upon first encountering Halide Edip's description, one might question the validity of the claim, but there are numerous accounts that

---

[29] FO371/544/25703, Lamb to Grey, 24 July 1908.
[30] Yalman, *Gördüklerim*, I, 68.
[31] Adıvar, *Conflict*, 71.

support this assertion, that the constitution, after the initial hesitation, was greeted with immense joy throughout the empire, and was well-received in Europe as well. The Young Turks were portrayed as the reincarnations of the French revolutionaries who were united by the call for *liberté, égalité, fraternité* (which in Ottoman Turkish was translated as *hürriyet, müsavat, uhuvvet,* respectively). However, in the Ottoman context, other concepts were also added, such as justice (*adalet*), unity (*ittihad*), order (*nizam*), progress (*terakki*), and homeland (*vatan*).[32] These concepts were not new to the Ottoman public at that time, as they had been central themes in the Young Ottoman movement.[33] Furthermore, the concept of *adalet* (justice) constituted a well-known and enduring principle with roots in Islamic political theory and classic Ottoman thought revolving around the notion of "the ideal order".[34]

In the aftermath of the "proclamation of liberty" (*hürriyetin ilanı*), the Ottoman capital witnessed a rapid proliferation of political and cultural clubs, along with a significant increase in the publication of newspapers and political pamphlets. According to Halide Edip, "It seemed as if the 'nationalities question' had been solved, social conventions and religious traditions had been shaken, and the Ottoman state had begun a process of revitalization".[35] The impact of the revolution was particularly evident in Macedonia, which had been embroiled in a territorial dispute since the Russian-Ottoman War of 1877–78, with Bulgarian and Greek bands

---

[32] These slogans and symbols of the revolution were most colorfully depicted in the postcards from this period. See in that regard Kutlu, *Didar-ı Hürriyet,* 97–125.

[33] The Young Turk self-image as someone taking over from earlier movements, such as the Young Ottoman and the Tanzimat reformer, is illustrated by a postcard with the heading "The revival of the Ottoman Sublime State" (*Devlet-i Aliye-i Osmaniye'nin İhyası*), depicting at the center a young woman on her knee chained up in arms and legs. She is surrounded by Namık Kemal, Prince Sabahaddin, Midhat Pasha and Fuad Pasha trying to help her up, while Enver and Niyazi with hammer and iron in hand are busy breaking her chains. Just above them is another female angel like figure holding over them a banner with the writing, *hürriyet, müsavat, uhuvvet* (liberty, equality, fraternity). For a reprint of this postcard, see Kutlu, *Didar-ı Hürriyet,* 105.

[34] Reinkowski, *The State's Security,* 204–205.

[35] Adıvar, *Conflict,* 71.

fighting among themselves and against Muslims.[36] In its immediate aftermath, the 1908 revolution resulted in a cessation of hostilities,[37] and Enver Bey, upon his return to Salonica, was greeted by "all nationalities in manifestations of popular rejoicing".[38] With an announcement that arbitrary government now had disappeared, he further claimed: "Henceforth, we are all brothers. There are no longer Bulgars, Greeks, Romans, Jews, Muslims; under the same blue sky we are all equal, we find glory in being Ottomans".[39]

In Serres a number of priests and officers, including the general in command of the garrison, reportedly made their way into the town hall, and swore an oath to the employees there that they would support the revolution on behalf of the constitution.[40] Meanwhile, in Istanbul, the district governor suggested that the head of the local Bulgarian committee and a Greek archbishop embrace each other, which they did. Additionally, the Bulgarian representative and the Greek consul were informed that violent activities that had been going on previously, would in the future be met with severe punishment.[41] According to Harry Lamb, British Consul-General at Salonica, a *mullah* proclaimed from a hotel window that a sultan who ruled unjustly could be legally dethroned.[42] However, it appears that not all individuals were in favour of the revolution. For instance, fellow officers escorted an officer who commanded the troops at Üsküb (Skopje) to the railway station after he refused to support the movement for a constitution.[43] He was forced to leave for Salonica.

On 25 July, Ottoman newspapers announced that the freedom of the press had been reinstated. Simultaneously, lengthy articles appeared that extolled the sultan for his wisdom and graciousness in restoring

---

[36] On the guerilla bands and violence in Ottoman Macedonia, see Yosmaoğlu, *Blood Ties*.

[37] FO371/544/27632, Lowther to Grey, 31 July 1908; FO371/544/28463, Lowther to Grey, 11 August 1908.

[38] FO371/544/25877, Lamb to Grey, 25 July 1908.

[39] Miller, *Ottoman Empire*, 476.

[40] FO371/544/25632, Barclay to Grey, 23 July 1908.

[41] FO371/544/25888, Barclay to Grey, 26 July 1908.

[42] FO371/544/25891, Lamb to Grey, 26 July 1908.

[43] FO371/544/25748, Barclay to Grey, 24 July 1908.

the constitution. These articles appealed to all of his subjects, regardless of their religion or ethnicity, to use their newly acquired freedom for the common good of all Ottoman citizens and to express the happiness felt by all classes for the beginning of this new era.[44] Some newspapers even referred to the date as "year one" (*sene bir*).[45] In Istanbul, a crowd of 50,000 people first proceeded to the Sublime Porte and then to the Ministry of War, the office of the *Sheikh-ul-Islam*, and finally to the Ministry of Finance. The *Sheikh-ul-Islam* offered a prayer for the sultan, and the ministers swore oaths to serve their country, remain loyal to the sultan, and uphold the cause of liberty.[46] Subsequently, the sultan declared an amnesty, and on 26 July, all political prisoners in Istanbul were released. In addition, the amnesty extended to all political exiles and fugitives, whose total count had reached 140,000, of which 60,000 were Muslim and the remaining were Armenian.[47] Nevertheless, the amnesty was not universal—the prisoners in Konya for instance were not as fortunate. Only the political prisoners were released there, which caused dissatisfaction among the ordinary inmates, who therefore rioted, resulting in the death of two prisoners at the hands of their guards.

The reality of the revival of the constitution was becoming increasingly evident as the inhabitants of the capital rejoiced, decorating the city with great care, followed by enthusiastic demonstrations at public places. The prevailing rhetoric emphasized that this was a manifestation of the general will to unite for the sake of the empire, with loyalty to both the sultan and the constitution. The grand vizier addressed a gathering of several thousand Muslims and Christians at the Sublime Porte (the office of the grand vizier) and was met with enthusiastic applause. One observer remarked that "The crowd is animated with good humour, and it is remarkable to see the fraternization of Moslems and Christians, especially Armenians".[48] Then a speech was delivered by members of the CUP declaring the dawn of a period of liberty and fraternity under the constitution, followed by a prayer by one of the Muslim clerics, and a Greek bishop addressing

---

[44] FO371/544/25885, Barclay to Grey, 25 July 1908.
[45] E.g. the Ottoman periodical, *Anadolu*.
[46] Kansu, *1908 Devrimi*, 138.
[47] Ibid, 140.
[48] FO371/544/25887, Barclay to Grey, 25 July 1908; FO371/544/25754, Barclay to Grey, 24 July 1908.

the people in both Greek and Turkish. The ceremony concluded with an artillery salute.

Since the public discourse frequently included affirmations of loyalty and respect for the sultan along with the praise of the constitution, the CUP, as the champion of the revolution, was eager to prevent the sultan from stealing the scene by claiming credit for reinstating the constitution. This fear was not unfounded; as Kazım Karabekir (1882–1948)[49] notes in his memoirs, many people saw the constitution as a gift bestowed by the sultan.[50] Even the students from the military academy, *Harbiye*, who demonstrated in the streets in support of the constitution, shouted along the way "long live the sultan!"[51] In response, Kazim Karabekir and his fellow officers, aided by members of the CUP, drafted and circulated a proclamation to students and the general public, emphasizing that "liberty" was not a gift bestowed by the sultan but had been attained through tremendous effort and sacrifice by the CUP.[52]

While not all officers shared Karabekir's patience in raising public awareness about the revolution's true leaders, some were willing to resort to violent means if necessary. At this point, it is interesting to follow the moves of a particular officer and his troops during the early days of the proclamation of the Constitution. On 23 July 1908, Ruşen Bey, a young *kolağası*,[53] arrived in Drama from Salonica with 100 soldiers and 20 officers under his command. Ruşen delivered a speech explaining the reasons for the rebellion, starting with the injustices of the current government. He emphasized the fraternity of all nationalities under the Ottoman flag and the urgent need to establish a constitutional government to save the Ottoman Empire from complete ruin. He presented the CUP's motto

---

[49] At the time of the revolution, Karabekir was a staff officer in the Third Army in Macedonia. He was a prominent member of the CUP, working closely with Enver to establish the crucial cell in Manastir, which became the driving force for the rest of the movement. He continued to play important roles throughout the Second Constitutional Period, the National Struggle, and the early republican period. For more detail on Karabekir, see Zurcher, *Legacy*, 19.

[50] Karabekir, *İttihat ve Terakki*, 339–341.

[51] Ibid.

[52] *Tanin*, 15 Temmuz 1324 (28 July 1908).

[53] A *kolağası* was an officer who ranked above a captain and below a major in the Ottoman army.

as "the fatherland, liberty, equality, fraternity", and stressed the importance of eliminating distinctions of race and religion under the Ottoman government. Ruşen concluded by instructing the soldiers to enter the town and proclaim a constitutional government, warning that anyone who resisted, regardless of rank or position, would be shot dead and their body left where it fell until evening.[54]

Furthermore, Ruşen's activities can be traced through British reports detailing his involvement in other incidents. In one case, Ruşen publicly exposed two police officers who had allegedly beaten a Christian while under the influence of alcohol.[55] They stood before a crowd of people as Ruşen announced that the CUP had condemned them to death but did not wish to dishonour the new liberty with such a violent act. Instead, the police officers had their buttons, badges, and stripes cut off with a pocketknife in front of the crowd, after which they were imprisoned and a telegram was sent to Hilmi Pasha requesting permission for further punishment. In another incident, Ruşen had a *hoca* (a Muslim cleric), who was accused of being a spy for fifteen years; confess his crimes under oath while a revolver was pointed at his head. After kissing him, Ruşen accepted him again as a *hoca*, read out his death sentence, but commuted it, stating that it was a day for the people, and they did not want bloodshed. In yet another case, a Muslim reportedly insulted a Christian in a café in the presence of several revolutionary officers and was immediately arrested and taken to prison. In another instance, Ziya Pasha, the district governor, was made to pay money to Ruşen's soldiers after Ruşen claimed that the conscience of Ziya Pasha had awakened and was demanding he return the gold he had stolen.

On 28 July, people in Edirne gathered to celebrate the reinstatement of the constitution and the proclamation of liberty. A group of Unionist officers from Salonica, including Ruşen, were present at the celebrations. When people began to cheer, "Long live the sultan!" the group from Salonica was surprised. Ruşen nervously gave a speech emphasizing that the reinstating of the constitution was not the work of the sultan, but of the CUP. He became so angry that he slashed at the pro-sultan bills with his sword. According to reports, the crowd, both civilian and military, became very excited and thought that the officers from Salonica intended

---

[54] FO371/544/26956, inclosure 1 in no. 1, Bonham to Barclay, 23 July 1908.
[55] FO371/544/26956, inclosure 3 in no. 1, Bonham to Barclay, 25 July 1908.

to overthrow the sultan. About 350 soldiers travelled to Istanbul by train to check if the sultan was still alive and, finding that he was, declared their support for the constitution and loyalty to him—whereupon the CUP also publicly declared loyalty to both the constitution and the sultan who had reinstituted it.[56]

As news about the "proclamation of liberty" spread from the focal point of the events, Salonica, Manastır, Edirne, and Istanbul, to other areas of the Empire, it became evident that there was a range of sentiments, including confusion, excitement, and anticipation. At the same time, differences emerged on various levels. In some cities, protests were accompanied by assaults on high-ranking officials of the previous regime, including governors, and resulted in their forced resignations.[57] While in some cities, such as *Avlonya* (Valona), the proclamation of the constitution was hailed with great enthusiasm, with Christians and Muslims embracing one another in the streets, at *Işkodra* (Scutari), for example, the Muslim Albanians received the news with indifference, perhaps, as Kansu notes, fearing that they would lose their privileges vis-à-vis the Christians. Kansu argues that the constitution was not so vigorously welcomed in the Arab provinces; however, examples provided by British reports suggest this was not the case in every province.[58] In Beirut, for instance, the rejoicing lasted for over a week, culminating in a grand celebration at which 15,000 people were present.[59] The British consul reports that it "terminated in a tableau in which a *hoca* and a priest embraced one another, while an Ottoman officer stood behind with a drawn sword signifying that he protected both alike".

In specific areas, such as Konya, which had a Muslim majority population and was known for its religious inclination, the CUP took additional measures to emphasize their reverence for the Ottoman throne and religious beliefs. The CUP delegation was greeted with enthusiasm, accompanied by cheering for the sultan, the army, and liberty.[60] In

---

[56] Kutlu, *Didar-ı Hürriyet*, 118.

[57] Kansu, *1908 Devrimi*, 150–51.

[58] Ibid.

[59] FO371/545/29292, Lowther to Grey, 18 August 1908.

[60] FO371/545//27649, inclosure in no. 1, Doughty-Wylie to Lowther, 1 August 1908.

Salonica, the Committee presented a flag to each man in the local regiment on which had been printed "liberty and progress" (*hürriyet ve terakki*) or "the nation and liberty" (*millet ve hürriyet*). The flags were attached to every rifle and the soldiers had been told to take them to their villages. The British consul reports that he was presented with two of these flags afterwards as souvenirs, which for him was above all a "proof of this clever means of spreading the Young Turkey idea".[61] The imams and *hatibs* (preachers) were instructed to preach in the mosques on the new constitution, and in favour of the "non-abuse of liberty, brotherhood with the Christians, equality, and the unchangeable law of religion".[62]

Freedom of the "People"?

"Freedom" (*hürriyet*) and "despotism" (*istibdat*) were the words most widely used in order to differentiate the new era of the constitution from the old. While "freedom" became synonymous with "constitution", epitomized by the common name given to the revolution of 1908 as the "proclamation of freedom" (*hürriyetin ilanı*), Abdulhamid's authoritarian rule stood for the "era of despotism" identified as the cause of all the shortcomings and injustices in the affairs of state and society, including problems relating to separatist nationalism.[63] Instead of providing clear definitions of the ideals of the revolution and a concrete policy roadmap, the overall rhetoric focused on what the revolution was reacting against, i.e. the Hamidian regime and its accumulated complex set of problems. Significantly, the early phase of the revolution created a political atmosphere where people now had the chance to raise their voices publicly, as shown by the sheer number of complaints sent to the newspapers asking for all wrongs to be corrected because the new era of freedom had arrived.[64] According to a prominent newspaper of the time, it was generally expected that people's wishes now would receive attention and that

---

[61] Ibid.
[62] Ibid.
[63] Hüseyin Kazım Kadri, *Hatıralarım*.
[64] Topuz, *Basın Tarihi*, 82–83.

the new constitutional government would remedy the wrongful restrictions of the old "era of despotism", which was remembered as a period when people were not allowed to criticize anything.[65]

Apart from framing the revolution as a contrast to the Hamidian regime and stating broad goals like justice, prosperity, and unity for all Ottomans, on a more concrete level the implications of the pervasive slogans of the revolution were far from clear. This ambiguity presented both advantages and disadvantages for the new regime, especially when faced with the challenges of realizing the grandiose goals promised. Hence, in public discourse, freedom and constitutional government had various meanings relating to national identity, state administration, local government, the economy, infrastructure, municipal services, education, judiciary, and more. As a British report states, for a peasant, it above all meant being exempt from taxes; for a townsperson, an end to bribery, and better municipal services; and an educated bureaucrat, promotion by merit not through favouritism.[66] For the urban population, it meant order and effectiveness in the bureaucracy, justice in the courts, improvement in agriculture and trade, good education for their children, similar concrete developments, and security from oppressive power-holders.

In connection with the parliamentary elections during the fall of 1908, the CUP launched various initiatives to demonstrate its popular and legitimate nature.[67] CUP delegations were dispatched to engage with local communities and disseminate information about the Committee and the new constitutional regime. The delegations' messages revolved around the advantages of constitutional government, the CUP's efforts to realize it, the importance of national unity and economic development, the rights and responsibilities of the state towards its citizens and vice versa, and the necessity for the public to elect suitable representatives to the parliament.[68]

During the elections, the reputation of the CUP as a liberator and the champion of the revolution had gained general recognition. In the absence of party politics and competing ideologies, as even the CUP named and presented itself as a "society" (*cemiyet*) with a sacred mission,

---

[65] *Ikdam*, 15 Ağustos 1324 (28 August 1908).
[66] FO371/544/26572, Barclay to Grey, 26 July 1908.
[67] Kayalı, "Elections and the Electoral Process", 271–272.
[68] Kansu, *1908 Devrimi*, 275–278.

the CUP was viewed as the all-encompassing representative body of the Young Turks and the primary advocate of the discourse of freedom and constitution.[69] Hence, during the elections, the CUP saw no need to present itself as a political adversary of a rival party. This, however, had the disadvantage that the CUP was unable to establish a specific political-ideological stance beyond the image as a champion of the constitution and "freedom", who had freed the country from despotism. This ideological and conceptual fluidity, and the corresponding greater emphasis on concrete action and a growing aversion to the opposition, based on a highly adjustable idea of a sacred mission to save the state, in the face of unfolding events, would constitute a recurrent and characteristic theme of the Unionist regime.

The pragmatism of the CUP was also demonstrated by the attitude of the delegations towards local power-holders, such as the *ulema* (the Muslim learned class), large landowners, merchants, and notables. Given the indirect, two-stage electoral system the outcomes of the upcoming elections would be highly dependent on the existing local power structures and socioeconomic conditions. Forging local networks and political alliances would therefore be critical to the future of the CUP.[70] With this in mind, the CUP pursued a primarily strategic course of action, as the delegations to the provinces sought to establish good relationships with those who were likely to win parliamentary seats, where the CUP was, as Kayalı points out, more interested in a pro-CUP parliament than a specific ideological makeup.[71] As it was far from clear what CUP exactly stood for ideologically, even whom the CUP actually consisted of and was led by,[72] a vastly heterogeneous group of people found themselves listed as CUP

---

[69] Although the Ottoman Freedom Party (*Osmanlı Ahrar Fırkası*), the single rival of the CUP, was established on 14 September 1908, it was, firstly, an early offshoot from the CUP, and secondly, could not organize in the provinces, see Rıza Nur, *Hürriyet ve İtilaf*. See also Kayalı, "Elections and the Electoral Process," 271.

[70] These local networks and alliances were to prove crucial during the armistice period (1918–22). Moreover, the same strategies were used by Atatürk's Republican People's Party, which worked closely with local power brokers in rural areas, regardless of whether they agreed with Kemalist principles and policies—which they often did not—but were loyal to the governing party.

[71] Kayalı, "Elections and the Electoral Process", 271.

[72] Thus, for a long time, it was far from clear who the CUP consisted of and who its leaders were. Its decision-making process and organizational structure were also shrouded in mystery. Answers to these questions were kept a secret until the very end, and were

candidates. This, in turn, resulted in a highly diverse and colourful parliamentary assembly filled with CUP list members opposing CUP Central Committee ideas and policies.

EARLY DISAPPOINTMENTS AND THE END OF EUPHORIA

While the parliamentary elections were still underway, and the CUP celebrating the ideals of the revolution in its campaigns, it was confronted by a number of shocking events putting an abrupt end to the initial optimism of the revolution. The first major crisis occurred in October 1908, when Bulgaria, which had gained autonomy according to the Treaty of Berlin in 1878, declared its independence from the Ottoman Empire.[73] The next day, Austria-Hungary announced its annexation of Bosnia-Herzegovina, followed soon after by Crete's decision to unite with Greece.[74] The bleak geopolitical Ottoman realities, not the least the part involving Great Power interests and interventions, were obviously catching up with the Young Turks at an alarming rate. As shown by British archival records, in fact, there had been ongoing diplomatic manoeuvring behind the scenes since the early days of the revolution.[75] Although the grand vizier, reacting to rumours in the press throughout September about a possible proclamation of Bulgarian independence, was quick to inform foreign diplomatic representatives that the Ottomans would never approve of such a thing, in reality, his government was highly limited in its ability to respond.[76]

only partially answered by the tribunals established after the end of World War I. For a discussion on the CUP leadership cadres, see Tunaya, *Siyasal Partiler*, III, 298–305.

[73] FO371/544/25969, Buchanan to Grey, 22 July 1908.

[74] According to the Berlin Treaty of 1878, Bosnia-Herzegovina was under nominal Ottoman sovereignty although occupied and governed by Austria. The same treaty granted Bulgaria—excluding Eastern Rumelia and Macedonia—a semiautonomous Bulgarian principality, again under nominal Ottoman sovereignty.

[75] FO371/545/29214, Grey to Lowther, 20 August 1908. According to a British report, a Bulgarian representative had given the British consul assurances that the Bulgarian Government would avoid doing anything that might increase the difficulties and uncertainties in the aftermath of the Young Turk Revolution, and would therefore make no attempt to take advantage of the Ottomans' situation (FO371/544/25627, Buchanan to Grey, 23 July 1908). See also FO371/544/25969 and FO371/545/27691 on Bulgaria's stance towards the Young Turk movement and the revolution generally.

[76] Ünal, "Ottoman Policy", 148, 162, 166–167.

Therefore, when Bulgaria finally declared its independence on 5 October 1908, the Ottoman government, unprepared for effective countermeasures, let alone war, not least due to the disorganization resulting from the revolution, could do little more than maintain an initial hesitant attitude. Indicatively, following an emergency meeting at the grand vizier's house, a telegraphic protest was sent to the great powers on 6th October, "asking them to safeguard the interests of Turkey".[77] In the meantime, this relative passivity was perceived as indifference by Ottoman minorities, including Albanians, as reflected by the memoirs of Ismail Kemal, an Ottoman Albanian politician at the time.[78] According to Ismail Kemal, Albanians saw it as a clear sign of indifference on the part of the Ottoman government to the interests of Albanians, highlighting the schism between the interests of Ottoman peoples and the power politics of the Unionists.

The Ottoman government on its part, unable to act more forcefully and effectively through diplomacy or by showing military muscle, turned, in a desperate attempt to compensate, to the "people" and sought to unite all Ottomans by appealing to patriotic feelings and emphasizing the danger posed by hostile European powers seeking to weaken and dismember the Ottoman homeland. What had been lost outwardly would be won inwardly. To that end, the government initiated a general boycott of Bulgarian and Austrian goods throughout the empire, lasting for about six months.[79] Local CUP cadres in provincial towns and cities, along with various organizations coordinating the boycott, such as the Boycott Society (*Boykotaj Cemiyeti*), Society for Economic Warfare (*Harb-i iktisadi Cemiyeti*), and the Ottoman Benevolent Society for Bosnia-Herzegovina (*Bosna-Hersek Cemiyeti Hayriye-i Osmaniyesi*), contributed to the movement.[80] Although the boycott movement did not result in the empire regaining lost territory, it provided the new regime with new economic tools, which were later used in service of the Unionist goal of creating a "national economy" (*milli iktisat*).[81]

---

[77] FO371/551/34753, Lowther to Grey, 7 October 1908.
[78] Ismail Kemal, *Memoirs*, 323–332.
[79] Cetinkaya, *Boycott Movement*, 111; Ünal, "Ottoman Policy", 158.
[80] Cetinkaya, *Boycott Movement*, 78, 111.
[81] Erol, *The Ottoman Crisis*, 140–143.

Additionally, it yielded valuable experiences in the dissemination of political propaganda and mass mobilization based on concepts such as nation, homeland, solidarity, and liberation. These insights into the mechanisms of arousing patriotic feelings on a greater political scale and gaining popular support were further developed during the Balkan Wars, World War I, and the War of Independence.

THE POLITICS OF REVOLUTION

The CUP list won a decisive victory in the first general elections following the revolution. However, as the new parliament that opened on 17 December was to prove the next four years, the election victory did not result in a CUP compliant assembly, far from it, fierce opposition soon surfaced from the parliamentary floor. Moreover, although this was the *second* constitution, the CUP soon found itself navigating unfamiliar political waters in terms of constitutional government, party politics, and a pluralist parliamentary system, which gave rise to dissident voices amplified by a lively press and a vibrant public life requiring persuasive and rhetorical abilities.

It remained to be seen therefore how the champions of the constitution, who had come to power through military means and violent tactics of guerrilla warfare in Rumelia, while legitimizing the political takeover through the representation of the "people", would adapt to this new environment. Nevertheless, the ensuing power struggle between competing factions, including those in Salonica and Istanbul, involving military officers and civilian politicians, new power-holders, and those who had lost their positions and influence made it evident that this would be a very difficult process of transition. While the takeover from the palace created a power vacuum not easily filled, the main contenders for power were the central bureaucracy led by the grand vizier and the ministries of government, and the CUP, relying on the army, which after many decades of restructuring since Mahmud II once again took the centre stage in Ottoman politics.

The political situation during 1908–13 bore interesting similarities to 1920–25. In both cases, different groups united under one overarching cause, but the original clusters of heterogeneous groups were gradually purged and reduced, resulting in the dominance of one of the factions after fierce power struggles. The heterogeneous group at the beginning of the revolution in 1908 was the Young Turk movement, although often used synonymously with the CUP, the former was the broader designation of a coalition, which gradually but definitively was supplanted by the Unionist faction. Similarly, in 1923 Atatürk's People's Party (*Halk Fırkası*) took over and monopolized the resistance movement, the Association for Defence of Rights of Anatolia and Rumelia.

In addition, similar to 1920–25, the period of 1908–13 was marked by conflict between a more radical activist group and a relatively moderate one, indicating the tension between the principles of a constitutional parliamentary regime and the actual power base made up by the army. This process translated itself into one of the enduring legacies of the late Ottoman Empire to the Kemalist republic, in the form of a distinction between the military-bureaucratic state elite on the one hand, and the elected politicians in parliament and government on the other, and a system characterized by political tutelage under the guardianship of a modernizing elite.[82]

This also highlights one of the effects of the Hamidian period on the Unionist generation in terms of political culture, emphasizing the value of secrecy and sacredness. In the self-image of the Unionists, they were the enlightened members of a secret organization entrusted with the sacred mission of saving the Ottoman Empire. A worldview[83] and a mind-set, stemming from a combination of the effects of their modern education, the aversion to the Hamidian regime and its support base, and the violent experiences from the Macedonian provinces.[84] These values continued to play a vital role throughout the second constitutional period, with the CUP asserting itself as "the sacred society" (*cemiyeti mukaddese*).[85]

On the practical level, the CUP faced a critical decision with regard to ruling the empire after the revolution: whether to form a cabinet consisting of its own leaders and thus assume direct rule, or to leave

[82] Heper, "Ottoman Legacy", 64–78; Weiker, *Political Tutelage*, 2–4; Akkoyunlu, *Tutelary Democracy*, 48–51.

[83] As Hanioglu has pointed out, rather than a well-defined ideology, the Young Turk opposition movement (1889–1908) was characterized by a set of ideas, wherein vulgar materialism, positivism and elitism figured prominently. When the movement was overtaken and spearheaded by the young officers of the Third and Second armies stationed in Ottoman Rumelia, the ideological aspects were further toned down, replaced by a much more activist and pragmatic instrumentalist approach. Hanioglu, *Opposition*, 203–212; Hanioglu, *Preparation*, 212–219.

[84] Zürcher, *Legacy*, 97–104, 110–114.

[85] Akşin, *Jön Türkler*, 21.

power and governance in the hands of the experienced statesmen of the older generation who were already known to the public.[86] The latter option was capable of instilling confidence both domestically and abroad, which the young regime needed to counteract the destabilizing effects of the revolution. Yet, such a move would also mean an unbroken continuity with the Hamidian regime, for these statesmen had established their careers under Abdulhamid II, a serious problem when considering the Young Turk movement had fought Abdulhamid for decades and sought to distance itself from all things Hamidian.

At this juncture, however, the CUP was presented with a recurrent problem of modernizing elites in modern Turkish history, the lack of personnel to implement their projected reforms on a wide scale. Hence, the CUP lacked the necessary cadres to replace the high-ranking officials of the previous regime.[87] The relative young age of the Unionists, their inexperience and lack of self-confidence in their ability to govern have been cited as contributing factors in that regard.[88] In the end, the CUP chose a third approach by opting to remain in the background and allow parliamentary politics to develop, while simultaneously attempting to govern from behind the scenes.[89] In this arrangement, prominent CUP members, including the hard-line leaders who controlled the army, worked behind the scenes and exerted pressure on the government to ensure that policies aligned with their own opinions and interests were implemented.[90]

Thus, when the CUP forced Said Pasha to resign as grand vizier shortly after the revolution,[91] the position was entrusted to another member of the old guard, Kamil Pasha.[92] Initially, the latter had been lenient towards the Unionists, refusing to take steps to dissolve the CUP now that its

---

[86] Among these the grandveziers of Abdulhamid, like Kamil and Sait Pashas. Akşin, *Jön Türkler*, 74–78.

[87] Zürcher, *Legacy*, 75.

[88] The leaders of the movement were at the time of the revolution in their 30s, one of the front figures, Enver Bey (1881–1922) being only 27. Other important names included Mehmed Talat (1874–1921), Ahmed Cemal (1872–1922), Dr. Nazim (1870–1926), Ahmed Niyazi (1873–1913). Zürcher, *Unionist Factor*, 19–44.

[89] FO371/545/29286, Lowther to Grey, 16 August 1908.

[90] Akşin, *Jön Türkler*, 21.

[91] Zürcher, *Turkey*, 99.

[92] Sohrabi, *Revolution and Constitutionalism*, 139.

declared goal of reinstating the constitution was achieved. Kamil Pasha's dealings with the CUP showed that the old guard had their own political interests within the equation between the palace, the Sublime Porte, and now the military. As a grand vizier, he saw the CUP, especially in the early days of the revolution, as an opportunity to strengthen the position of the bureaucratic apparatus. Thus, in Kamil Pasha's reasoning the sultan posed a real danger as he might attempt to regain power and reverse the political situation. This suggests that for Kamil Pasha and other experienced statesmen who thought themselves in a position to reassert the dominance of the central bureaucracy, the immediate concern was to maintain the weakness of Abdulhamid and secure the new political system, with the CUP acting as a strong guarantee against reversal vis-à-vis the palace.[93]

Nevertheless, signs of disagreement soon emerged as it became increasingly challenging to determine where the real power lay.[94] The government therefore decided to assert its authority drawing upon oppositional support in parliament, which proved to be a pivotal struggle for survival of both the government and the CUP, ultimately resulting in the CUP's triumph against the old guard within the bureaucratic apparatus and shaping the political trajectory of the second constitutional period.[95] Kamil Pasha's downfall established a form of governance in which the Central Committee (*Merkezi Umumi*), operating from the CUP headquarters in Salonica, continued to function as a non-accountable political body while at the same time wielding substantial powers to influence and constrain the legitimate government.[96]

The side-lining of the old guard did not mean, however, that the CUP had overcome the opposition. On the contrary, the complaints were many and involved different sections of society and population elements.[97] More significantly, the high promises of the revolution regarding good governance, economic development, technological advancements, improved infrastructure, and general welfare for all Ottomans had not

---

[93] Ismail Kemal, *Memoirs*, 323.

[94] FO371/561/43986, Lowther to Grey, 13 December 1908; FO371/760/6295, Lowther to Grey, 11 February 1909.

[95] FO371/760/5984, Lowther to Grey, 14 February 1909.

[96] Turfan, *Rise of the Young Turks*, 147–156, 172–182.

[97] Ibid, 145–148, 156–159.

materialized.[98] Although the end of the era of "despotism" had been proclaimed, the problems of maladministration persisted, with unpopular bureaucrats being appointed to local administrative positions based on the patronage of various pashas and increasing authoritarian tendencies of the new regime.[99] Many individuals had lost their positions as a result of the Revolution, leading to widespread unemployment in the capital, including dismissed spies and officials, who were disgruntled and eager to support any opposition to the CUP regime.[100] The fate of members of the palace's inner circle, through whom Abdulhamid had ruled,[101] remained uncertain, and social unrest was on the rise, finding expression in the form of an increasing number of strikes and protests.[102] Furthermore, the plans for compulsory military service for Muslims and non-Muslims raised issues, not least among the *medrese* students (Islamic schools) formerly exempt from military service, who were apprehensive about the prospects of conscription.[103] Moreover, while the Ottoman administration found itself in a state of confusion, the oppositional factions were forming within the military as well, aggravated by the discharge of thousands of officials and military officers since the revolution.

The Counterrevolution Attempt

Eventually, the widespread discontent in the capital culminated in the dramatic events of March–April 1909, as a violent showdown between the CUP and the opposition in what is commonly known as the "31 March incident" (*31 Mart olayı*). Significantly, this counterrevolution attempt was to deliver one of the key components of political discourse and symbolism of the second constitutional period and the Kemalist republic: the notion of *irtica* (Islamic reaction), portrayed subsequently as the main antagonist of progress and modernity, and thus the counter-image of the reformist Unionist/Kemalist elites.[104] Despite the traditional labelling as

---

[98] FO371/545/29286, Lowther to Grey, 16 August 1908.
[99] Şerif, *Bir Muhalifin Hatıraları*, 20–29.
[100] Knight, *Awakening*, 233–238.
[101] Sohrabi, *Revolution and Constitutionalism*, 139–140.
[102] Knight, *Awakening*, 237–239.
[103] FO371/107/108, 13/14 April 1909.
[104] Tunaya, *İslamcılık Cereyanı*, vol. II, 39–41, 62–67.

a blueprint of Islamic reaction, the narrative has been seriously questioned by later scholarship, drawing a much more complex picture.[105] While the actual organizers and connections in the counterrevolution attempt remain uncertain, it is evident that several factors and factions were involved, hardly surprising as numerous groups at this point were highly antagonistic to the CUP for different motives. Not restricted to the Islamic-oriented groups, it for instance also included the liberal opposition.[106]

More importantly, the 31 March incident laid bare the new political role of the military and the power dynamics within the new regime. During the incident, the known faces among the Unionists were forced to flee the capital to Rumelia, a clear indication of the geographical aspect of the CUP regime. From their power base in Rumelia, Unionist officers formed the Action Army[107] (*Hareket Ordusu*), launching a full-scale military operation to retake the capital. Crushing the uprising, the CUP at the same time gained a pretext to carry out sweeping purges against opposition groups. Among those targeted, however, Abdulhamid II was singled out as the mastermind orchestrating the counterrevolution behind the scenes. Despite his new position as a constitutional monarch whose powers were seriously curbed, Abdulhamid's continued presence clearly unsettled the Unionists. As the Unionist fleeing from the capital had shown, the CUP regime was still unstable, especially in the imperial centre, where a central figure such as Abdulhamid could still step

---

[105] Sohrabi, *Revolution and Constitutionalism;* Türesay, "Political Victims", 78–86.

[106] While Kansu describes the counterrevolution as a "well-organized monarchist scheme to restore the absolutist regime" and, therefore, not a "spontaneous outburst of religious reaction," Zürcher points to the liberal opposition, *Ahrar*, as "the original instigator" who intended to "use the religious groups" against the Unionists but lost any control whatsoever soon after the start of the revolt. Kansu, *Post-Revolutionary Politics*, 118; Zürcher, *Young Turk Legacy*, 81.

[107] Led by Mahmud Şevket Pasha, the Action army included among its commanding officers included Mustafa Kemal (Atatürk) and Kazım Karabekir.

in to regain some of his power.[108] Thus, the incident provided a valuable opportunity to remove Abdulhamid and replace him with a more compliant ruler, Mehmed Reşad.[109]

Consequently, the CUP's grip on Ottoman politics was strengthened with the support of the Action Army, effectively making the Central Committee (*Merkezi Umumi*) in Salonica the dominant force in Ottoman political life. Now there was a grand vizier appointed and directed by the Unionists and a sultan whose position relied entirely on their support. At the same time, the CUP assumed a more active and responsible role in government affairs, with two of its prominent members, Cavit and Talat, becoming Minister of Finance and Minister of the Interior respectively, in Hilmi Pasha's cabinet.[110] Additionally, a plan was implemented to hire Unionist supporters as undersecretaries in various government departments.[111] To gain more effective control in parliament, the CUP also formed its own political party, the Union and Progress Party (*Ittihad ve Terakki Fırkası*), which, however, remained subordinate to the real power still held by the Central Committee, a situation that persisted until the end of the Unionist era.[112]

Moreover, a new instrument of power was introduced, martial law, another lasting legacy to the Turkish republic, enabling the military-bureaucratic establishment to intervene in governance outside of the ordinary constitutional channels. Also, a variety of strategies was employed by the CUP to maintain its dominance against the opposition, ranging from appeals to patriotic sentiment to more aggressive tactics such as intimidation, accusations of "reaction", and later even kidnapping, assault, and murder.[113] The CUP saw these measures as necessary for securing the

---

[108] Abdulhamid had indeed tried very early on to retain some of his power by insisting on his right to appoint the minister of war and navy, which the Unionists perceived as an alarming attempt to regain control. See in this regard FO371/545/27647, Lowther to Grey, 4 August 1908; FO371/545/27648, Lowther to Grey, 5 August 1908; FO371/545/27647, Lowther to Grey, 4 August 1908; FO371/545/28455, Lowther to Grey, 10 August 1908.

[109] *Geveze*, 19 Nisan 1324 (2 May 1908).

[110] Subsequently, Gabriel Efendi (Nouradoungyan), a politician loyal to the old regime, was replaced by Hallajyan Efendi, another Unionist politician, in the autumn 1909.

[111] Turfan, *Rise of the Young Turks*.

[112] Tunaya, *Siyasal Partiler*, III, 252–263.

[113] *Geveze*, 1 Nisan 1325 (14 April 1909).

constitution and ensuring a majority in parliament, as was reflected in articles written by Hüseyin Cahit (Yalçın) in the leading Unionist newspaper, *Tanin*, which branded parliamentarians who sought to pursue independent policies and to persuade others to vote against the Unionist party as enemies of the constitution.[114] While the debates in the parliament and press grew more intense and unruly, and the CUP increased its repressive measures, the opposition gained strength as well, both in parliament and outside it.

---

[114] *Tanin*, 26 Ağustos 1325 (8 September 1909).

CHAPTER 5

Identity Policies in Action

It is said that the use of the term "ethnic nationality" constitutes an opposition to Ottoman unity. However, whether an Ottoman is Bulgarian, Arab, or Turkish is not a barrier to unity. If there is something that drives us towards unity, it is our common interests. When our interests are mutual, unity can still be achieved even though the concept of ethnic nationality is retained.[1]

There should be consensus among the citizens on issues regarding the life of the state. This means they must view and envision the future of the state in the same manner and be trained accordingly. Naturally, this is the objective sought by the government and the constitution. The aim is to standardize education and training. All Ottomans should learn Ottoman history in the same way. Whenever something related to our national heritage is mentioned, everyone's heart should beat with the same passion. Is it not so? This is an important goal.[2]

These statements made on the parliamentary floor by Hristo Dalcef Efendi, a Bulgarian Ottoman MP representing Seres, and Ibrahim Hakkı Pasha, a prominent Ottoman general of Turkish origin and an MP representing Amasya, serve to illustrate some of the distinct notions and discourses surrounding Ottoman unity. These views varied widely

---

[1] MM ZC, D: 1, S: 2, Cilt. 2, 30 Kanunusani 1325 (12 February 1910), 265.
[2] MM ZC, D: 1, S: 3, Cilt 1, 25 Teşrinisani 1326 (8 December 1910), 467.

depending on the sociopolitical interests and groups involved, while also highlighting the dividing lines between them. The surge in the establishment of numerous newspapers and journals in the aftermath of the revolution, paving the way for intense debates and dialogues on critical matters affecting the country, was indicative of the public's eagerness to express their views on issues related to national identity and regarding the conditions for keeping together a multinational empire. The dynamics of the second constitutional period also found its manifestation in the new parliament, which reconvened on 17 April 1908, after a 30-year suspension.

After examining the parliamentary debates and media coverage, it becomes evident that the central point of contention was not the desirability of Ottoman unity itself. The minutes from the sessions demonstrate that both Unionist and opposition parliamentarians, Muslim and non-Muslim members alike, repeatedly expressed their patriotic commitment to the Ottoman cause, while public discourse attests to different population groups readily identifying themselves as "Ottoman". This inclusive sense of Ottomanness was one of the most significant features of Ottomanism, enabling it to adapt and endure according to circumstances and sociopolitical groups. Despite scholarship focusing primarily on separatist ethnic identity formations, the Ottomanist approach presents an alternative aimed at unifying diverse ethnic identities, at least on discursive and imaginary levels.

The disagreement, however, revolved around what this unity required and actually meant on concrete political, social, cultural, and economic levels. Was it to be built on common interests, for instance, in a framework able to include, and respect, various ethnic and national identities, as Dalcef Efendi suggested? Or, did it require something more, such as the homogeneity of education and training mentioned by Ismail Hakkı Pasha, to mould all Ottomans into one nation loyal towards the Ottoman state and safeguarding *its* interests and united on the basis of shared patriotic feelings and perceptions of a national past and future? Not surprisingly, the latter option, representing a more interventionist approach in the lives of Ottoman citizens, was laden with the most potential to cause friction in relation to the population elements of the empire.

In addition, this difference resounded one of the enduring disagreements within the Young Turk movement, which eventually caused it to split at the Young Turk conference in 1902, between the group associated with the positivist intellectual Ahmet Rıza and that supporting

Prince Sabahaddin respectively.[3] The former group later merged with the activist officers in Ottoman Rumelia who subsequently constituted the core of Unionist leadership. In the second constitutional period this divide continued in the main political grouping, the CUP and the liberal faction of the Young Turk movement, which organized itself first in the Ottoman Freedom Party (*Osmanlı Ahrar Fırkası*) and later in the Liberal Alliance Party (*Hürriyet ve Itilaf Fırkası*). As reflected by its party program, the latter viewed Ottoman unity primarily through the lenses of economic and political liberalism, as well as decentralization.[4] In *Tanin*, the CUP's main mouthpiece, Sabahaddin explained the liberal opposition views on Ottoman unity as:

> If there is any preparation in the Ottoman Aegean islands towards throwing themselves into the arms of Greece, it is not centralization that will prevent it, but military force. Military force, however, is increased by national wealth. What increases national wealth? Private initiative! What kind of administration facilitates private initiative? Decentralization! Human history underlines and proves this fact with countless examples. Will we still not see or understand that centralization means taking away freedom, letting the majority trample down the minority and crushing the spirit of private initiative? Decentralization, on the other hand, will bind the Ottomans to the Ottoman state with all their hearts, not only in Istanbul through the parliament, but also in the provinces through provincial councils. Moreover, as it will cause our national trade to expand continuously, it will become evident that we must act in unity against foreign powers, which in turn will serve as a powerful means of mitigating nationalist rivalries. Thus, implementing administrative decentralization and eliminating political centralism will foster greater Ottoman unity and turn it into a formidable force.[5]

Sabahaddin's views sharply contrasted with the prevalent perspective within the CUP Central Committee (*Merkezi Umumi*), with its headquarters in Salonica. With the self-imposed image as the guardians of the constitutional regime, which practically meant actively intervening in the affairs of government behind the scenes, the Central Committee espoused

---

[3] Hanioglu, *Opposition*, 197.

[4] Tunaya, *Siyasi Partiler*, 338–342.

[5] *Tanin*, 26 Teşrinisani 1324 (9 December 1908). See also Sabahaddin, *Türkiye Nasıl Kurtarılabilir*, 64–68, 10–101, 191–192; and Sabahaddin, *Teşebbüs-ü Şahsi ve Adem-i Merkeziyet*.

an increasingly hard-line centralist approach. Highly critical towards this development in Ottoman politics, Sabahaddin repeatedly addressed the issue in the press. In an open letter to the CUP in 1910, for instance, he warned that centralism would bring about nothing but harm to the country, as it was "turning all of Turkey to a graveyard of misery" (*Türkiyeyi baştan başa bir kabristan-ı sefalete çeviren*).[6]

Hence, the content of national identity construction in the second constitutional period would depend highly on the political development and the intricacies of power politics, and thus which groups held state power. The CUP gradually strengthened its rule, especially after the failed counterrevolution attempt in 1909, therefore marking a significant shift towards the centralist perspective, wherein the survival and security of the Ottoman state had top priority. As such, it constituted a coherent element in Unionist thought both before and after the revolution.

As discussed in previous chapters, the Unionist elite, belonging to the military-bureaucratic educational and institutional structure, was preoccupied with the question of how to save the Ottoman state. This was to be accomplished by implementing far-reaching reforms to strengthen and broaden the central authority and at the same time consolidate the new regime, thus establishing a more centralized and unified political structure that could effectively safeguard the empire against external threats and ensure internal stability. In that sense, the centralization drive of the Unionist regime was a continuation of a long trend in Ottoman governance. As mentioned in Chapter 2, throughout the nineteenth century, the empire had already undergone various processes of centralization and restructuring of imperial control. These included attempts by the central government to incorporate remote or less controlled regions into the imperial core, framed as a "civilizing" (*medeniyet*) mission and as a means of disseminating the (new) symbols, traditions, and ideas of the imperial centre to other parts of the empire.[7]

Similarly, the Unionist military and bureaucratic elite pursued a strategy of consolidating state power and extending central authority throughout the empire, hoping to unify the diverse territories and peoples under the imperial political core. Despite opposition at the local level and in parliament, the Unionists believed that centralism and local concerns

---

[6] Sabahaddin, *Mesleğimiz Hakkında Üçüncü ve Son Bir Izah*, 23.
[7] Deringil, *Domains*, 41, 67, 94, 99–103, 151–158, 168–171.

were not mutually exclusive, since integrating the empire would benefit all.[8] They argued that parliamentary representation would ensure regional interests were represented in government and lead to a stronger and more cohesive Ottoman state, able to mobilize resources and manpower more effectively, and thus provide security and prosperity for all its citizens. The Unionist regime then linked centralization of state power and standardization of administrative and fiscal practices with Ottoman nationalism, aimed to foster loyalty and legitimacy among the population through education and language policies in particular, seeking to create a shared sense of national identity that transcended local, ethnic or religious differences.[9]

In practice, however, contemporary critics saw many of the nation-building policies of the CUP regime as cultural, educational, and linguistic homogenization favouring particular population elements. In historiography, these policies are often labelled "Turkification" and regarded as a clear indication of the Unionists'Turkism and chauvinism.[10] Although there is ample evidence for the latter, particularly during the second half of the CUP rule (1913-1918), the exact boundaries, implications, and the timeline of Unionist Turkism and their "Turkification" agenda are still highly debatable, as the scholarship has shown. When did the Unionists become Turkists, and how decidedly so?

Dündar, for instance, sees the Unionists' transition from Ottomanism to Turkism as an evolutionary process, closely linked with the continual loss of territory and the need for readjustment and imaginings of what constituted the "homeland" (*vatan*).[11] Turkism became the Unionists' dominant thought only after the Balkan Wars, Dündar notes, when the loss of the European provinces redirected their attention, by necessity and pragmatism, to Anatolia.[12]

According to Hanioglu, on the other hand, "in the beginning", meaning from the founding of the CUP in 1889 and the early 1890s,

---

[8] Mardin, *Jön Türklerin Siyasi Fikirleri*.

[9] Toprak, *Milli Burjuvazi*, 12-20.

[10] Erol, "'Macedonian Question' in Western Anatolia"; Üngör, *Making of Modern Turkey*, 25-33.

[11] Dündar, *Iskan Politikası*, 36-37.

[12] Ibid, 31.

"the Young Turks advocated Ottomanism".[13] Subsequently, though, they began turning to Turkism sometime at the turn of the century, and decidedly so between 1902–1907.[14] Thus, Hanioglu adds, they were already convinced Turkists at the time of the revolution in 1908. They had a "strong nationalist sentiment", but, as a "tactical stroke", they "sidelined their Turkist ideology into the background out of political opportunism" because such ideas and sentiments were ill-suited to bringing about a successful revolution in the Ottoman imperial setting.[15] Instead, Hanioglu concludes, they promoted Ottomanism as "a useful shield to prop up the decadent Ottoman Empire".[16]

Şerif Mardin, however, points to the Unionists' incoherence and uncertainty, attributing their failure to establish a unifying national identity to their lack of clarity about the national issue even before and during World War I. Despite the growing emphasis on the concept of "Turk" and their increased interest in the Turkish element within the Ottoman population, Mardin argues, they still believed in the unifying power of Ottomanism and Islam.[17]

Centralization and the Nationalities

A notable example of a correlation between centralization and nation-building was the Law on Associations (*Cemiyetler Kanunu*), which was enacted on 16 August 1909 after two months of extensive deliberations in the Assembly of Deputies.[18] The context of the new law was the multitude of organizations, which sprang up in the wake of the 1908 revolution, in the process taking advantage of the newly expanded public freedoms and new channels of communication. Some of them were previous secret revolutionary committees, which were now able to function more openly and legally. However, this development also led to the

---

[13] Hanioglu, "Turkish Nationalism", 87.
[14] Ibid, 95.
[15] Ibid, 94.
[16] Ibid.
[17] Mardin, *Jön Türklerin Siyasi Fikirleri*, 268.
[18] For the law text see *Düstur*, 2. Tertip, vol. I, 604–608.

government's efforts to regulate and monitor the organizations, hence introducing the issue to parliament to establish the legal framework.[19]

The law had far-reaching implications. Notably, Article 6 made it "strictly forbidden to establish secret societies" and introduced extensive measures of state control. Although societies could be established without prior permission, notifying the authorities was required after establishment (Article 2), whereas failing to do so would lead to termination of said society (Article 12).[20] Additionally, Article 7 made it compulsory for societies to keep records of their members, decisions, correspondence, and public announcements, as well as their income and expenses, subject to inspection by judicial and administrative authorities when necessary. Furthermore, Article 14 empowered the government to close down and seize the assets of any society that was found to have been established for subversive or illegal purposes.

As an indication of such purposes were cited activities that posed a threat to the internal or external security of the state. Article 3 stated, "It is impermissible to establish societies based on unlawful principles that contradict the laws and public morality, violate public order and territorial integrity of the state, and aim to change the existing government system or politically separate the various Ottoman population elements from each other".[21] The last part was made more specific by Article 4, according to which it was "forbidden to establish political societies based, in name or essence, on ethnicity[22] or race".[23]

Article 4, which initially was rejected, not once but twice, by the assembly, without much debate, ended up as one of the most controversial

---

[19] MM ZC, D: 1, S: 1, Cilt 4, 6 Haziran 1325 (19 June 1909), 470–471; MM ZC, D: 1, S: 1, Cilt 5, 13 Haziran 1325 (26 June 1909), 27.

[20] A such notification had to contain the society's name, purpose, and administrative centre, as well as the names, professions, and addresses of those members holding responsibility for the society.

[21] *Ahkamı Kavanine ve adabı umumiyeye mugayir bir esası gayrı meşrua veya asayişi memleket ve tamamiyeti mülkiyei Devleti ihlal ve şekli hazırı Hükümeti tağyir ve anasırı muhtelifei Osmaniyeyi siyaseten tefrik maksadına müstenit olmak üzere cemiyetler teşkili caiz değildir.* Düstur, 2. Tertip, vol. I, 604.

[22] Importantly, while the Ottomans constituted a millet, the other nationalities were designated a "kavim".

[23] *Kavmiyyet ve cinsiyet esas ve unvanlarıyla siyasi cemiyetler teşkili memnudur.* Düstur, 2. Tertip, vol. I, 605. See also MM ZC, D: 1, S: 1, Cilt 5, 13 Haziran 1325 (26 June 1909), 27.

issues related to the new law, causing heated debates and staunch opposition, revolving around the concept of Ottomanness and its relationship to ethnic and religious identities within the empire. This dramatic shift from consensus to polarization came about after the persistent efforts of the government to convince the assembly to retain the Article 4. To inform and defend the government's viewpoint on the issue, the Ministry of the Interior sent its undersecretary, Adil Bey, to the Assembly of Deputies with a detailed statement in hand, describing why the government was vehemently opposed to the removal of Article 4 from the Law on Associations. Upon the second down vote, Adil Bey protested.[24] Asked by the president of the Assembly why Article 4 was necessary, Adil Bey responded:

> Adil Bey (Continuing)—It is necessary indeed. Because there are many elements in our country. They have conflicts in their minds. Therefore, it is absolutely impossible to give such permission.
>
> Seyyit Bey (Izmir)—The third and sixth articles are sufficient.
>
> Adil Bey (Continuing) —The opinion of the Ministry is that it is not permissible to establish societies based on ethnicity or race.
>
> Kozmidi Efendi (Istanbul)—Then, how can they preserve their ethnicity?
>
> Adil Bey (Continuing) —They can indeed preserve their ethnicity. However, establishing a society based on ethnicity is harmful for the country.[25]

Adil Bey then read the government's statement on the issue, according to which political societies formed on the basis of ethnicity and race would be detrimental to the country, and that associations highlighting the differences between the various elements of the Ottoman Empire would inevitably lead to divisions and undermine its unity. At that point, the government's concept and perception of "association" (*cemiyet*), and in a

---

[24] Despite objections, that the vote to remove the Article 4 had already passed, the President of the Assembly, had revoked the decision and returned it to the law commission for reprocessing, as a result of the insistence of the Minister of interior, Ferid Pasha, who stated that Article 4 was crucial for the very existence of the Ottoman nation. On 19 July 1909, the Article 4 was rejected a second time, to be revoked yet again. MM ZC, D: 1, S: 1, Cilt 5, 13 Haziran 1325 (26 June 1909), 27; MM ZC, D: 1, S: 1, Cilt 5, 6 Temmuz 1325 (19 June 1909), 437.

[25] MMZC, D: 1, S: 1, Cilt 5, 6 Temmuz 1325 (19 June 1909), 437–438.

wider sense of civil society, was revealed, framed as a fundamental difference between private interests, held by individuals or particular groups in society, and the public interest, represented by those working for the well-being of the Ottoman nation as a whole and the Ottoman state. Defining an association as "a gathering of individuals who, collectively or individually, are engaged in the dissemination of ideas to achieve a specific goal", the statement further claimed that because associations represented private interests and "forces that might even oppose government authority", they "sometimes pose a very serious and constant danger to the peace and stability of a country and its institutions".

Although admitting that Ottoman experiences with political associations based on ethnicity were "not very old", the statement nonetheless listed a number of potential dangers of allowing such associations to form in a multiethnic empire such as the Ottoman. Alluding to the liberal opposition's principles of private initiative and decentralization, the statement claimed that while "some individuals may imagine the granting of the right of association to ethnic and national groups as a step forward towards decentralised rule, it will rather result in the disintegration of the country's organizational structure". Not only that, the statement added, "granting the right of association to various ethnic groups and religious communities will be equivalent to preparing the downfall of the constitution and the partitioning of the Ottoman Empire".

To prevent this from happening, the statement found precedence in the French Revolution, which it repeatedly used as a point of reference, thus apparently suggesting that the general state of affairs in the Ottoman Empire was still that of an ongoing revolution. "In order to create a new order in France", the statement claimed, "The French Revolution first of all sought to establish on a firm basis the unity of the country. It therefore abolished all privileges and associations", and "the National Assembly of the revolution dissolved all associations of the ancien régime, and subsequently allowed the establishment of new associations".

These measures were taken, according to the statement, even though the conditions in revolutionary France were not as critical as in the Ottoman Empire, because:

> the French nation was composed of different ethnicities, but had a shared language and religion, and were enlightened by knowledge (...) in the Ottoman Empire, there are 20 nations, 20 creeds, and 20 languages, most

of whom are submerged in oppressive ignorance and always separate themselves from each other along all kinds of creeds. (...) But let us assume that various elements were allowed to form certain associations. It cannot be expected that these societies will work for the common good of the country. Their goals are naturally limited to protecting their own interests. They will strive to attain domination over other elements and an elevated position for their own kind and nation against the central administration.[26]

Against "some individuals" (*Bazı adamlar*), who "imagined" (*tahayyül*) decentralization but brought disintegration, the statement placed the "patriots" (*Vatanperveran*, lit., the lovers of the homeland), whose primary objective was "to transform the various population elements comprising the state into a unified Ottoman nation". To achieve this, the government claimed, "actions should correspond to the circumstances" (*ef'al, ahvale tevafuk eylemelidir*), and efforts "be made to end conflicts among the children of the homeland (*evladı vatan*) and to eliminate the conditions causing divisions between children of the same country (*aynı memleket evladını*)".

In this respect, the government criticized previous policies of "allowing the various elements to remain divided and live separately", all the while trying to create unity. In this case, the realignment between action and circumstances entailed a readjusted approach to Ottoman unity, this time more keen on eliminating alternative definitions and political manifestations of the nation. As such, it represented a less tolerant and more aggressive variant of Ottoman nationalism. The government defended a prohibition as if it was to combat any division between the elements, and preventing them from organizing politically as a separate millet, even as "Muslims" or as "Turks". Accordingly, only the Ottoman millet was to be promoted by the state.

Overall the CUP did not want nationalist parties and associations to be formed and was especially opposed to the kinds of committee activities that it itself came from and knew all too well. Interestingly, though, the Unionist leadership seemed to ignore the fact that the CUP itself was a secret "association" (or "society") (*cemiyet*). Thus, throughout the constitutional period it maintained the secrecy surrounding its members,

---

[26] Not surprisingly, though, the statement mentioned nothing about another highly relevant principle of the French Revolution in this regard, namely the right to self-determination of peoples.

leadership, operations, finances, and internal structure while situating itself beyond the reach of the very restrictions imposed on societies by the constitution and the Law on Associations. While itself avoiding compliance with said restrictions, however, the CUP used them to suppress its political opponents, as The Law on Associations also applied to political parties, which too were considered societies[27] in the absence of a separate law on political parties. When confronted with criticism on the issue, Unionist spokesmen defended the CUP with the argument that the committee had not conducted its opposition against Abdulhamid II with a Turkish ethnic agenda and that the constitutional revolution had been a collective undertaking of groups and individuals of diverse ethnic origins.[28]

The tone and atmosphere of the discussions, as well as the result, changed drastically after the government intervention through Adil Bey, which was highly indicative of the dynamics and relations between the CUP-backed government and the parliament, and of the attempts to silence or repress alternative representations of Ottomanness and other modes of nationalism, than those sponsored by the governing elite. Further discussions revealed one of the primary aims with Article 4 as the curtailment of nationalist or separatist movements in the empire, particularly the revolutionary armed bands in Rumelia.[29] Following the revolution, these groups had reestablished themselves as "constitutional clubs",[30] but their activities were deemed a threat to the state's unity and security, making them a main target in relation to the new law. Indeed, "clubs" were specifically pointed out in a separate Article.[31] As expected, the government subsequently took extensive measures to suppress the clubs and dismantle their means of resistance, which included disarming procedures in various parts of Rumelia.

The government's statement regarding Article 4 faced criticism from many MPs, however, who argued that it contradicted the fundamental

---

[27] MM ZC, D: 1, S: 1, Cilt 5, 16 Haziran 1325 (26 June 1909), 91.

[28] MM ZC, D: 1, S: 1, Cilt 5, 6 Temmuz 1325 (19 July 1909), 465.

[29] MM ZC, D: 1, S: 1, Cilt 5, 6 Temmuz 1325 (19 July 1909), 440.

[30] Yosmaoğlu, *Blood Ties*, 222–286.

[31] Article 15 stated, "Clubs are also included within the scope of the societies mentioned in this section" (*Kulüpler dahi, işbu fasılda münderiç cemiyetler kabilindedir*). *Düstur*, 2. Tertip, vol. I, 607.

principles of the constitution and Ottomanism, which as a unifying principle transcended ethnic and religious differences. For instance, MPs such as Yorgo Boşo Efendi, Kozmidi Efendi, Ohannes Varteks Efendi, and Zehrap Efendi contended that this article would ultimately harm Ottoman unity. Varteks Efendi emphasized that he was an Armenian Ottoman devoted to Ottomanism. When challenged on the sincerity of his claim, he remarked that he was more pro-Ottoman than those who considered themselves Turkish and that Armenians could not live anywhere else other than within the Ottoman lands.[32]

Yorgo Boşo Efendi, one of the most outspoken and keen discussants on issues pertaining to Ottoman nationhood, wanted clarification of the relation between the diverse ethnic and religious identities held by Ottoman population elements and Ottomanness as a general marker of national identity. More concretely, he asked if one could be an Ottoman with a name like Yorgi, and whether distinct national identities such as Albanian, *Rum*, and other elements prevented them from being Ottoman, which he believed was not the case. He then pointed to the dominant role of Islam and Muslims, and how the non-Muslim elements could continue their existence as Ottomans on equal footing.

Kozmidi Efendi, declaring himself a supporter of complete Ottoman unity, stated that such a unity could not be achieved by trampling on the rights of different elements.[33] In his opinion, organizations such as the *Rum* Ottoman Political Club would not be detrimental to the integrity of the state. In any case, he claimed, no one could deny their own nationality. In addition, if there were distinctions within society, Muslims were already going to the mosque and Christians were going to the church, so associations based on ethnicity, he believed, were an actual necessity.

Tarayan Nali Efendi noted that while the existence of societies, or clubs, based on ethnicity and race, there also existed union clubs (*ittihat kulüpleri*), disseminating the idea of Ottoman union all over Rumelia. While the Committee of Union and Progress played a prominent role, Tarayan Nali Efendi added, the union clubs also included members of various elements and clubs, *Rum*, Albanian, Serbian, Bulgarian alike.[34]

---

[32] MM ZC, D: 1, S: 1, Cilt 5, 6 Temmuz 1325 (19 July 1909), 448.
[33] MM ZC, D: 1, S: 1, Cilt 5, 6 Temmuz 1325 (19 July 1909), 441.
[34] MM ZC, D: 1, S: 1, Cilt 5, 6 Temmuz 1325 (19 July 1909), 440.

Some MPs claimed that the situation was similar to the one in revolutionary France, to which Hallacyan Efendi protested asking what that revolution had produced: "The despotism of Napoleon Bonaparte. Napoleon (noises)".[35] While non-Muslim MP's mostly took the lead in objecting to Article 4, they also did their utmost to make clear their commitment to Ottoman unity and Ottoman identity. Those who objected to the Article repeatedly emphasized the wish to freely practice and express their ethnic identities—the concept of "race" (*cinsiyet*), however, did not draw specific attention during the discussions—while maintaining their Ottomanness. According to several MPs, if this was part of the government's attempt at Ottomanization, it would be understandable, but even if the case, that using coercion in order to inculcate Ottoman unity among the elements would be the wrong method to use, which would only breed staunch resistance and push activities underground. As Kirkor Zöhrap Efendi put it, "You cannot make someone to love by legislation" (*kanunla sevilmez*).[36]

Despite the general dissatisfaction and the ensuing protests, the government's insistence finally paid off, as the parliament passed Article 4, which it had rejected twice before. The price, however, was an agitated and split parliamentary assembly along with issues pertaining to ethnicity and national identity.[37] Then, a few days after the enactment of the Law of Associations, on 21 August 1909, amendments were made to the Ottoman Constitution. Article 120, guaranteeing the right to establish societies, laid down at the same time restrictions similar to those stated in the Law on Associations:

> With the condition of compliance to the law on the subject, the Ottomans have the right of assembly. It is forbidden to establish societies that violate the territorial integrity of the Ottoman state, seek to alter the form of the constitution or government, act against the provisions of the constitution, aim to divide the elements of the Ottoman Empire politically, or are contrary to public morals and manners. Establishing secret societies in general is forbidden.[38]

---

[35] MM ZC, D: 1, S: 1, Cilt 4, 6 Haziran 1325 (19 June 1909), 482–483.

[36] MM ZC, D: 1, S: 1, Cilt 5, 7 Temmuz 1325 (20 July 1909), 462.

[37] The Article passed with 90 votes in favour and 69 against (out of 159 cast votes). MM ZC, D:1, S:1, Cilt 5, 7 Temmuz 1325 (20 July 1909), 468.

[38] *Düstur*, 2. Tertip, vol. I, 644.

Ottoman Unity Through Education

On the educational and language front, the Unionist policies resembled the ideas suggested by Ibrahim Hakkı Pasha on creating Ottoman national unity through homogenization and standardization. Hence, the state introduced educational reforms highlighting national identity construction. The period also witnessed the early attempts at unification of education (an objective fully implemented only after the republic) to reduce educational institutions functioning independently within the Ottoman millet framework. Furthermore, civic education programs and textbooks were introduced to cultivate a sense of Ottoman patriotism and solidarity.[39] Such a textbook used in primary schools of the Second Constitutional Period was the "Guide to Unity" (*Rehber-i Ittihad*), a citizenship handbook, published in 1910, one year after Abdulhamid was deposed.

A comparison with another textbook from 1908, when Abdulhamid was still on the throne, provides an interesting insight into the difference between Hamidian identity policy and that of the Young Turks respectively. Simply titled *İlmihal Kitabı* (Catechism Manual) this book was written by a major in the Ottoman army as a religious handbook for military cadets. Apart from religious instruction in the doctrines of Islamic faith, worship, and ethics, the book also contained a wide range of themes and principles regarding national identity and obligations towards the homeland and the state, all formulated within a religious framework, illustrating the Hamidian regime's emphasis on Muslim nationalism.[40] According to the *İlmihal Kitabı* one's primary community was the religious one, in this case, the Muslims within the Ottoman Empire constituted a single national community, as a separate *millet*, while the allegiance was owed to the sultan-caliph and the Ottoman state. Hence, when asked "To which religion and which nation do you belong?" the military cadet was expected to give the following answer: "I belong to Islam, the religion most highly esteemed by God, and God be praised, I'm a Muslim".[41]

---

[39] Üstel, *Makbul Vatandaş*, 32–40.

[40] Mustafa Hamdi, *İlmihal Kitabı*.

[41] The original text reads, —*Hangi dindensin ve ne milletdensin?* —*Allah indinde en yüce din olan Islam dinindenim, ve elhamdulillah müslümanım!*. Mustafa Hamdi, *İlmihal Kitabı*, 13.

Compared to the *İlmihal Kitabı*, the "Guide to Unity" (*Rehber-i Ittihad*) reflected another approach, more in line with the Tanzimat Ottomanism and the principles greeted by the Young Turks in the early phase of the revolution. Replacing the emphasis on Muslimness, the students were now expected to be proud to call themselves Ottomans, regardless of religious affiliation, and to love *everyone* living in Ottoman territory as Ottomans and as family:

- Thus, you love all villagers, city-dwellers, and all our citizens living inside the Ottoman domains.
- But sir, how can we love people we never met?
- I will tell you how. Ahmet, do you love your grandmother who died when you were only six months old?
- Yes, I do. I didn't know her, but my mother always tells me she never met a better person. She loved me very much, and I love her.
- You see, Ahmet, how you love your grandmother. When she is mentioned you get tears in your eyes. But you just said you never knew her. So, exactly like that, you love all your fellow citizens, and all the children living inside the Ottoman territory.[42]

These two textbooks reflect a remarkable shift, not so much in tone, because they both are filled with patriotic zeal but in terms of the redefinition of the "nation". Who was to be counted as part of the "nation" had changed and, thus, whom to "love" and on what grounds. Now the Ottomans had to love each other as fellow citizens. What was to be deemed sacred had also changed. The constitution was sacred, and so was the Committee of Union and Progress with its "sacred" mission to save and reform the state and country.[43] The basis of legitimacy and allegiance now inhered in concepts like "constitution", "freedom", "the fatherland", and the Ottoman state. The sultan-caliph, once the foundation of traditional Islamic legitimation, had been pushed into the background—only to be revitalized in the years following 1910.

The most striking element of the second text, however, seems to be its definition of the Ottoman nation, the Ottoman homeland (*vatan*), as something to be imagined in its entirety, with its domains, cities, and

---

[42] Müstecebizade İsmet, *Rehber-i Ittihad*, 9–10.

[43] Akşin, *Jön Türkler*, 21.

villages. Yet it was certainly no easy task to unite, in the minds and imaginations of its dwellers, a vast empire and all its peoples stretching over Southeast Europe, the Middle East, and North Africa. Everyone living within this territory was to be envisaged as part of a single nation and loved as one loves one's grandparents. Thus, close emotional links were sought, and the connection between ancestors and younger generations was illustrated.

The weak link, however, was the absence of common identity markers and bonds of belonging between members of the Ottoman nation—other than that of sharing same territory. The question asked by Ahmet was raised by the strange notion of loving "all villagers, city-dwellers, and all our citizens living inside the Ottoman domains"; as the children had learnt that the Ottoman domains were vast and filled with a difference, Ahmet's question seems quite reasonable. It is hard to guess whether the teacher's answer satisfied Ahmet (and all the Ottoman pupils he represented). Although the teacher presents an impressive argument, defining the nation in a form that resonates with the work of Benedict Anderson[44]—invoking the power of the imagination and the love of ancestors and the unknown dead—the links are not elaborated and the argument is left where the question started, as a matter of territory: one had to love all "fellow citizens, and all the children living inside the Ottoman territory". Yet Namık Kemal, as a prominent member of the Young Ottoman movement and a pioneer of Ottoman patriotic nationalism, had criticized the mere territorial definition of the "homeland" (*vatan*), as places of birth or geographic location and territorial boundaries, which he claimed lacked the emotional appeal that would make the Ottomans die defending even remote portions of it.[45]

Nevertheless, beginning and ending with territory was not surprising at all, given the Ottoman elite tradition and its imperial context. In accordance with this tradition, Unionist Ottoman nationalism was state-centred and closely linked to territory, the preservation of which gained paramount importance for Ottoman rule. As such, during the late Ottoman period and in the early years of the Republic, the primary focus of government leaders continued to be the state's territorial integrity rather than the ethnic or racial composition of the population. In light

---

[44] Anderson, *Imagined Communities*, 9–12.
[45] Namık Kemal (1872), *Vatan Yahut Silistre*.

of the nineteenth-century territorial losses, the concept of territorial indivisibility was coined, becoming a central notion of Ottoman polity and a defining element of the worldview of Ottoman statesmen, which was passed on to the leaders of the Turkish Republic.[46] Territorial indivisibility also became a central principle of Ottoman imperial and Turkish republican constitutions respectively. Thus, the first article of the Ottoman constitution of 1876 read: "The Ottoman State, consisting of distinguished provinces and domains, is a unified entity and never accepts any form of division for any reason whatsoever".[47]

The stress on indivisibility stood in dire contrast to realities on the ground, however, as late Ottoman history was filled with territorial losses since 1774 in particular, making the redrawing of borders the norm rather than the exception. Not surprisingly, though, the Ottoman state responded by accentuating the idea of indivisibility. This was also the earliest recognizable principle of the Young Turk movement. From the outset, the CUP had pledged itself to withstand territorial loss and outside interference. As will be remembered, the revolution itself was triggered by such an occasion marked by the Reval meeting.[48]

Reactions to Centralization and Homogenization

Before long, it became increasingly obvious that the realities on the ground were not shaping according to the expectations and promises of the revolution. Both in and outside parliament, therefore, widespread criticism was voiced against the new regime. While some MPs noted that this had not been what they had signed up for when running for a seat in the Assembly,[49] others still expressed that the constitution had created conditions worse than before.[50] In his memoirs, Lermioğlu, as a contemporary observer, noted that the constitutional revolution before long became unwanted not only by the majority of the population but also by a large portion of Ottoman intellectuals.[51] The government's efforts to exert

[46] Tunaya, *Türkiye'de Siyasal Partiler*, III, 476.
[47] *Düstur*, 1. Tertip, vol. IV, 4.
[48] FO371/1017/46560, Marling to Grey, 20 December 1910.
[49] MMZC, D: 1, S: 4, Cilt 2, 29 Kanunuevvel 1327 (11 January 1912), 466–467.
[50] MMZC, D: 1, S: 4, Cilt 2, 28 Kanunuevvel 1327 (10 January 1912), 437.
[51] FO371/999/28568, enclosure 1 in no. 1, Hough to Lamb, 31 July 1910.

direct control throughout the empire, in addition to the general disappointment with the new regime's failure to implement significant reforms to improve social, economic, and administrative conditions,[52] contributed greatly to that end, and began causing widespread unrest in Anatolia, Albania, Syria, Libya, and Yemen.[53]

While the primary catalysts for the uprisings in Albania and Crete in the first half of 1910 were the radical political changes occurring in Rumelia, in the Arabic-speaking provinces, rebellions were especially fuelled by local leaders' concerns about increased foreign intervention and the expansion of central government authority, leading to a decline of local autonomy and privileges.[54] While the policies implemented by the new regime were a significant factor in the discontent among the local population and contributed to the growth of nationalist tendencies, loyalty to the Ottoman state still existed in different forms, particularly among the Muslim local elites, although not directed towards the Unionists as such.[55]

Ottoman Yemen constituted such an example, where the CUP's policies of centralization met staunch resistance, backed with a religious colouring.[56] While British reports attributed the unrest in Yemen to dissatisfaction with the constitution on religious grounds, based on the claim that the Arab element considered it incompatible with the sharia,[57]

---

[52] Lermioğlu, *Halkın İstemediği İnkılap*, 28.

[53] FO371/1249/19795, Lowther to Grey, 16 May 1911.

[54] Gawrych, *The Crescent and the Eagle*, 176–179.

[55] Gawrych notes on the conflict in Albania, that although the advocates of Ottomanization and Albanianization engaged in a violent conflict, Ottomanism remained a viable ideology even by the time of the Balkan Wars,

as local groups, including the Albanian nationalists achieved recognition for their ethnicity and the right to their local customs within the Ottoman Empire. Gawrych, *The Crescent and the Eagle*, 3–4, 197–202.

[56] Throughout the nineteenth century, Yemen experienced various degrees of rebellion, occupying Istanbul's political and military agenda, particularly after the Zaidis rebelled in 1889, demanding to be governed by their Zaidi Shiite imams rather than the Ottoman sultan-caliph. The Hamidian government was in the midst of peace negotiations regarding a similar Zaidi rebellion at the time of the Young Turk Revolution. With the change of government, the Zaidis resumed their armed uprising, and in 1909, Sheikh Idris's rebellion in Asir escalated under the leadership of Imam Yahya. For more on Ottoman rule in Yemen see Farah, *The Sultan's Yemen*.

[57] FO371/1245/6164, Lowther to Grey, 14 February 1911; FO371/1491/25598, Kitchener to Grey, 9 June 1912.

as Farah notes, other factors were at play as well.[58] Restoring the constitution meant increased central government control over the provinces, which concerned local elites seeking to protect their positions and privileges. A military expedition in 1910 had failed to resolve the issues causing unease.[59] Faced with even greater resistance in the subsequent year, the Ottoman government saw no other option but to seek a truce and adopt a more moderate approach.[60] Hence, it introduced administrative reforms that granted greater autonomy to the local notables of Yemen, returning to a better-known model, where the notables would nominally rule the province in the name of the Ottoman government.

An important aspect of the religious arguments directed against the Unionist regime must also be sought in the utility of such arguments to render the new regime illegitimate, while at the same time illustrating how religion also played a significant role in shaping local resistance to government attempts to impose more direct and effective control. The leaders in Benghazi, for instance, is reported to have refused to obey the Unionist government on the grounds that they only recognized three authorities: God, the Prophet, and the caliph, none of which the Unionists were considered to represent.[61]

Similar disturbances arose in Macedonia, where the non-settlement of the church dispute, the strict application of the Law on Associations,[62] the suppression of constitutional clubs, and, above all, the disarmament procedures were given as the main grievances.[63] According to British reports, the government's disarmament methods displayed an "excessive brutality towards the Bulgarians, Serbians, and *Rum*s in Macedonia",

---

[58] Besides religious motivations, Farah cites such reasons for the uprisings in Yemen as maladministration leading to the impoverishment of the regions involved, incompetence of state officials and their ignorance of local affairs, and the local elite's loss of privileges and power. Farah, *Sultan's Yemen*, 272-273.

[59] FO371/1244/3439, Lowther to Grey, 25 January 1911.

[60] Farah, *Sultan's Yemen*, 269-271.

[61] FO371/760/404, Fontana to Grey, 21 December 1908.

[62] MM ZC, D: 1, S: 1, Cilt 5, 6 Temmuz 1325 (19 June 1909), 437.

[63] FO371/999/28568, enclosure 1 in no. 1, Hough to Lamb, 31 July 1910.

with the use of torture to obtain information concerning the whereabouts of materiel.[64] The highly unstable conditions notwithstanding, the CUP congress in 1910 decided that disarmament in Macedonia had to be completed by whatever means necessary.[65] The general result of this policy was a state of affairs in Macedonia that was as uncertain as that in Albania after the Ottoman army expedition. British reports further observe that the Bulgarians, who turned to the establishment of secret organizations after the suppression of their constitutional clubs,[66] were further antagonized by the disarmament methods,[67] leading to the increase in activity of armed bands. This in turn led the government to encourage the arming of Muslims and the formation of Muslim bands.[68]

This would prove of little use, however, as discontent with the Unionist government had spread among Rumelian Muslims as well. The developments in Albania in particular were to have traumatic consequences for the future of Ottoman nationalism. Albanian unrest constituted a prime example of local discontent and alienation vis-à-vis the regime that had stemmed from the CUP's centralizing and unifying policies.[69] The Albanians appealed for officials who could speak their language, and demanded special treatment in regard to military service and taxation. The uprising of April 1910 was brought about by the imposition of a special duty tax, the attempt to enforce conscription and to levy taxes regularly, and the appointment by the Ottoman government of officials who were ignorant of local conditions—thereby alienating local power-holders increasingly worried about their future positions and fearing the weakening or removal of their traditional privileges.[70] The extent of the insurrection was such that the Ottoman government experienced great difficulty in overcoming

---

[64] FO371/1000/40426, Lowther to Grey, 31 October 1910; FO371/1000/40429, Lowther to Grey, 31 October 1910; FO371/1000/40431, Lowther to Grey, 31 October 1910.

[65] FO371/1017/44796, Marling to Grey, 7 December 1910; FO371/1017/46560, Marling to Grey, 20 December 1910.

[66] See further on these clubs in Tunaya, *Siyasal Partiler,* I, 514–519.

[67] FO371/999/33846, Lowther to Grey, 13 September 1910.

[68] FO371/1000/43057, Marling to Grey, 19 November 1910; FO371/1000/43073, Marling to Grey, 23 November 1910.

[69] FO371/998/926, Lowther to Grey, 4 January 1910.

[70] Gawrych, *The Crescent and the Eagle,* 177–179.

it.⁷¹ At the beginning of June 1910, Ambassador Lowther stated his conviction that the real state of affairs was being concealed, that the Ottoman losses had been greater than what the government was willing to admit, and that, despite Mahmut Sevket Pasha's triumphant entry into Djakova, the insurrection was far from over.

In addition, the government defeated its own ends with the severity of applying repressive measures. The government's activities in Albania were not calculated to create the impression that their difficulties in that regard were at an end because, although the Ottoman army subdued the province, it evidently stirred up deep resentment against the central government while doing so. According to a British report, the methods of the Ottoman army created an Albania more united than it had been for many years.⁷² The report further states that at the end of 1910, the insurgents rejected an offer of amnesty, declaring that it was the Ottoman government that had driven them to the mountains, and that they were there to express their dissatisfaction. They repeated their demands for the freedom of all Albanians to be educated in their native language, the reopening of Albanian schools, the removal of the embargo on printing presses and publications, the appointment of Albanian officials, and permission to use the Albanian alphabet.⁷³

Thus, far from succeeding in stamping out unrest in the Albanian provinces, the government was forced to withdraw and adopt conciliatory measures already towards the end of 1910. For instance, the schools at Elbassan and Koritza were reopened, the option of using the native alphabet in schools was offered, and a general amnesty was declared for all those accused of political offences. This policy of appeasement was carried several steps further when a decision was made by the government to permit the reopening of the schools closed the previous year and the opening of other schools in which Albanian was to be taught in Latin characters, on the condition that the schools were subject to government control.⁷⁴

---

⁷¹ FO371/1003/17337, Lowther to Grey, 3 May 1910.

⁷² FO371/1246/11077, Lowther to Grey, 21 March 1911.

⁷³ Ahmad, *Ottoman Nationalities*, 58–59.

⁷⁴ The policy of accommodation was also applied towards the Arab population, with increased parliamentary representation for the Arab provinces, compliance with some of the claims for the use of Arabic in local administration and educational institutions, and demands that bureaucrats stationed in Arabic provinces spoke the language.

Return to Ottoman Muslim Nationalism

The armed uprisings from 1910 onwards, especially those in Albania and Yemen, marked an alarming development in the eyes of Unionist leaders as an indication that the Ottoman state was losing legitimacy among the Muslim population and local elites, whose loyalty to the sultanate-caliphate had hitherto been taken for granted but might now aspire to break free from Ottoman rule altogether.[75] These concerns were discussed in the annual congress of the CUP in 1910. In this case, the concept of Ottoman unity was restated, but it was argued that moderate measures alone would not be sufficient to achieve it.[76] Hence, it was decided to suppress all separatist nationalist aspirations, using force if necessary. Talat, Minister for the Interior at the time, claimed that it had not been possible to gain the loyalty of non-Muslims, why the focus must now be redirected towards those elements that only owed political allegiance to the Ottoman State, meaning the Muslim elements in particular.[77]

The central role of Islam in dealing with the Muslim population of the empire was emphasized, in which case Muslim domination was considered to be essential, as well as the uniting and legitimizing role of the caliph as head of the Ottoman nation. Consequently, Ottoman Muslim unity would gain more ground in state policy and national identity discourses, especially regarding the unrest in Albania.[78] To illustrate this new line of policy, the CUP regime organized for the sultan a reconciliation tour through Rumelia to Kosovo in June 1911, making overtures to local elites on his way.[79] The press in Istanbul compared the tour to the conquering sultans' campaigns in the heydays of the empire, when they returned

---

During Cemal Pasha's draconic rule as governor in Syria (1914–17), however, many of these accommodating changes were reversed. Kayalı, *Arabs and Young Turks*, 135–137, 193–196.

[75] Sümer, Çağdaş, "What Did the Albanians Do?" in Yavuz & Blumi, War and Nationalism, 727–736.

[76] FO371/1017/44796, Marling to Grey, 7 December 1910.

[77] FO371/1017/44796, Marling to Grey, 7 December 1910; FO371/1017/46560, Marling to Grey, 20 December 1910. For Talat's speech, see also Gingeras, Fall of the Sultanate, 45.

[78] Ahmad, *Ottoman Nationalities*, 58.

[79] Gawrych, *The Crescent and the Eagle*, 186.

home with the keys to the conquered cities. In the opinion of the press, however, Sultan Resad's tour in Rumelia represented another kind of conquest; he brought back with him the keys to people's hearts. Nonetheless, the intentions were made amply clear: reinstating the legitimate rule of the sultan-caliph—that is, the Ottoman State—over Albanians, the majority of whom were Muslims.

The symbolism and the rhetoric used were also clearly Islamic, although mixed with the ideals of the constitutional revolution. The sultan was accompanied by the local heroes of the revolution, like Niyazi of Resne, the descendants of the influential and ancient Evranos family, and members of parliament from Rumelia. They were to serve as an intermediary link between the central state and the local elites and population. The tour itself was a clear sign of the intention of the central government to mobilize support at the local level. Furthermore, the sultan's participation in the tour was quite a novelty in Ottoman political traditions, as the Ottoman sultans, with very few exceptions—like Sultan Abdulaziz who visited Paris in 1867—had almost never left the capital since the early seventeenth century.[80]

Yet, in relation to political developments around Europe at the time, these attempts of the Ottoman government were quite comparable to other countries, where the basis of political legitimacy had changed, placing the concept of "people"—or the "nation" as its politically charged twin—at the centre of legitimacy, meaning that national identity construction and the control of public discourse had become crucial. Although Islamic symbols and rhetoric were used, the idea that a sultan had to go and meet the people in their own locality and appeal to their feelings and support was reflective of this new state of things. However, as legitimacy requires at least a minimal degree of acceptance of those who seek it,[81] the Unionists were soon forced to acknowledge the difficulty of obtaining this acceptance in the first place, let alone controlling it. Thus, even though the sultan managed to gather considerable crowds and awoke public interest wherever he stopped along the way, it is difficult to measure the overall impact of the tour. A report of a remarkable incident seems to shed some light on the question of success, and the conquering of hearts. As Packham, the British Vice-Consul wrote:

---

[80] Zürcher, *The Young Turk Legacy*, 85.

[81] Weber, Theory of Social and Economic Organization, 324–328.

> When the Sultan was here last year he deposited a relic, in the shape of the prophet's beard, in the tomb of Sultan Murad at Kossovo Polye. Within the last two months a rumour has got about that this hair grew on the chin, not of Mohammed but of Mahmud Shevket. The Albanians demanded a trial by fire, the prophet's beard being apparently, fireproof. The local authorities refused, and were forced to surround the tomb with a cordon of soldiers to prevent the Albanians making a trial for themselves. ... The refusal of authorities, who presumably know of no method of making hair fireproof, tends to convince the Albanians that a trick has been played on them, and I fear that in the event of disorders, appeals for loyalty to the Caliphate will be disregarded.[82]

Contrary to the formulated goals of the central government to inspire the local populace with religious and national zeal, the incident seems to have led to a religious boycott of the mosque and its holy shrine. The Unionists had obviously not yet mastered the ability to communicate and manipulate public opinion as effectively as they would have liked, symbolized in this case as a "trial by fire", which at the same time lay bare the shortcomings of the Ottoman government in terms of resources, technology, and methodology necessary to make the propaganda work as intended. Evidently, mere religious propaganda did not suffice. The incident exposed the great challenges faced in that regard. Local actors demanded to be heard and wanted to see convincing policies and arguments, making it amply clear that their loyalty would not come automatically but had to be earned.

These government initiatives, and the ensuing rhetoric, are particularly interesting as they took place before the Balkan Wars. Consequently, they render questionable the argument that the Balkan Wars—wherein the Ottoman Empire lost nearly all its European provinces and, with them, most of its non-Muslim population and consequently much of the reason for pursuing an inclusive, civic Ottoman nationalist policy—marked the beginning of the CUP's Islam-oriented nationalism,[83] what Üngör calls "Muslimism". Instead, what we see is yet another instance of Unionists deploying different kinds of policies and nationalist discourse, shaped according to place and circumstance and characterized more by

---

[82] FO195/2422/1217, Packham to Lamb, 11 March 1912.

[83] Erol, "'Macedonian Question' in Western Anatolia"; According to Üngör, this marked the shift between Ottoman nationalism and "Muslimism", to later conclude with a final stage, Turkish nationalism (Üngör, *The Making of Modern Turkey,* 29).

ambivalence than a clear-cut succession of "isms". The CUP regime's identity policies thus tended to change over time and to differ according to regions and circumstances.[84] What is undeniable, however, is the crucial importance of events that were changing the Ottomans' world, and creating the conditions for different modes of adaptation. War and its consequences soon became the all-pervasive determinant, fundamentally reshaping the territorial and population composition of the empire.

THE BALKAN WARS

The beginning of the Balkan Wars coincided with political turmoil shaking the Unionist regime in its very core, the Ottoman military. Under severe pressure from a rapidly mounting opposition and a highly volatile political atmosphere, the Unionist regime faced a choice that would also present itself to Mustafa Kemal a decade later. Against the prospect of losing power, would they hold to the professed ideals of the constitution, based on civil rights and freedoms, political representation, and a parliamentary government, which they had presented as the very legitimizing foundation of the CUP regime? The notorious 1912 parliamentary elections, known as "the elections with the stick", made the CUP's preferences clear on the matter. Using violent means against their opponents and critics—beatings, intimidations, even murder—the CUP manipulated the electoral process in order to secure its victory against growing opposition, which by then had united under the banner of the Liberal Alliance Party (*Hürriyet ve Itilaf Fırkası*— HIF).[85] As the new party was not allowed to organize properly or participate in the elections freely, it was hardly surprising that the CUP "won" in 1912. This did little to calm the storm, however, as the opposition, frustrated by the unlawful means deployed by the Unionists to hinder the advancement of opposition forces, responded with their own underground methods.[86]

Lending support to the Liberal Alliance (*Hürriyet ve Itilaf*) and calling themselves "The Saviour Officers" (*Halaskar Zabitan*), a faction within the Ottoman army began making announcements in the press and issuing

---

[84] Ülker, "Contextualising 'Turkification'".

[85] FO371/1494/17830, Lowther to Grey, 18 April 1912. Among those assaulted were the prominent figures of the opposition, Riza Nur and Riza Tevfik (Riza Nur, *Hayat ve Hatiratim*).

[86] FO371/1496/31978, Marling to Grey, 23 July 1912.

memoranda to the military high command.[87] Alarmed by the threat of political divisions within the officer corps, which would have compromised their power base,[88] the CUP, rather than risking such a split, ceded the reins of government to members of the liberal party.[89] This, however, was followed shortly by the Unionist efforts to regain power.[90] Before the new anti-CUP government could take effective action against the CUP, it became fully preoccupied with the devastating outcome of the First Balkan War, resulting in a humiliating Ottoman defeat at the hands of Greece, Serbia, Montenegro, and Bulgaria, whereby most of Rumelia, including Edirne, the Ottoman capital prior to Istanbul, was lost.[91]

The ensuing turmoil presented the CUP with a much sought-after opportunity. Holding the HIF-led government responsible for the disastrous defeat, the Unionists staged a violent takeover in 1913, remembered in Turkish military history as "the raid on the Sublime Porte" (*Babıali baskını*).[92] The "raiders", under the leadership of Enver Bey (later Enver Pasha), attacked the office of the grand vizier, in the process mortally wounding their much hated political rival, the Minister of War and the Navy, Nazım Pasha.[93] The group finally forced grand vizier Kamil Pasha—at gunpoint—to resign.[94] With the coup, the CUP at last attained undisputed power, with a docile parliament and one-party rule that very soon turned into a one-party state.[95] It was the first

---

[87] FO371/1495/33863, Marling to Grey, 4 August 1912.

[88] According to Marling "the army is aware of its power. In other words, the pretense that the Chamber is the dominant power in the State is destroyed, and in future rival parties will undisguisedly compete for the support of the army" (FO371/1496/32930, Marling to Grey, 26 July 1912).

[89] FO371/1496/31978, Marling to Grey, 23 July 1912; FO371/1496/32924, Marling to Grey, 25 July 1912; FO371/1496/32942, Marling to Grey, 30 July 1912.

[90] FO371/1496/33869, Marling to Grey, 6 August 1912.

[91] Hall, *The Balkan Wars*, 22–44.

[92] FO371/1788/4358, Lowther to Grey, 24 January 1913; FO371/1788/4851, Lowther to Grey, 26 January 1913.

[93] Ibid.

[94] In his resignation letter, Kamil Pasha wrote: "I bed humbly to inform your Majesty that at the instance of the military it has become necessary for me to place my resignation in your Majesty's hands", whereupon Enver insisted the Grand Vizier to add above the line and before the word "military" the words "of the people and of the" (FO371/1788/4854, Lowther to Grey, 28 January 1913).

[95] FO371/1788/6200, Lowther to Grey, 5 February 1913.

but not the last of its kind in modern Turkish history, and was later to be emulated by the Kemalist republic under Atatürk. Coupled with the growing authoritarianism of the government and strict censorship, political dissent and its expression became practically impossible.[96] Thus, equipped with new powers granted by martial law proclaimed on the grounds of wartime security, the CUP crushed the opposition organized under the umbrella of the Liberal Alliance, thereby breaking up the political alliance between the liberals and various ethnic and religious elements, forcing the remaining opposition to either go underground or abroad.[97]

The new Unionist government then entered the second Balkan War, taking advantage of the conflict among the Balkan allies, who had begun fighting each other. The Ottoman forces, led by Enver, retook Edirne without much difficulty, allowing Enver to title himself "conqueror of Edirne" (*Edirne fatihi*). The consolation of retaking Edirne notwithstanding, the loss of nearly all Ottoman Rumelia instigated mass trauma and suffering, accompanied by vast streams of destitute Muslim refugees making their way—much like the mass exodus after the Ottoman-Russian War (1877–78)—to the capital and further into Anatolia. Indeed, it has been suggested in recent scholarship that the concomitant psychological impact on the Anatolian population and Unionist elite was one of the main reasons for the disastrous events during World War I.[98] Numerous books and highly heated debates in the Ottoman press during and after the Balkan Wars support this suggestion.[99]

Üngör, taking 1913 as a point of departure in his highly influential work on the Unionist and Kemalist policies of nation-building and demographic engineering, discussing the devastating effects of the Balkan Wars, places special emphasis on these psychological aspects, referring

---

[96] Turfan, *Rise of the Young Turks*, 210–213, 326–329.

[97] Tunaya, *Türkiye'de Siyasal Partiler*, III, 520–523.

[98] Kieser, Öktem & Reinkowski, *World War*, 15–22; See also Toprak, "Balkan Harbi, İntikam ve 'Ötekileştirme' Süreci", 42–53.

[99] Works encapsulating the Ottoman desperation to cope with and understand what and why the things were happening as they were include: İbrahim Hilmi, *Balkan Harbinde Neden Munhezim Olduk* (1329 [1913]); İbrahim Hilmi, *Balkan Harbinde Askeri Mağlubiyetlerimizin Esbabı* (1329 [1913]); İbrahim Hilmi, *Milletin Hataları. Felaketlerimizin Esbabı* (1328 [1912]); Ömer Faruk, *Enkaz-ı İstibdad İçinde Züğürdün Tesellisi* (1329 [1913]); Mehmed Fetgerey, *Eşkali Hayat* (1331 [1915]); Hüseyin Kazım Kadri, *Arnavudlar ne Yaptılar* (1330 [1914]).

to an uprooted, disillusioned, and bitter Unionist elite with a revanchist attitude.[100] Indeed, the loss of Ottoman Rumelia meant that the CUP, with headquarters in Salonica, not only lost its hinterland and base of operations, the majority of the Unionist leadership lost their native country in Macedonia and Thrace as well.[101] Consequently, as Zürcher has pointed out, the Unionist leadership suddenly found itself technically in the category of immigrants, a fate they shared with thousands of Ottoman Muslims from the lost Balkan territories.

Amidst these traumatizing experiences, dramatic changes took place in public attitudes and discourse, as feelings of loss, helplessness, and frustration were translated into resentment towards the Great Powers, Balkan countries, and the Ottoman non-Muslim population.[102] While most of the resentment was directed towards non-Muslims, some Ottoman Muslim elements were also criticized, sowing doubt on the extent of Muslim unity. As the revolt in Albania was followed up by a delegation of Albanian leaders declaring independence on 28 November 1912, while the first Balkan War raging on,[103] seemed to have a particularly negative impact on Ottoman public opinion,[104] also fuelling anti-CUP sentiments.[105] Albanians, as is often pointed out, were largely Muslim, hence part of the "dominant nation", whose loyalty to the Ottoman

---

[100] Üngör, *The Making of Modern Turkey*, 43–46; See also Erol, "'Macedonian Question' in Western Anatolia".

[101] Zurcher, *Legacy*, 99–100.

[102] İbrahim Hilmi, *Zavallı Millet. Felaketlerimizin Esbabı*, 1–2.

[103] FO371/1495/28612, Lowther to Grey, 1 July 1912; FO371/1495/28730, Lowther to Grey, 3 July 1912; FO371/1495/28734, Lowther to Grey, 4 July 1912; FO371/1495/29820, Lowther to Grey, 9 July 1912.

[104] Sümer, Çağdaş, "What Did the Albanians Do?" in Yavuz & Blumi, War and Nationalism, 727–736. On the Albanian uprising, see also Ahmad, Ottoman Nationalities, 59–64; see also Gawrych, *The Crescent and the Eagle*, 170-202.

[105] This especially made itself felt as general unrest in the Ottoman army. A British report claimed that "Constantinople is of course teeming with reports of an impending military coup d'Etat and the dissolution of the Committee" (FO371/1495/29823, Lowther to Grey, 10 July 1912). According to another report, this crisis, which might, in case CUP instead of giving in to the opposition chose to step up the conflict, spill over to the provinces and "result in civil war" (FO371/1495/32290, Cartwright to Grey, 30 July 1912). Consequently, CUP, facing a split within the Ottoman army, indeed gave in to the opposition, who took the reins of government, temporarily at least (FO371/1495/33863, Marling to Grey, 4 August 1912; FO371/1496/30863, Marling to Grey, 16 July 1912; FO371/1496/30870, Marling to Grey, 17 July 1912).

throne was widely trusted, had occupied prominent positions within the Ottoman central bureaucracy and the army.[106] The charm offensive of the sultan in 1911 had clearly not worked.

WORLD WAR I

It was against the backdrop of these dramatic events that the Unionist top leadership began discussing its future course of action. A radically new situation was at hand. With the loss of nearly all of Ottoman Rumelia—apart from the Arabic-speaking provinces—only Anatolia was left in Ottoman hands. It is not surprising therefore, that the Unionists turned their attention to Anatolia, especially to areas with sizeable non-Muslim populations, such as the Aegean coast of Anatolia. Memoirs of some of the leading Unionists provide crucial information in this respect.

Kuşçubaşızade Eşref, one of the leading figures of the Special Organization (*Teşkilatı Mahsusa*),[107] and one of Enver Pasha's very close assistants within the CUP, mentions in his memoirs some highly secret meetings which took place among such select echelons of CUP hierarchy that even several cabinet ministers were excluded.[108] At these gatherings, remedies for future problems "outside the scope of usual affairs of government" (*Hükümetin normal faaliyeti dışında*) were discussed, one of which—"a deadly sorrow" (*öldürücü dert*) in Eşref's words—was depicted as the non-Turk elements of the empire (here Eşref uses "Turk" as synonymous with "Muslim", non-Turks in this case thus being Ottoman non-Muslims). According to Eşref, Talat and Enver expressed the opinion that the highest threat to remaining Ottoman lands, Anatolia in particular, was the non-Muslim population, who were "treacherous" and could no longer be trusted.

---

[106] Karpat, *The Politicization of Islam*, 171, 369–370.

[107] The infamous *Teskilatı Mahsusa* was a secret organization made up largely of military officers (often referred to as *fedai-i zabitan*—self-sacrificing officers). It was founded by the leading Ottoman military officer of the Second Constitutional Period, Enver Pasha, to function directly, and secretly, under him as a paramilitary force dedicated to intelligence-gathering, warfare, propaganda, political assassinations, and the suppression, and later still mass-killings, of the empire's non-Muslim population. For more on the Special Organization see Safi, "History in the Trench", 89–106.

[108] Eşref's memoirs are lost, although preserved in parts in the autobiography of Celal Bayar, the Unionist boss in Izmir, later to be Prime Minister and then President of the Turkish Republic. See Bayar, *Bende Yazdım*, vol. V, 102–124.

With Eşref's full concurrence, these were depicted as "ungrateful elements who had eaten for centuries the bread and food of our state" (*asırlarca devletimizin ekmeği ve nimeti ile beslenmiş bu nankör unsurların*) (p. 103). The main theme of the secret meetings, according to Eşref was to "purge" (*tasfiye*) the clusters of non-Muslims in strategic places, the Aegean region in particular, "as these constituted a strategic problem and a threat to national existence". Izmir and its surrounding area were singled out as being "seriously in great danger" (*cidden büyük bir tehlike içindeydi*), because of the "treacherous and shameless ambitions" (*hain ve hayasız ihtiraslar*) of "un-national elements" (*menfi ve gayri milli unsurların*) who were "threatening to bring devastation and ruin to the national existence and unity of the country" (*memleketin istiklal ve birliğine yapabileceği tahrip*). Eşref attributed the serious proportions attained by this "national threat" to the "totally unnational policies of Abdulhamid". Now, he claimed, the *Rum*s, under the banner of the secret Greek nationalistic society, *Ethniki Etairia*, were so absorbed by the *Megali Idea* (The Great Idea), the policy of Greek irredentism, that they had made preparations verging on armed rebellion, thereby posing the threat that "they would suddenly rise up and strike our army from behind".[109]

Subsequently, Eşref was allegedly tasked by Talat and Enver with undercover reconnaissance in the area in order to draw up solutions that would further the purposes discussed. In this respect, Eşref writes, he told Enver and Talat firmly that nationalizing efforts in Izmir must be executed by "persons of uncontaminated patriotism", with a "firm conviction, strong-willed and determined". The nationalization of Izmir, or, to put it more clearly, the conquest of Izmir to change it from "infidel" Izmir to "Turkish" Izmir, would then form a part of a countrywide struggle for existence.[110]

In accordance with the issues and measures discussed in the secret meetings, "nationalizing activities" (*millileştirme faaliyetleri*) gained "countrywide" proportions, as envisaged by Eşref. Towards this end, having categorized the non-Muslim populations as disloyal and unwanted,

---

[109] Ibid, 104.

[110] *Bu itibarla İzmir'deki millileştirme hareketlerinin, değerleri ciddi, azimli, iradeli ve tertemiz vatanseverler elinde tatbiki şarttı. İzmir'in millileştirilmesi, daha açık tabiriyle gavur İzmir'in Türk İzmir olabilme fetih hareketi, bütün memleketi şamil bir hayat davası mahiyetini alınca.* Bayar, *Bende Yazdım*, vol. V, 108.

the Unionists launched a project of bolstering the Muslim element while eradicating the non-Muslim.[111] This, among other things, entailed the "nationalization" of the economy, for instance by excluding the non-Muslim commercial classes from the economic sphere.[112] As shown by Göçek, Toprak, and Keyder, the Ottoman economy, its trade and financial sectors in particular, had long been dominated by the Ottoman non-Muslim commercial classes.[113] In light of this, the so-called "national economy program" sought to replace these groups with a new Muslim bourgeoisie.[114] According to Celal Bayar (third President of the Turkish Republic), the Izmir party boss who had attended the secret meetings mentioned by Eşref, this was an important move towards making the Muslim element master in its own house, and of its own economy.

It was with the outbreak of World War I, however, that the Unionists gained the opportunity to Implement their economic scheme on a vast scale, starting on 1 October 1914 by unilaterally abolishing the capitulations[115] (*ahdname*) that had granted special rights and privileges to European tradesmen, and their Ottoman brokers, for centuries.[116] Until this point, the CUP had maintained an earlier Ottoman policy of open

---

[111] Grandits, *Conflicting Loyalties in the Balkans*, 179–181.

[112] Toprak, Zafer (1982). *Türkiye'de Milli Iktisat, 1908-1918*.

[113] Keyder, *State and Class in Turkey*, 78–79; Göçek, *Rise of the Bourgeoisie*, 115; Toprak, *Türkiye'de Milli Iktisat*, 19–21.

[114] Göçek, *Rise of the Bourgeoisie*, 134–137; Toprak, *Milli Burjuvazi*, 3–9, 101–124; Keyder, *State and Class*, 61–69. Interestingly, as A. H. Başar has pointed out, this process was continued in the republican era, to create a Muslim commercial and industrial middle class, which in turn made the state - and a career within politics and bureaucracy - one of the main sources for gaining economic wealth, with detrimental effects on Turkish democracy, however (Başar, *Hürriyet Buhranı*).

[115] Yavuz, *War and Collapse*, 5; Toprak, *Milli Burjuvazi*, 52–53.

[116] Originally, capitulations were the rights and privileges the Ottoman sultans assigned foreign, non-Muslim merchants conducting business in Ottoman territory in order to ensure their security of life and property. During the nineteenth century, with growing Ottoman weakness vis-à-vis the great powers, capitulations became a means of political intervention and bringing about advantageous economic conditions for European tradesmen and manufacturers, with highly negative effects on their Ottoman, especially Muslim, counterparts; many Ottoman critics came to view them as a tool of economic colonization of the empire. Many previous attempts by Ottoman governments to abolish capitulations had been unsuccessful because of Great Power resistance. The capitulations were finally abolished by the Treaty of Lausanne in 1923. On the capitulations and Ottoman views of them see Ahmad, F. (2000). "Ottoman Perceptions of the Capitulations". *Journal of Islamic Studies*, Vol. 11, No. 1 (January 2000), 1–20.

economy along liberal lines in which non-Muslim commercial classes had flourished.[117]

Among the measures taken under the new "national economy" were boycotts against non-Muslims and the compulsory use of Turkish in business. Hence, local non-Turkish names were changed to Turkish and firms were forced to conduct their transactions only in Turkish.[118] Non-Muslim company owners were also forced to take Muslims onto their boards of directors.[119] As a result, nearly 130,000 *Rums* from Western Anatolia left the country, as did many Armenians, whose companies were then taken over by Muslims.[120] To strengthen Muslim businesses, the Unionist government organized Muslim traders and artisans' guilds. These groups were then provided with government support to accumulate capital by taking advantage of the favourable wartime market conditions and government connections, resulting in substantial profits being generated. This process took pace especially after the 1915, leading to a vast number of new companies starting up with government backing.[121] The support of the latter was crucial, as the war created huge demands for goods, especially food, and those who had access to transport (which was under government and army monopoly) and enjoyed political connections, managed to get their goods, most importantly wheat, to the major cities.[122] Following this model, Unionist officials and Muslim landowners in Anatolia were enriched at the expense of *Rum* and Armenian businessmen.[123]

While economic restructuring in full play, some of the other measures indicated during the Unionist secret meetings went into effect, aimed

---

[117] According to Toprak, the Young Turks initially believed that economic development would come from implementing free market policies, but as their trust in liberal European countries diminished, and German influence grew, they gradually transitioned towards embracing economic nationalism. Toprak, *Türkiye'de Milli Iktisat*, 23–29.

[118] Keyder, *State and Class in Turkey*, 62–66.

[119] Zürcher, *Turkey: A Modern History*, 126.

[120] Ibid.

[121] Toprak, *Milli Burjuvazi*, 113.

[122] Ibid., 151–153.

[123] This arrangement was in fact continued by the Kemalist regime in the republican era, to such a degree that the backbone of the political and economic structure of the early Kemalist republic was created in this way. The foundation led to a solid alliance between the Unionist/Kemalist state elite and the large landowning class in the countryside.

to reshape Anatolia along ethnoreligious lines, whereby the "unmixing" of populations reached new levels of radicalization and violence.[124] This began with a population exchange with Bulgaria in 1913, resulting in the deportation of 48,570 Muslims from Bulgaria and 46,764 Bulgarians from Ottoman Thrace.[125] The Unionist government proposed in May 1914 a similar exchange with Greece about the *Rum* population on the Aegean coast of Anatolia. To exert pressure on Greece, systematic persecution was initiated against the *Rum* inhabitants of the Aegean coast and Thrace. Although Greece subsequently agreed to a population exchange, the plans were shelved as the Ottoman Empire entered World War I on the side of the Central Powers.[126] While expelling non-Muslims from Anatolia, the Unionist government at the same time tried to strengthen the Muslim demographic component in different parts of Anatolia.[127] This included attempts to bring Muslims living outside Ottoman borders to settle in strategically important areas in order to boost the Muslim population there. Muslim immigrants were also settled in non-Muslim villages, particularly *Rum*,[128] whereas some were relocated to the inner regions of Anatolia, while others were forced out to Greece.[129]

Then, in May 1915, the government passed a law regulating the relocation of groups it saw as potential traitors, as a means of justifying deportations, with the tragic outcome for the Ottoman Armenians.[130] During the early stages of World War I, the Unionist regime, considered the Ottoman Armenians as a strategic threat, particularly after the Ottoman army's defeat in Sarıkamış in January 1915 resulting in a decimated Ottoman 3rd army and an exposed Anatolia to the risk of invasion, began a policy of extermination. Claiming that the Armenians were collaborating with the Russian enemy behind the lines, the Ottoman government thus decided to deport the entire population away from

---

[124] Hirschon, *Crossing the Aegean*.

[125] Dündar, *Modern Türkiye'nin Şifresi*, 228–229, 182–191.

[126] Dündar, *Modern Türkiye'nin Şifresi*, 228–229.

[127] According to estimates, around 435,000 Muslim immigrants arrived in Ottoman territories between the Balkan Wars and the end of World War I. Dündar, *İskan Politikası*, 66–70.

[128] Dündar, *Modern Türkiye'nin Şifresi*, 216–225; Ladas, *The Exchange of Minorities*, 15–16.

[129] Ladas, *The Exchange of Minorities*, 14–17.

[130] Dündar, *İskan Politikası*, 62–63.

the war front and into the Syrian desert and Mesopotamia. However, the scope of deportation extended far beyond the war-front area and encompassed Armenians living in different parts of western Anatolia as well.

This process, termed *tehcir* (deportation) by the Ottoman government, running mostly from May 1915 to mid-1916, turned into systematic extermination and mass killings amounting to genocide,[131] which, when completed, had resulted in the near destruction of the Armenian population of Anatolia.[132] Although some officials in the Ottoman provinces and military reportedly opposed the killings, the radical activist group within the CUP leadership, provincial party bosses, and the "special representatives" of the CUP headquarters (known as *katib-i mesul*), carried the policy through.[133] The actual killings, however, were mostly done by the *fedai*s (lit. "those that self-sacrifice"), the fighting force of the Special Organization trained in guerrilla warfare and band activity. As Zürcher strikingly points out, these were convinced that what had occurred in the Caucasus and Balkans would happen again in Anatolia.[134] This perception, with related narratives of national ruin and partitioning of Anatolia, continued to shape the actions and rhetoric of the ruling elite, providing one of the most effective tools for mobilizing Muslims in Anatolia for yet another war, this time for national independence.

---

[131] Akçam, *Crime against Humanity*, 183–193, 198–199; See also Gingeras, *Sorrowful Shores*, 41-45.

[132] The Armenian genocide has generated a significant and contentious amount of literature, with deeply entrenched viewpoints from both the Armenian and Turkish perspectives. The debate is highly politicized and controversial, making it challenging for the historical community to engage in critical analysis. However, in recent years, a substantial amount of scholarly work has been published, among which especially must be mentioned: Akçam, *From Empire to Republic*; Akçam, *Crime against Humanity*; Bloxham, *The Great Game of Genocide*; Üngör, *The Making of Modern Turkey*; Kieser, Anderson, Bayraktar & Schmutz, *The End of the Ottomans*.

[133] According to Eşref, the presence of these representatives in local areas became all the more crucial for the party, as it was almost impossible to find the right personnel in the provinces willing and sufficiently able to grasp fully what the administrative party centre expected done and wanted to achieve, in order to "bring about the brave and new atmosphere the country especially needed". Bayar, *Bende Yazdım*, vol. V, 108.

[134] Zürcher, *Legacy*, 221.

CHAPTER 6

Claiming the Homeland?

The Turkish portion of the present Ottoman Empire should be assured a secure sovereignty, but the other nationalities which are now under Turkish rule should be assured an undoubted security of life and an absolutely unmolested opportunity of autonomous development.[1]

This chapter deals with the period of Turkish history generally designated by historiography as "The Armistice Period" (*Mütareke Dönemi*), "The National Struggle" (*Milli Mücadele*), "The Independence War" (*Istiklal Harbi*), or "War of Liberation" (*Kurtuluş Savaşı*). The word "Turkish" in this context should, however, also be understood as meaning Ottoman, although ambiguity and conflict over what, exactly, the term subsumed was a problem encountered by contemporaneous actors and one that has dogged historians ever since. As the period and the crucial events taking place within it constitute the history, legitimacy, even the very identity of the Republic of Turkey, official Turkish historiography presents it as the early history of the Republic.[2] Therefore, a tendency to read and write the basic characteristics and self-image of the Kemalist republic during this

---

[1] Woodrow Wilson, 8 January 1918. For the full text of the "Fourteen Points" see MacMillan, *Paris 1919: Six Months That Changed the World*, 495–496.

[2] Atatürk, for instance, in his opening speech at the congress of the Republican People's Party in 1927, referred to the congress as RPP's second, counting the Sivas Congress in 1919 as its first. "Our Party", he added, "came into being nine years ago, in the years

period is quite common. Yet of considerable concern here is the question of the "nationalist" character of the resistance movement, which turned into an alternative power base, then into a new parliament in Ankara, eventually leading to the proclamation of the Republic of Turkey. Evidently, this is the period that produced the myths, not only of the republican state but also its "founding father" and saviour figure, Mustafa Kemal Atatürk; thus, close attention is necessary in order to navigate the murky waters of accumulated source material and historical literature.

The first question that greets us is whether this period belongs to Ottoman or republican history. Regarding the period and the actors living it as the point of departure, however, means that the issue becomes more or less irrelevant. Contemporaneous actors were interested in and concerned with their own current situation. Hence, while many scholars argue that the Ottoman Empire had virtually ended by autumn 1918 with its defeat in World War I, it is crucial to remember that, from the perspective of the Ottomans themselves, it had not. As a stage of contemporary Ottoman realities, considerable effort was actually being directed towards securing its future existence. Furthermore, it is important to keep in mind that it was not at all obvious during the Armistice period that events were going to result in a Turkish nationalist, secularist Republic with Mustafa Kemal as its indisputable leader.

Even though Turkish official history commences the history of the Turkish Republic with Atatürk's landing in Samsun on 19 May 1919—celebrated today as a national holiday—contemporary accounts placed emphasis on different events. This is demonstrated in a booklet issued by the Grand National Assembly in April 1922.[3] Titled "The April 23 Calendar", to commemorate the second anniversary of the GNA, it provided a listing of significant events that occurred following the signing of the Armistice of Mudros. Notably, the Calendar did not mention any of the resistance leaders, including Mustafa Kemal, with the exception of a dedication: "to all the heroes who contributed and made sacrifices". Instead, the Calendar presented the "nation" as the protagonist, highlighting that the nation "saw its very existence threatened and threw itself

---

of suffering, for the sake of our nation's existence and honor." For the full speech, see *Cumhuriyet Halk Fırkası Büyük Kongresi, 1927*. BCA 490.01 / 22.840.2.

[3] Türkiye Büyük Millet Meclisi, *23 Nisan Takvimi*.

into a struggle for the liberation and independence of the homeland".[4] According to the Calendar, the "National Struggle" (*Milli Mücadele*) began when the Armistice of Mudros was violated by the Entente, resulting in "transgressions against the homeland" and leaving "resistance as the only option".[5] The Calendar identified the most significant events as the signing of the armistice (30 October 1918), the occupation of Izmir, the resistance congresses, the National Pact, the establishment of a new parliament in Ankara, the wars with Greece and Armenia, and treaties and peace negotiations.

A "Nationalist" Movement?

Additionally, when analysed in relation to Ottoman nationalism, a critical examination of this period must also include a discussion of the general claim in traditional Turkish history writing of a Turkish nationalist movement and a rebirth and awakening of "the Turkish nation" under Atatürk's leadership during the "national struggle".[6] In this context, the key concept to examine is "nation" (*millet*), and its various derivative adjectives attributed to the resistance movement, by both the members of the movement themselves and others.

In historiography, the general tendency among scholars is to refer to the members of the movement as "the nationalists", or "Turkish nationalists".[7] One possible reason for this is that the resistance movement throughout the armistice period referred to itself as "national" (*milli*), although not "nationalist".[8] Additionally, the label used by the Entente and the European press was also "the nationalists", and even

---

[4] Ibid. 2.

[5] Ibid, 2–4.

[6] Darendelioğlu, *Türkiye'de milliyetçilik*, 12–13.

[7] Prott, while admitting the problematic aspect of defining the resistance movement in ethnolinguistic terms, nonetheless uses "Turkish nationalists" very consistently in his work. Prott, *The Politics of Self-determination*, 83–110.

[8] The word normally used today for "nationalist" (*milliyetci*) had not yet been coined— the closest probably being *milliyetperver* (love for the nation) or *milli his* (national feeling)—the (Pan-)Turkist movement on the other hand, called themselves "Turkists" (*Türkcüler*). In a letter Kara Vasif told the resistance leaders that the Americans saw the resistance movement as an expression of "radical nationalism and religious fanaticism" (*müfrit milliyetperverlik ve taassubi din*), which he rejected. Kirzioglu, *Erzurum*, II, 276.

"Turkish nationalists".[9] However, upon closer examination of the actions and rhetoric of the resistance movement, it becomes evident that this definition falls short of capturing the intricate complexities at play.

Firstly, the tendency to define the resistance movement as solely "nationalist" or "Turkish nationalist" obscures the complex sociopolitical makeup of the movement and its ideas and aims. One particular challenge in this regard is how to place the extensive use of Islamic rhetoric and religious symbolism within the framework of "nationalism". Historians have often resolved this issue by referencing the pragmatism and instrumentalism of the resistance leaders. According to this argument, the resistance leaders, although nationalist, had to act and express themselves along Islamic religious lines in order to secure popular support and mobilize for war. It presupposes that the leadership was nationalist, but the local supporters were not—meaning that the resistance movement contained only one type of nationalism—and further, that the leadership *was* the resistance movement. This is highly problematic when considering the complex composition of the resistance movement, which underwent several stages of power struggles and purges within its ranks, and corresponding significant shifts and changes in the processes of national identity formation, as well as in the rhetoric surrounding the concepts of "nation" and "nationality".

Erik J. Zürcher, in his seminal work on the role of the Unionists in the resistance movement described the movement as "Turkish nationalists".[10] In his later works, however, he nuanced this considerably by exploring further into the rhetoric of the movement. In his "Vocabulary of Muslim Nationalism" for instance, he pointed to the fact that the term "Turk" was indeed used at the local resistance congresses, especially those held in Western Anatolia, but that it was synonymous with "Muslim".[11] Similarly, Mete Tunçay argued that the resistance movement was not pursuing Turkish nationalism in the ethnolinguistic sense, but rather "Muslim nationality". By this choice of word, Tunçay aligned himself with the resistance movement's own conceptual usage, as the movement

---

[9] See for example *Daily News* (London): 24 January 1921; 21 June 1920; 10 December 1920. *Le Temps*, 11 December 1919. *The New York Times*: 15 October 1919; 17 June 1920; 19 August 1920; 3 October 1920; 25 April 1921; 9 November 1921. See also various British reports enclosed in FO 371/4162/174172.

[10] Zurcher, *Unionist Factor*, 23.

[11] Zurcher, *Young Turk Legacy*, 223.

did not call itself "nationalist" but "national" (*milli*). The "national" in this context, as will be analysed further below, functioned as a broader identity marker that was able to include various other ethnic elements. In other words, the *milli* of the resistance movement was more closely aligned with the classic Ottoman understanding of a religiously defined communal entity. It is important to note, however, that the early uses of "Turk" and "Turkish" within the conceptual framework of the "national" and its development in this period must be examined in relation to the specific instances of change, adaptation, and multiplicity of interpretations, expressions, negotiations, and tensions involved, which is often overlooked in scholarship.

ARMISTICE AND THE NEW OTTOMAN REALITIES

It is appropriate to begin the history of the period with the Ottoman defeat, followed by the signing of the Armistice of Mudros on 30 October 1918. With the armistice, a radically new situation emerged as Istanbul came under Entente control, and the CUP lost its power in the capital, soon to be replaced by an anti-Unionist government under *Damat* (Imperial Son-in-Law) Ferid Pasha. Amid the gloomy atmosphere of defeat and unease, however, the Ottoman Government and the public at large also showed signs of hope that the Ottoman state would retain its independence and territorial integrity within Anatolia. These hopes were largely fuelled by American President Woodrow Wilson's 14-point peace program,[12] which envisioned "secure sovereignty" for what he referred to as "the Turkish portion" of the Ottoman Empire—thereby making an unusual semantic differentiation between what in Europe had hitherto been used synonymously, "Turkey" and the "Ottoman Empire" respectively.[13]

---

[12] In January 1918, President Woodrow Wilson presented a proposal to the US Congress, known as the 14-point program for peace, to serve as the basis for peace negotiations at the end of World War I, with the declared goal of ensuring world peace in the future. Among other things, the program advocated the removal of economic barriers between countries and emphasized the principle of self-determination in the post-war peace settlement. Prott, *Politics of Self-determination*, 22.

[13] The usage of "Turkey" in place of "Ottoman Empire" was prevalent in contemporary Europe and the United States, as evident in various sources such as the following titles: Abbott, G. F. (1909). *Turkey in Transition*; Knight, E. F. (1910). *Turkey. The Awakening of Turkey. The Turkish Revolution of 1908*; Ferriman, Z. D. (1911). *Turkey and the Turks*;

Yet, certain provisions within the armistice agreement caused Ottoman concerns, with Article Seven granting the Entente powers the right to occupy any territory deemed a threat to their security being one of them.[14] Another provision, Article 24, referred to the provinces of Erzurum, Sivas, Diyarbekir, Van, Bitlis, and Harput in Eastern Anatolia as "Armenian", and stated that the Entente reserved the right to occupy any part of them "in the case of disorder".[15] Also, a particular concern raised by the Ottoman delegation during the armistice negotiations pertained to Greek military presence within Ottoman territorial waters, fuelling fears of the possibility of Greek occupation.[16] In the following months these concerns, coupled with the Ottoman experiences of territorial loss since the constitutional revolution, put Muslim groups in both the eastern and western regions of Anatolia in a state of high alert. As a result, pockets of resistance began to form in areas perceived to be at risk of occupation or secession.[17]

While the fate of the Ottoman territories yet to be decided in the near future by the Entente powers constituted the most pressing matter, another significant aspect of the new Ottoman realities was the highly unstable political situation—specifically, the future of the Unionist regime. The interaction between these two factors would prove crucial to the dynamics of the Armistice period.

Eddy, D. B. (1913). *What Next in Turkey*; Brailsford, H. N. (1916). *Turkey and The Roads of The East*; Eversley, G. Shaw-Lefevre (1917). *The Turkish Empire—Its Growth and Decay*; Earle, E. M. (1923). *Turkey, The Great Powers, and The Bagdad Railway*.

[14] Article 7: The Allies to have the right to occupy any strategic points in the event of any situation arising which threatens the security of the Allies.

[15] Theese provinces were Erzurum, Sivas, Diyarbekir, Van, Bitlis, and Harput. Article 24 stated, "In case of disorder in the six Armenian vilayets, the Allies reserve to themselves the right to occupy any part of them".

[16] Orbay, *Cehennem Değirmeni*, I, 101, 116, 129–130, 148.

[17] The associations for "Defense of National Rights" (Mudafaa-i Hukuk-i Milliye) began emerging relatively early after the Armistice. For instance, 26 November in Eastern Anatolia, 1 December in Edirne, and 4 November in Istanbul.

The Political Situation: Unionists and Resistance

Immediately after the Ottoman surrender and the subsequent Armistice, the CUP held its final annual congress (1–5 November 1918), during which it officially dissolved itself.[18] While the congress was still ongoing, the top echelon of the CUP fled the country aboard a German submarine.[19] From that point on, it became nearly standard procedure for individuals with a Unionist background to deny any association with CUP, as they not only faced the prospect of shouldering the burden of defeat but also prosecution for the massacre of the Armenian population.[20] The Entente had already announced during the war that those responsible for the massacres would stand trial. The Unionist strategy was to evade responsibility for both defeat and the massacres, starting with the dissolution of the CUP.

In reality, though, the Unionist organization, with its comprehensive networks extending across the state apparatus, particularly the military-bureaucratic establishment, and wider society, was still intact and active.[21] The CUP, described by Şükrü Hanioglu as the strongest political organization in the country, had built this vast organizational structure during its ten years in power—the last five of which constituted a virtual party dictatorship—involving comprehensive purges within the military and bureaucratic ranks, which in turn led to a high degree of convergence between party and state. As seen in previous chapters, the personal and professional connections of the leadership cadres went back even further. When considering what made up Unionism (*Ittihatçılık*), arguably, it was above all these personal and professional networks, and, especially true

---

[18] Tunaya, *Siyasal Partiler*, II, 74-75.

[19] Ertürk, *İki Devrin Perde Arkası*; Karabekir, *Istiklal Harbimizin Esasları*, 33; Tunaya, *Siyasal Partiler*, III, 677–679.

[20] In a joint address to the Ottoman Government the Allies stated that "In view of these new crimes of Turkey against humanity and civilization, the Allied governments announce publicly to the Sublime Porte that they will hold personally responsible [for] these crimes all members of the Ottoman Government and those of their agents who are implicated in such massacres" (The Ambassador in France (Sharp) to the Secretary of State, *Papers Relating to the Foreign Relations of the United States, 1915, Supplement*. https://history.state.gov/historicaldocuments/frus1915Supp/d1398). This assertion had a follow up in the Armistice period by the attempts of the Entente and the central government in Istanbul to set up tribunals to try the individuals responsible for the massacres.

[21] Criss, *Istanbul under Allied Occupation*, 94–105.

for the leadership cadres represented strongly in the Ottoman military and bureaucracy, a shared sense of purpose (as guardians and owners of the state), rather than a well-defined ideology. In addition, the organization further down through the channels of provincial administration resulted in strong provincial networks between party branches, local power-holders, and merchant guilds.[22]

At this point, the course of action chosen by the unionist cadres was of utmost importance. Their immediate move to found a new party, which they tellingly named the Renewal Party (*Teceddüt Fırkası*) indicated that their bid for power had not ended. Their actions ultimately brought alignment between resistance to the Entente's plans for Anatolia, thereby aiming to achieve the liberation of the country and the independence of the state, and their survival strategy as political elite in the armistice setting. Hence, autobiographical sources reveal Unionist plans of adaptation to the new situation at hand. In Husamettin Ertürk's memoirs, for instance, we learn that Enver Pasha held a meeting with Ertürk shortly before leaving the country, at which he outlined the current situation. He told him that the Unionist leaders were leaving as a temporary measure[23] and the Special Organization, now in Ertürk's care, would be transformed into a new secret organization,[24] to help organize resistance in Anatolia and, apparently, prepare the ground for the return of the leaders.[25] In the following months, a new Special Organization, called Karakol, indeed materialized, founded, however, by two other influential Unionists, Kara

---

[22] The internal correspondence of the resistance movement contains ample evidence of the imprint of local Unionist networks, causing conflicts between Unionists and anti-Unionists at the local level. Atatürk, *Nutuk, III:* Vesikalar. For a discussion of the CUP organisational structure and networks, see Tunaya, *Siyasal Partiler*, III, 253–258.

[23] Bleda, a member of the CUP Central Committee, was originally set to depart with the other leaders, as a temporary measure, "until circumstances became calm and the foreign occupation lifted". He was then allowed to remain, because, as he claims, he had had "nothing to do with" (*o hiçbir şeye karışmadı*) the "deportation" (*techir*) of Armenians, indicating that the prospect of prosecution for the Armenian massacres constituted the primary motivation behind the flight of the top-leaders of the CUP. The fact that Bleda remained, did not mean, however, that the Entente was convinced about his non-involvement in the genocide. Following the Armistice, he was arrested along with several other leading Unionists and eventually interned in Malta. Bleda, *İmparatorluğun Çöküşü*, 121–130.

[24] Ertürk, *İki Devrin Perde Arkası*, 165.

[25] Ibid, 168.

6 CLAIMING THE HOMELAND? 133

Kemal and Kara Vasıf[26], who belonged to Talat Pasha's group within the CUP.[27] Initially, Karakol's mission was to safeguard Unionists persecuted for their role in the Armenian massacres.[28] Then, as the resistance began to take shape, it was assigned additional tasks, such as protecting Muslims in occupied areas and smuggling men and arms out—especially from Istanbul.[29]

Mustafa Kemal Pasha's position and actions following the Armistice were indicative of the situation of the Unionist political elite in general, and the military officers in particular, as they found themselves increasingly powerless in the capital. Relieved of his command when the war ended, he came to Istanbul, evidently trying to find a way to influence events.[30] He participated in the debates in the Ottoman press, and actively wrote about the post-war situation, the state and fate of the country, and the possible paths to follow in order to conclude a favourable peace agreement.[31] At the same time, he tried to obtain a governmental post, even proposing himself as Minister of War in the Izzet Pasha cabinet. When that did not materialize, he reportedly tried to be appointed governor in Anatolia with British backing.[32]

Disappointed in all these efforts, after a series of negotiations and meetings with army commanders and Unionist networks, Mustafa Kemal was offered the leading role in the emerging resistance.[33] His standing within the army (and the Unionist cadres)—in addition to his wartime record as an officer who had increasingly distanced himself from the top leadership of the CUP (because of personal grievances)[34]—proved useful

---

[26] Ibid, 205–212.

[27] Criss, *Istanbul under Allied Occupation*, 97–99.

[28] Ertürk, *İki Devrin Perde Arkası*, 205.

[29] Indeed, according to Yerasimos, it was also Karakol, which established contact between the Soviet government and the resistance movement, through the members of the Special Organisation, who had been active in Azerbaijan and Elviyei Selase, and still were in the region. Yerasimos, 107.

[30] Cebesoy, *Milli Mücadele*, 51–56; Orbay, *Cehennem Değirmeni*, I, 222–231; Okyar, *Üç Devirde bir Adam*, 258–261, 274–275.

[31] Zürcher, *Unionist Factor*, 108.

[32] Zurcher, *Unionist Factor*, 107.

[33] Karabekir, *Istiklal Harbimiz*; Cebesoy, *Milli Mücadele*, 50–54; Orbay, *Cehennem Değirmeni*, I, 222–234.

[34] Bleda, *İmparatorluğun Çöküşü*, 102-104; Cebesoy, *Milli Mücadele*, 50–51.

in that regard.[35] As a result, he became commander of the third, and most important, general inspectorate in Anatolia, with vast authority—the golden rope attached to his uniform meant he was officially *fahri yaver-i şehriyari*: that is, honorary personal adjutant of the sultan.

However, his mission as general inspector in Eastern Anatolia was to secure peace in the region, put an end to the increasing unrest, and implement the demobilization of Ottoman forces, which meant, in practice, dissolving the only remaining military force left intact. Enver Pasha had transferred this army corps from the southern front to the Caucasus to conquer territory in the region while the Russian army was crippled by the Bolshevik revolution.[36] The direct cause of Mustafa Kemal's appointment, however, was the reports of mounting regional unrest and massacres of the *Rum* population along the eastern Black Sea coast, for which the Entente demanded immediate action from the Ottoman government.[37] In this respect, the latter set out to suppress any tensions that could technically warrant initiation of the clause in the Armistice agreement giving the Entente powers the right to occupy any territory deemed a threat to their security. Furthermore, the government, believing that resistance through renewed armed struggle would be futile, led a policy of cooperation with the Entente, in the hope of working out a lenient peace agreement.

Coinciding with Mustafa Kemal's departure for Anatolia, news of the Greek occupation of Izmir on 15 May 1919 reached the capital, marking one of the main events of the armistice period. Received as devastating news by the general public, the resulting momentum marked a turning point for the embryonic resistance movement. Consequently, building on an atmosphere of fear and resentment, the occupation arguably

---

[35] His appointment, which Zürcher has ascribed to the Unionist networks especially within the Ottoman army, was the result of a complex set of negotiations between various actors. For a detailed discussion on the issue, see Zürcher, *Unionist Factor*. See also Cebesoy, *Milli Mücadele,* 54–57. Ahmet Izzet Pasha claims the Unionists had approached him, before Mustafa Kemal, to lead the Unionist efforts for resistance in Anatolia, which he allegedly declined. Ahmet Izzet Paşa, *Feryadım*, II, 62–63.

[36] According to Ali Fuat Cebesoy, Enver Pasha told him, during a meeting in Moscow, that it had been his plan with the army he sent to the Caucasus, depending on the severity of the conditions imposed by the Entente, to establish a provisional government in Baku and with that army to spearhead the resistance and to "restore the homeland." Cebesoy, *Milli Mücadele,* 59–60.

[37] Cebesoy, *Milli Mücadele,* 80.

provided the resistance with the most effective instrument for mobilizing general support, which found its immediate expression in widespread demonstrations, the biggest of which took place in Istanbul.[38]

According to some accounts, the demonstrations drew in as many as 200,000 participants and continued at intermittent intervals until January 1920.[39] The speeches delivered during these demonstrations reveal that intellectuals, particularly those affiliated with the Turkish Hearth (*Türk Ocağı*),[40] played a dominant role. One of the most prominent figures in this regard was Halide Edip, who called for national solidarity in "the dark hour of the nation" and delivered several emotional and patriotic speeches focused on the argument that the Ottomans were victims of injustice. This indeed became the common theme of the demonstrations and was expressed through two main accusations against the Entente powers. The first accusation was that the latter had violated their agreements by allowing the Greek occupation of Izmir, which had no justification according to the terms of the Armistice. The second accusation was that Greece had not been engaged in war with the Ottomans and had not won battles against them; thus, it was argued that they had no right to be awarded territory in Anatolia.[41]

Commenting on the demonstrations, Mustafa Kemal wrote to Halide Edip and others, stating that protests would not accomplish any great goals, while the "national forces" (*kuva-i milliye*) would.[42] He was referring to the resistance taking shape since the signing of the Armistice, initially organized as local associations to resist a possible occupation or annexation, which then evolved into armed resistance. In Western Anatolia, it manifested as armed bands aiming to halt the advancement of Greek troops, which, after their landing in Izmir, began moving further

[38] Arıburnu, *Istanbul Mitingleri*, 39.

[39] Ibid.

[40] The Turkish Hearth was a Unionist association founded in 1912, with Ahmet Ferit (Tek) and Yusuf Akçura as its president and vice-president respectively. Declaring itself a non-political organization, and promising it would "never support any political party", it had the declared aim of highlighting Turkish culture and language, and to work for the advancement of the social, intellectual and economic life of the Turkish people. The Turkish Hearth association was transformed in 1931 into Atatürk's People's Houses (*Halkevleri*) which disseminated national culture in the provinces. For the text of the Turkish Hearth's regulations from 1912, see Üstel, *Türk Ocakları*, 100–103.

[41] Arıburnu, *Istanbul Mitingleri*.

[42] Atatürk, *Nutuk*, III: Vesikalar, 917.

inland in the Aydin province. Until a regular army could be deployed, these "bands" (*çete*) became the front line of the resistance, relying heavily on local forces and popular support.⁴³

The Officers Make Their Move

As the army constituted the dominant power in the country, Mustafa Kemal's leadership role within both the military-bureaucratic apparatus in Anatolia and the resistance movement, which had already begun by organizing locally in different parts of Anatolia and Thrace, depended heavily on commanders in the field recognizing him as a leading figure.⁴⁴ An early sign of this recognition occurred when military commanders took their first decisive action after a meeting with Kemal in Amasya in June 1919.⁴⁵ Subsequently, they issued the famous Amasya Circular (*Amasya Tamimi*), announcing coordination among commanders, agreement, and plans for further action.

The Circular, parts of which were kept secret, including the section revealing the names of the commanders participating in the endeavour,⁴⁶ further declared that Istanbul was under Entente control, the sultan virtually a captive in his own capital, and the government unable to safeguard the interests of the nation. "This situation makes our nation appear nonexistent", the Circular further stated, which is why it was necessary to "make the world hear the rightful voice of the nation".⁴⁷ Therefore, the Circular added, a "national committee" (*heyet-i milliye*), "free from all interference" would be formed and a "national congress" convene in Sivas, within the organizational structure of the associations for the

---

⁴³ Cebesoy, *Milli Mücadele Hatıraları*, 151–166.

⁴⁴ Zürcher, *Unionist Factor*, 119.

⁴⁵ Cebesoy, *Milli Mücadele*, 89–96; Akşin, *İstanbul Hükümetleri*, I, 424–425.

⁴⁶ The names provided were Mustafa Kemal (Atatürk), Hüseyin Rauf (Orbay), Kazim Karabekir, Ali Fuat (Cebesoy), Refet (Bele), Cevdet (Ahmet), Cemal (Mersinli), Selahattin (Mehmet), Cafer Tayyar (Eğilmez), Bekir Sami (Günsav), Hamit Bey" and "other military and bureaucratic personnel of importance" (*diğer bazı mülki ve askeri mühim zevat*). Among the names mentioned in the circular, only Hamit Bey, the governor of Canik, was non-military. Cebesoy, *Milli Mücadele*, 93–94.

⁴⁷ Cebesoy, *Milli Mücadele*, 93–94; Atatürk, *Nutuk*, III: Vesikalar, 915–916. Circular (*Tamim*), dated June 22, 1919.

"Defence of National Rights" (*Müdafaa-i Hukuk-i Milliye*) and "Rejection of Annexation" (*Redd-i Ilhak*). The general congress in Sivas was to build upon the existing resistance organizations and thus consisted of delegates sent by the local branches of resistance.

This radical move by the military commanders to challenge the central government immediately raised the question of legitimacy, as their actions, without providing a just cause, would appear as little more than a military rebellion. In this context, representing the nation became the focal point of departure. However, this also raised the next line of questions: who was this "nation" and how and by whom would it be represented? According to the Amasya Circular, the representational platform was the congresses, both regional and national, while the local resistance associations were to function as the organizational body. Thus, at the end of the line stood the local resistance networks already in existence, the support which the military-bureaucratic elite desperately needed, not only for legitimization purposes but also in relation to mobilization of popular support and participation in the resistance.

An indication of the significance of local power groups in the resistance movement was demonstrated by the regional congress in Erzurum (held between 23 July and 7 August 1919), which was called by the local resistance associations in Eastern Anatolia to be held prior to the general congress announced by the military-bureaucratic leadership. This was something Mustafa Kemal had to reckon with and incorporate into his plans for uniting the resistance efforts under one rule and direction. Thus, the first major gathering of the resistance, which figures prominently in the official narrative in Turkey about the resistance movement and Mustafa Kemal's originating role in it—was actually organized locally. In fact, he was only able to participate as a member of the congress after some behind the scenes discussions[48] and the intervention of General Kazım Karabekir,[49] which provides an insight into the emerging power dynamics within the resistance movement. The actual state authority in the region was vested in the military, commanded by General Karabekir, who intervened on behalf of another general to establish a prominent role for the latter in relation to local groups.

---

[48] Dursunoğlu, *Milli Mücadelede Erzurum*, 98.
[49] Karabekir, *Istiklal Harbimizin Esasları*, 73–75.

The dependence on local support, in turn, necessitated cooperation and negotiation, and, more importantly, sharing power, by the inclusion of local elites, such as landowners, professionals, merchants, and religious leaders, into the leadership of the movement. As a result, an alliance was forged between the military-bureaucratic elite and the local groups, which would determine the dynamics within the resistance movement, as well as the characteristics and the vocabulary of national identity during the Armistice period. By opening up the political process, giving the resistance movement a more democratic character in terms of a plurality of opinion and possibility of opposition consequently created a highly dynamic and fluid process, where the local communal viewpoints often dominated the rhetoric. Mustafa Kemal's statements can shed important light on this issue. At a meeting held by the executive branch of the Sivas Congress, the Representative Committee (*Heyeti Temsiliye*), he spoke of two possible paths to choose from, "one is to move forward according to the true wishes and opinions of this nation, and the other is to act according to our own ideas. It is necessary to proceed not according to personal convictions, but by considering the opinions, feelings, and sentiments of the people".[50] While Mustafa Kemal did not make clear what he meant by "our own ideas", and to whom it exactly referred, the formulation made it apparent that it was not identical with "the people". However, it was clear that in the current state of affairs, local tendencies and power groups would have a greater influence.

The Sivas Congress, held from 4–11 September 1919, served as an indication of this fact. On the one hand, it was an expression of the military-bureaucratic leadership's efforts to bring the locally organized resistance associations under one roof and central authority. As such, although covering a broader geographic area and having delegates from various parts of Anatolia and Thrace, the Sivas Congress was less local and more under the control of the military-bureaucratic elite.[51] The same applied to the Representative Committee (*Heyeti Temsiliye*), tasked with implementing the decisions of the congress after its adjournment. When it came to basic principles, rhetoric, and goals, however, the Sivas Congress continued those decided in Erzurum, thus building upon a template

---

[50] Mustafa Kemal's speech at a Representative Committee meeting (17 November 1919). Tunçay, *Tek-Parti*, 216.

[51] Gologlu, *Erzurum*, 206. Tanör, *Anayasal Gelişmeleri*, 224–225.

established by a regional congress based on local and regional concerns in Eastern Anatolia. As a result, the decisions made at the Erzurum Congress were carried forward through the Sivas Congress, the last Assembly of Deputies, and the new parliament in Ankara, creating an enduring effect.

The general agreement of the congresses does not imply, however, that complete concurrence existed among all factions and individual members of the resistance movement. On the contrary, there were significant differences in opinions that coexisted and collided, not least issues pertaining to the national question, where perspectives and positions varied considerably based on factors such as location, group affiliation, individual viewpoint, particular interests, and points of reference. Furthermore, discourses on nation and national identity were particularly influenced by three major impulses, characterized as arising from governmental, societal, and external factors—or, put differently, impulses from above, from below, and from the outside. Although the distinctions between these impulses were not always clear, a thorough examination of the sources, actors, and discourses involved reveals a discernible pattern.

WILSON AND NATIONAL SELF-DETERMINATION

The external factor was born out of the new Ottoman realities following defeat in WWI, leaving the Ottomans in a highly weakened state and dependent on the wishes of the victors, the Entente. In this juncture, where the very existence of the Ottoman state was threatened, the proposals for a post-war peace settlement presented by the American President, Woodrow Wilson, based on self-determination,[52] created hope and expectations on the Ottoman side. This idea of the right of nations to determine their own fate, meaning governing themselves and forming their own states,[53] would, if applied, of course, entail vast implications, especially for the defeated multiethnic empires, the Austro-Hungarian and the Ottoman.[54] Empires dismantled, qualifying as a "nation", and laying claim to a given territory on the basis of a "national" population majority, would thus gain great importance. The twelfth of Wilson's Fourteen

---

[52] Manela, *The Wilsonian Moment*, 17.

[53] Fisch, *The Right of Self-Determination of Peoples*, 32; Sterio, *Right to Self-determination*, 16.

[54] Not to mention the implication of such a principle for the imperial Entente powers, the British in particular. See in that regard Liebich, *Cultural Nationhood*, 73.

Points, guaranteeing "Turkish" sovereignty, placed the national question at the centre of Ottoman discussions relating to the fate of the Empire in the upcoming peace negotiations.

The relevance of Wilson's peace program for this study, however, lies not so much in its implementation, or the lack thereof[55], but its effects on the Ottoman attempts at bringing into alignment the existing concepts of "nation" (*millet*) with what was thought and understood to be the meaning contained in the Fourteen Points. Functioning as a central point of reference, the idea of nations having the right to self-determination had a direct impact on the way Ottomans' framing "nation" and national identity in the new setting of the Armistice period. To illustrate, two concepts that dominated the rhetoric regarding the national question in this period, "national rights" (*hukuk-i milliye*) and "national sovereignty" (*hakimiyet-i milliye*), respectively, were both closely linked to the principle of self-determination, although operating in different contexts.

Measured by the frequency of use of these two concepts in the source material point to a sequential shift occurring at some point during this period, divided between the two phases of the resistance, marked especially by the opening of the new Parliament in Ankara. In the first phase, "national rights" dominated the vocabulary of the resistance movement. The importance ascribed to the concept was shown from the very beginning by the names given to the resistance branches taking shape in Anatolia and Thrace soon after the signing of the Armistice.[56] They were commonly called "Association for Defence of National Rights" (*Müdafaa-i Hukuk Cemiyeti*) followed by their respective geographical designation.[57] Thus, when these local organizations became united under one roof at the Sivas Congress, the resistance movement called itself Association for the Defence of Rights of Anatolia and Rumelia (*Anadolu ve Rumeli Müdafaa-i Hukuk Cemiyeti*) (hereafter referred to as ADR)—a name retained until 1923. The type of defence of this right

---

[55] For in the end, Wilson's idea to incorporate the principle of self-determination, which had become synonymous with his name as *Wilsonism*, into the League of Nations Covenant was unsuccessful, and so was the realization of the political ideals in practice. Getachew, *Worldmaking after Empire*, 39; Liebich, *Cultural Nationhood*, 73–75.

[56] The earliest of these began springing up in late 1918, Kars, Erzurum, Thrace, all areas thought to be in immediate danger of occupation or secession. Zürcher, *Unionist Factor*, 89–91.

[57] Another common name used was "Rejection of Annexation" (*Redd-i İlhak*).

was contingent on the particular stage of the struggle at hand. In the formative phase, the resistance was operating from a position of weakness, lacking resources, military power, legitimacy, and legality. As a result, the defence of rights during this stage took the form of organization building, mobilization, and formulation of objectives and aims.

From the start, the resistance movement was highly conscious and direct in its appeal to the right to self-determination. The congresses in Erzurum and Sivas stated explicitly "the right of nations to determine their own destiny is a well-established principle in the entire world" and the fundamental principle of civilized countries.[58] Furthermore, self-determination not only served as a means of claiming ownership of a given territory, it also provided justification for resistance. The congresses in Sivas and Erzurum declared that in case the Ottoman state was forced to secede territory inhabited by the "nation" resistance "by all means" would be legitimate and there would be established a provisional government to keep the ties with the Ottoman state. An example was given in Kars, where, as the Ottoman army was forced to withdraw from the region, a provisional republic, the so-called Islamic National Council (*Milli Islam Şurası*), had been proclaimed on 5 November 1918 based on the principle of self-determination.[59]

The main task, then, was to demonstrate the existence of the "nation" by categories accepted by "the entire world", which in this case meant the Entente powers. That, however, proved difficult, first because such definitions would have to satisfy not only the external audience but also the internal coalition comprising the resistance movement. Hence, it had to be in accordance with the requirements of self-determination, while at the same time safeguarding—at least not disturbing—the internal cohesion of the resistance coalition. Consequently, the resistance movement engaged in a complex endeavour to incorporate existing markers of identity into a workable conceptual framework able to meet different needs and goals.

The movement found the external audience hard to convince, however. "Seeing that the general public in Europe is very much against us", one delegate said, "our only option is to tell and demonstrate thoroughly that

---

[58] While the proceedings of the Erzurum Congress are documented in Kırzıoğlu's *Bütünüyle Erzurum Kongresi*, for the transcripts of the Sivas Congress see Iğdemir's *Sivas Kongresi Tutanakları*.

[59] Balistreri, *Provisional Republic*, 65–69. Uran, *Hatıralarım*, 96–109.

the people are united in opinion".[60] In order to sway the European public it was thought necessary to demonstrate the existence of a national entity in Anatolia and Rumelia.[61] In order to achieve this, expert commissions were assembled to examine the issue from various perspectives and present the results to foreign visitors. The Erzurum congress placed a significant emphasis on the communication skills of those responsible for interacting with these visitors, stating that fluency in French was essential and not just "half-way" understanding (*yarım yamalak*).[62] These efforts were especially aimed at convincing the King-Crane commission, tasked with conducting inquiries concerning Ottoman territories including Anatolia, whose findings were to be submitted to the Paris Peace Conference.[63] To bolster its claims, the movement conducted inquiries of its own, such as demographic surveys, interviews, and conferences to demonstrate that Eastern Anatolia belonged to the "nation".[64] To accomplish this, a connection had to be established between territory, population, nation, and representation. As Milena Sterio concisely summarizes:

> For a group to be entitled to exercise its collective right to self-determination, it must qualify as a "people." Traditionally, a two-part test has been applied to determine when a group qualifies as a people. The first prong of the test is objective and seeks to evaluate the group to determine to what extent its members "share a common racial background, ethnicity, language, religion, history, and cultural heritage," as well as "territorial integrity of the area the group is claiming." The second prong of the test is subjective and examines "the extent to which individuals within the group self-consciously perceive themselves collectively as a distinct 'people,'" and "the degree to which the group can form a viable political entity."[65]

The process analysed here aligns well with this template, forming a two-stage development divided by the opening of the new parliament in April 1920. In the first phase, the emphasis was on identifying the group, its shared characteristics, and its territory. What was the geographical extent

---

[60] Kırzıoğlu, *Erzurum*, I, 33.
[61] Ibid.
[62] Kırzıoğlu, *Erzurum*, Belgeler, XII, 24–26.
[63] Heater, *National Self-Determination*, 63.
[64] Kırzıoğlu, *Erzurum*, Belgeler, XI, 23.
[65] Sterio, *Right to Self-determination*, 16.

of the new territory imagined and claimed? In the Fourteen Points President Wilson spoke of the "Turkish portion of the present Ottoman Empire". While it is highly doubtful, whether the resistance movement understood the same thing as Wilson regarding the "Turkish portion", early conceptualizations of the idea seem to have occurred nonetheless. The opening ceremony of the Erzurum Congress, for example, contained a prayer for victory to the "Islamic Government of Ottoman Turkey" (*Islam hükümetinin Osmanlı Türkiyesi*).[66]

In a memorandum to Wilson, reminding him that the Greek occupation of Izmir was incompatible with his principles, the congress expressed another variation of the concept. Submitted in Turkish, the congress changed, by translation, Wilson's original formulation "the Turkish portion of the present Ottoman Empire" to "the portions of the Turkish Empire inhabited by Turks",[67] thus using Turkish and Ottoman synonymously, while at the same time defining "Turkish portion" as areas populated by "Turks". Whether the "Turkish" population then also meant "Ottoman", was not specified by the memorandum, although Wilson's term "nationalities" was translated as "elements" (*anasır*), which, as will be remembered, was the concept used by the Ottomans to differentiate the *millet*s—thus complicating the matter even further as "Turks" did not constitute an "element" (*unsur*), while Muslims, Armenians and *Rum*s did. Nor was it clear what this "Turkish" population territorially corresponded with exactly.

The general congress in Sivas provided a more concrete demarcation. Debating what parts of the Ottoman Empire the resistance movement was representing and fighting for, it was finally defined as "Anatolia and Rumelia" (*Anadolu ve Rumeli*).[68] In a public speech explaining the decisions of the congresses in Erzurum and Sivas, Mustafa Kemal provided further geographical details. Speaking in December 1919, Kemal announced the new "national" borders to the South East as Antakya, Dirizor (Deir ez-Zur), Musul (Mosul), Kerkük (Kirkuk), Süleymaniye (Sulaymaniyah), as such drawing a line further into what is now Syria and Iraq. "These borders, which are defended with arms by our army,

---

[66] Kırzıoğlu, *Erzurum*, II, 9.

[67] *Türk İmparatorluğu'nun Türklerle meskun olan aksamında*. Kırzıoğlu, *Erzurum*, II, 155.

[68] "Rumelia" in this case referring to southeastern Thrace, including Edirne.

and include the areas inhabited by Turks and Kurds, delineate our homeland", Kemal said, and "are inseparable from the Ottoman community" (*camiai Osmaniyeden layenfek*).[69]

Ultimately, though, the extent of the "national" borders was determined, as also alluded to by Mustafa Kemal, by the more realistic criteria: what can be "defended with arms?" A reference to something as tangible as the territory still held by the Ottoman army at the time of the signing of the Armistice. "Outside these borders" (*hudud haricinde kalan*),[70] Mustafa Kemal said, "are our Arabic speaking fellow Muslims"[71], thus pointing to an emerging conceptual divide between "people of Anatolia" and that of "Arabia", and an indication that the view on the Arabic regions of the Ottoman Empire as now lost was taking root. On the issue of an American mandate and its territorial extent, the leaders of the resistance movement questioned whether people of Anatolia had any right to speak on behalf of "Arabia".

From Population to Nation

Population, on the other hand, posed a greater difficulty to define and defend in Wilsonian terms. Within the territory drawn up, the population needed to be presented as a nation with a political "national will" (*irade-i milliye*) deserving of independent government according to international norms.[72] In its first declaration, the Defence of Rights Society for Eastern Anatolia refuted the Armenian claims to Eastern Anatolia based on population, religion, culture, traditions, history, geography, communal and family bonds, and a sense of unity in thought and feeling.[73] The Erzurum and Sivas Congresses, presented as platforms representing the "national will"[74], using concepts such as "the Ottoman homeland" (*Osmanlı vatanı*), "the Ottoman Domains" (*Memalik-i Osmaniye*) and

---

[69] Atatürk, *Söylev ve Demeçleri*, II, 12.

[70] Ibid.

[71] Ibid, 15.s.

[72] Ibid, 77.

[73] The first declaration of the Association for the Defense of National Rights of the Eastern Provinces (*Vilayat-ı Şarkiye Müdafa-i Hukuk-ı Milliye Cemiyeti*), 3 March 1919. Kırzıoğlu, *Erzurum*, I, 10–11.

[74] Iğdemir, *Sivas Kongresi*, 111, 115.

"the Ottoman society" (*camiai Osmaniye*) unified as "full brothers" (*öz kardeş*) "fully committed to" (*tamamiyle riayetkar*) "feelings of mutuality and sacrifice" (*hissiyat-ı mutekabile ve fedakarlık*), "ethnic rights" (*hukuk-i ırkiyye*), and "conditions of locality" (*şerait-i muhitiye*).[75] When trying to narrow down the definition of the nation, however, all these categories led to one dominant group: Muslims of the remaining Ottoman lands, Anatolia and Rumelia. The main argument, therefore, was that the Muslim population of Anatolia and Rumelia constituted "one nation" (*millet-i vahide*),[76] whose rights as such should be established according to principles of national self-determination.[77]

Despite the prominence of Islamic identity, themes, and language in the resistance movement, caution should be taken when assessing the extent of its Islamic nationalism. Although the notion of "one nation" (*millet-i vahide*) used by the Erzurum branch of the ADR exhibits similarities with the Quranic concept of *ummah wahidah* ("one community"), the usage was adapted to the specific needs of the ADR, in this case referring to a community of Muslims in a particular area. As such, the Muslim "nation" advocated by the movement did not encompass all Muslims worldwide and did not aim to unite the Islamic *ummah*. The movement's reference to an anti-imperialist struggle for all Muslims was sporadic and not accompanied by additional commitment or concrete actions.[78] Most indicative in that regard was the stance towards the Arabic regions of the Ottoman Empire, as expressed by Mustafa Kemal as a hope that they might one day gain independence, but on the concrete level, they had to fend for themselves within "their own interior" (*kendi dahillerinde*).[79] Within that framework, the "nation" of the resistance movement was not just Muslims, but Muslims with a specific territorial and sociopolitical affiliation. In this regard, it bore a high degree of resemblance to the Hamidian territorial Islamic Ottoman nationalism.

---

[75] Ibid, 113.
[76] Kırzıoğlu, *Erzurum*, I, 86.
[77] İğdemir, *Sivas Kongresi*, 115.
[78] Kırzıoğlu, *Erzurum*, II, 49–52.
[79] Atatürk, *Söylev ve Demeçleri*, II, 15.

The Ottoman non-Muslims and the Resistance Movement

While the resistance movement made ample use of religious themes and vocabulary to mobilize popular support and foster unity within the ADR, another unifying element was found in the construction of an enemy image projected as the nation's other. This projection depicted both an external and an internal adversary—the Entente powers and the Ottoman *Rum*s and Armenians, respectively. The latter was increasingly portrayed as collaborators with Greece and Armenia. The occupation of Izmir was highly instrumental in that regard, contributing effectively to the redefinition of the threat and its source. In short, the processes of inclusion and exclusion placed the *Rum*s and Armenians, and thereby religious communal affiliation, at the centre, serving as an important element in the construction of "us" vs. "them".

Hence, the "national struggle" (*milli mücadele*) was increasingly framed by the resistance movement as a conflict between Muslims and non-Muslim "elements" of the Ottoman Empire.[80] At the Erzurum Congress the central argument was that the resistance was an act of self-defence against the aggression from *Rum*s and Armenians who acted as instruments of the Entente powers. While clearly defined as the other, the *Rum*s and Armenians were not "foreigners" (*ecnebi*),[81] which in turn made it possible to portray them as an internal enemy, accused of ingratitude and betrayal. According to Mustafa Kemal:

> The *Rum* and Armenian elements, although Ottoman subjects, embarked, with the encouragement and support from the Entente powers, on some outrageous transgressions, starting with displays of insolence deeply wounding our national honor, that continued until reaching a tragic and bloody stage.[82]

---

[80] While the adversary was defined as the *Rum* and Armenians, other non-Muslim population elements were not mentioned at the congresses of Erzurum and Sivas, however.

[81] According to Suleyman Bey the danger came from the Armenians, the *Rum*, and "the foreign elements" (*unsur-i Ecnebi*)—one of which was identified by Avni Bey as "the English". Kırzıoğlu, *Erzurum*, II, 76.

[82] *Tebaai Osmaniye'den olan Rum ve Ermeni anasırı Düveli Itilafiye'den gördükleri teşvik ve müzaheretin netayiciyle de, namusu millimizi cerihadar edecek taşkınlıklardan başlıyarak, nihayet hazin ve kanlı safhalara girinceye kadar küstahane tecavüzata koyuldular.* Kırzıoğlu, *Erzurum*, II, 16.

The designation of the *Rum*s and Armenians as *tebaa*, meaning subject—but also used to denote citizenship—set up against "our national" (*millimiz*) constitutes a striking example of framing nationality as different levels of belonging. Furthermore, the ADR spoke often of a *Rum* and Armenian "creation", meaning independence or autonomy to said populations in Anatolia, which it described as a threat to the national existence of the Muslim population. The final declaration of Sivas Congress stated that intervention of any kind would be seen "as actions serving the goals to create *Rum* and Armenian independence within our homeland", against which a unified defence and resistance would be formed. Evidently, there was a deep-felt fear of occupation and secession, which explains why the resistance associations first emerged in the eastern and western parts of Anatolia. However, the reactions and the rhetoric used indicate that the prospect of *Rum* and Armenian rule over the said territories acted as a strengthening factor in that regard. Arguably, a result of highly complex issues with many dimensions, not the least the experiences of the immediate past, the Balkan Wars and WWI, but also the strong claim of the *Rum*s and Armenians to territory in Anatolia, reinforced by the recognition by the European powers of such claims.

At the Erzurum Congress, fear of Armenian rule over Eastern Anatolia was presented as one of the primary reasons for resistance. In a communique issued by the Erzurum branch of the ADR, it was claimed that "an Armenian rule of any kind, even if autonomy, would mean the annulment of the right of Muslims in these lands".[83] The policies of the Entente powers were interpreted as a "clear indication that our country will be put under Armenian rule", why it was necessary to "unite in order not to perish under Armenian tyranny".[84] The perception of danger was not limited to loss of sovereignty and territory, however. One of the delegates at the Erzurum Congress worriedly pointed out, that there was a risk that those who had "taken part in the plunder" (*yağmalara iştirak edenler*) and had "benefited from the abandoned properties" (*emval-i metrukeden*

---

[83] Kırzıoğlu, *Erzurum*, I, 34.

[84] *Memleketlerimizin Ermeni idaresine terkedilebileceğine dair artık kat'i emareler zuhur ettiğinden ... Ermeni zulmü altında mahvolmamak için birleşmek.* Kırzıoğlu, *Erzurum*, I, 34–35.

istifade edenler)⁸⁵ if annexation by Armenia became a reality, would face the prospect of punishment and loss of their material gains.⁸⁶

Considering the future of non-Muslims and the possibility of coexistence after the coming of peace, both the Erzurum and Sivas Congresses stated that they would be allowed to stay within the Ottoman borders, but no special rights and privileges would be granted to them.⁸⁷ However, discussions during the congresses made it clear that the delegates leaned more towards envisioning a future without the non-Muslim population. In pursuit of this vision, considerations of population politics and demographic engineering were never far away. For instance, in a report presented to Mustafa Kemal in Erzurum, Kara Vasıf suggested plans for a population exchange with Armenia. According to Vasıf, it was a "necessity" (*lüzumlu*) to exchange Armenians of Eastern Anatolia with Turks and Kurds from Armenia.⁸⁸ Although finding the idea desirable, one delegate pointed out that its implementation was impossible, as, according to his estimation, there was not a Muslim population of equal size on the opposite side for such an exchange.⁸⁹

Kurds, Turks and Ottoman Muslim Unity

In the process of reimagining and conceptualizing the nation in accordance with the principle of self-determination, the resistance movement soon encountered discrepancies. While advocating self-determination, the movement had to contend with the inescapable fact that the Ottoman Muslim "nation" it claimed to represent, still had a multiethnic character. More importantly, in Southeast Anatolia Kurds constituted a majority. Consequently, if the "Turkish portion" of the Fourteen Points meant self-determination of "Turks" as a distinct ethnic entity, separated from the other ethnic components of the movement, then, by implication, the ADR's primary goal of preserving the territorial unity of the Ottoman state within Anatolia would be unattainable. It is telling in this regard, that the term "Turk" was rarely used during the congresses of Erzurum

---

⁸⁵ Meaning the properties of Armenians left behind during the deportations.
⁸⁶ Kırzıoğlu, *Erzurum*, I, 85–86.
⁸⁷ Kırzıoğlu, *Erzurum*, II, 252; Iğdemir, *Sivas Kongresi*, 114.
⁸⁸ Kırzıoğlu, *Erzurum*, II, 278.
⁸⁹ Ibid, 188.

and Sivas. When it occurred, it was often in connection with Wilson's principles. Although gaining relevancy for formulating the claims of the resistance movement in a relatable language towards European and American audiences, internally the ADR-members toned down such references as much as possible.

Characteristically, the occasional references came with an attachment of semantic fluidity, such as "Turk" meaning "Muslim" or "Ottoman Muslim". For instance when the Defence of Rights Society for Eastern Provinces stated that the principle of self-determination "would recognize no other nation's right to sovereignty over these lands than the Turks'" the given reason was that the "Muslim population" (*Islam nüfusu*) constituted the majority in comparison to the Armenian, thereby using "Turk" and "Muslim" synonymously, in contrast to "Armenian".[90] Not surprisingly, one of the greatest challenges posed by the idea of self-determination, and the implications of defining the nation based on contemporary European categories, involving the ethnolinguistic aspects in particular, was in relation to the preservation of Ottoman Muslim solidarity within the movement generally, and between Kurds and Turks in particular.

As revealed by a confidential report submitted to the Erzurum Congress by the Erzurum branch of the ADR, there was a noticeable difference between the outward language and the internal communications. While promoting the principle of self-determination of nations, internally the implicit meaning and concrete application of this principle was seen as highly dangerous and divisive, as it was a double-edged sword, which also could, and did, mean the self-determination not only of Armenians and *Rum*s, but also of Kurds, within Anatolia. In that case, the rhetoric could quickly turn into criticism of ethnic nationalism, denigrated in that case as "Turkishness-Kurdishness propaganda" (*Türklük-Kürtlük propagandası*). According to the report, this was a method of "divide and rule" (*Tefrika düşür, sonra zabt-et*), devised by Europeans "to sow discord" (*fitne*) within the "Muslim countries (*Islam ülkeleri*) under the guise of "representing the fundamental population element" (*Unsuri asliyi temsil etmek*), while in fact trying to "make void their fundamental

---

[90] Kırzıoğlu, *Erzurum*, I, 10–11.

traditions of religion and language in order to cause their disintegration".[91] Then the report went on to explain what made a people and a nation, and on what grounds, providing valuable insight into what the Erzurum branch of the ADR understood by contemporary European concepts related to nationalism.

The report began by rejecting the validity of racial divisions; "as there is no pure race in the world, and the racial theory, has been disproved by all the scholars of sociology".[92] "What makes a people differ from another", the report continued, "is differences of religion, moral disposition, tradition, and language". It then went on to illustrate why the Turks and Kurds belonged together, while Armenians did not, according to the criteria it deemed viable, as such turning to some of the categories it previously claimed were instruments of Europeans to create discord between Muslims by invalidating "their fundamental traditions religion and language". At that point, though, the purpose of the report became clear. Worried about the influence of nationalism on Kurds in Eastern Anatolia, the ADR Erzurum branch sought to refute claims of separateness between Turks and Kurds based on contemporary European concepts related to nation and nationality. While trying to find commonality between "Turks" and "Kurds" on the accounts considered, the report encountered serious difficulties, however, especially when it came to language. Admitting that they belonged to separate families of languages, the report concluded ambivalently that, compared to the Armenian language, Turkish and Kurdish had more in common, as there between them "possibly" (*belki*) existed "a great connection of language and custom".[93]

Importantly, to distinguish between Turk, Kurd and Armenian, the report chose the term *kavim*, meaning people or ethnic group, and not *millet*. The latter term it used to express national belonging, as in "our nation" (*milletimiz*), thereby tacitly including "Turks" and "Kurds" into one category. Accordingly, while Kurds and Turks could be differentiated as ethnic units, as a "nation" they were one. In this setting, the "nation" was narrowed down to "Muslim" and "Ottoman", portraying the non-Muslim population "elements" as the nation's other. Referring

---

[91] Kırzıoğlu, *Erzurum*, I, 90.
[92] Ibid.
[93] Kırzıoğlu, *Erzurum*, I, 95.

to the Muslim population in the former Ottoman territories in Europe, the report claimed, "the non-Muslims made us emigrate, and have thus become the majority",[94] and emphasized the significance of the existing situation of preserving Ottoman unity (*vahdeti Osmaniyye*) and maintaining the Muslim majority in each area as "the foremost patriotic and religious duty".[95]

Not surprisingly, the importance of Muslim unity and solidarity as a patriotic and religious obligation was particularly emphasized in regard to Kurds. According to the Erzurum congress: "The historical and national duty to defend and maintain the sacred rights of Muslims has befallen the Turk and Kurd who by their shared blood, history and religion are as one".[96] In an appeal to Kurdish notables of Diyarbekir and Mardin in Eastern Anatolia, the Erzurum branch of the ADR sent a telegram asking for their support, claiming that the "Armenian nation" (*Ermeni milleti*) was trying to undermine the rights of Muslims as a "nation made up of Kurds and Turks constituting the majority in our Eastern Provinces". Next, the telegram laid out the arguments why it was "vitally important for all the sons of the Eastern Provinces to unite in language and purpose".[97] According to the Erzurum branch of the ADR:

> You surely cannot sacrifice the religious, patriotic and traditional duty at the inculcation of the enemies of Islam. Especially when, among the population of the seven provinces, which is projected to be placed under Christian rule, there are no others than the Turk and the Kurd,[98] who have become an inseparable family, as each other's brothers, sons-in-law, maternal and paternal uncles etc.
>
> Centuries of intermixing of blood and social life has produced moral and material ties between the Turk and the Kurd in our Eastern Provinces, bringing them together by a shared existence and fate. We are convinced that external inculcations cannot dissolve this fellowship and unity.
>
> The time is short; our common homeland is in danger. If the currents of division and dissent that our enemies want to instigate here are not

---

[94] Ibid, 101.
[95] Ibid, 101–102.
[96] Ibid, 57.
[97] Ibid, 66–68.
[98] Apparently, a reference to the demographic composition of Eastern Anatolia after the destruction of the Armenian population.

rejected, we ourselves will have handed over the supremacy and victory to the Armenians, in which case we see it as our brotherly duty to remind you that we will not be able to escape responsibility neither in this world nor in the next.[99]

The involvement of Kurds in the resistance movement indicates that the movement was ultimately successful in securing the support of Kurdish leaders, despite the activities of Kurdish nationalist currents in Eastern Anatolia,[100] and also that Ottoman Muslim solidarity was not just empty rhetoric, but rather a potent tool for popular mobilization and the formation of solidarity.[101] However, the Eastern Anatolian Muslims also had common interests, especially the local elite groups of the region, an aspect often overlooked. The perceived threat posed by the possibility of an independent Armenian state encompassing significant portions of Eastern Anatolia, including areas primarily inhabited by Kurds, was a significant factor in motivating Kurdish groups to participate in the resistance. While the Kurds of Eastern Anatolia generally joined forces with other Muslim groups in the region, the Treaty of Sevres offered the possibility of an independent Kurdistan, as stated in Article 64, which allowed for the "Kurdish peoples" to gain independence from Turkey if they so desired.[102] At the same time, the treaty envisioned a larger Armenia that also included areas in Eastern Anatolia densely populated by Kurds.[103] According to a confidential report from the Erzurum branch, "as long as Kurds and Turks stand united, an Armenian formation is impossible".[104]

---

[99] Kırzıoğlu, *Erzurum*, I, 68.

[100] Olson, *Emergence of Kurdish Nationalism*, 22–23. Bruinessen, *Agha, Shaikh and State*, 278.

[101] A thankful Mustafa Kemal wrote that even Kurds, who previously had propagated independence for Kurdistan, now responded positively to ADR's call to gather around the sultanate-caliphate. Letter dated 21 June 1919, from Mustafa Kemal to "important figures in Istanbul". Atatürk, *Nutuk*, III: Vesikalar, 916–917. See also Atatürk, *ATTB*, IV, 36–37, 48, 64, and 71.

[102] For the full text of the Treaty, see https://treaties.fcdo.gov.uk/awweb/pdfopener?md=1&did=63986.

[103] Based on the Treaty of Sevres, for instance, President Wilson, as the appointed arbiter, announced that most of the provinces of Erzurum, Trabzon, Van, and Bitlis would be ceded to Armenia. https://history.state.gov/historicaldocuments/frus1920v03/d949.

[104] Kırzıoğlu, *Erzurum*, I, 97.

The Central Government and the Resistance Movement

While the ADR claimed to be fighting for independence and national rights, from the government's perspective it was a sign of an impending takeover by the Unionists and the army.[105] As will be remembered, this was not the first time the military led by Unionist officers rebelled against the sultan and his government, even marching on the capital in 1909. The resistance movement criticized the government for its inability to defend the country's territories, its appeasement policy, and its attempts to suppress the resistance. However, the prospect of antagonizing Istanbul caused unease within the resistance ranks. While reactions to the government were generally negative, the viewpoints on the Ottoman monarchy and the institution of the sultanate-caliphate constituted quite another matter. Many members contended that the purpose of the resistance was not to destroy the Ottoman state or create an alternative government but to save it.[106] Thus, both individual members and local ADR branches frequently conveyed their loyalty to the Ottoman monarchy and reverence for state institutions.[107]

The resistance movement therefore found itself in a difficult dilemma: they did not want a direct confrontation with the sultan and his government. However, they did not want to refrain from continuing the resistance either. Consequently, the language used by the ADR reflected a balancing act, in which was adopted a mild tone towards the Istanbul

---

[105] Famous in that regard is the Grand Vizier Ferid Pasha's appeal to the Entente to save the Turks from the Unionists as they were trying to save the Slavs from the Bolsheviks. In a statement presented at the Paris Peace Conference on 17 June 1919, Ferid Pasha claimed the following: "Europe and America are endeavouring at the cost of immense sacrifice to deliver the Slav people, whose ostensible attitude towards the Entente is scarcely different at the present time from that of the Turks, for both have been reduced to silence and both paralysed by an unheard-of tyranny. The Turks, who thus find themselves, under the domination of the Committee, in the same situation as that of the Russians under the Terrorists, deserve the same sympathy and the same humanitarian and kindly assistance at the hands of the rulers of the Great nations which hold the destinies of the world in their hands." *Papers Relating to the Foreign Relations of the United States, The Paris Peace Conference, 1919, volume IV.* https://history.state.gov/historicaldocuments/frus1919Parisv04/d30.

[106] Kırzıoğlu, *Erzurum*, II, 52, 84, 102. Iğdemir, *Sivas Kongresi*, 80–83, 89, 99.

[107] Kırzıoğlu, *Erzurum*, II, 41.

government and expressions of loyalty to the Ottoman State. To counteract the government's attempts to render the movement illegitimate and in opposition to the sultan's wishes, the movement promoted the argument, that the Ottoman capital was crippled by foreign occupation, and the sultan-caliph was virtually a captive and unable to act freely for the true interests of the nation. Hence, the movement claimed that it was necessary for the "nation", or rather the ADR on its behalf, to take matters into its own hands to save the homeland *and* free the sultan-caliph.[108] The prayer at the end of the Erzurum Congress read:

> My God! Make our sultan, Mehmed Vahideddin, the caliph of all Muslims, endure on his caliphal throne. Raise, o Lord, the sound of his might, for the sake of the trustworthy Spirit, to the highest levels of heaven, while You reverse the judgement of the foreigners. My most merciful, most loving, God! Just as Your enemies, the tribes of 'Ad and Thamud, were destroyed by disasters, make the people persistent in cruelty lose as well. Increase the strength of the Ottomans' government, bolster the security of their borders, solidify their defensive structures, make them prevail when concluding peace treaty, grant them plenty of money and higher vigilance.[109]

While publicly maintaining the assurances of loyalty and respect towards the sultan, though, the movement blamed the government for sowing discord between the sultan and the movement.[110] Based on the claim that the ADR constituted the rightful representatives of the "nation", and at the same time portraying the existing government as illegitimate,[111] the movement demanded new elections and the reopening of the Ottoman parliament, which had been dissolved by sultanic decree on 21 December 1918.[112] At this point, the Istanbul government found itself in an impossible position, as demonstrated by frustrations expressed by the rapidly changing cabinets.[113] Deprived of influence in Anatolia and unable to resist the pressure any longer, the government finally yielded,

---

[108] Ibid, 17, 33-41, 95-96.
[109] Ibid, 236–237.
[110] Iğdemir, *Sivas Kongresi*, 88–89.
[111] Ibid, 74–77, 80–82.
[112] Akşin, *Istanbul*, I, 135.
[113] Atatürk, *Nutuk*, III: Vesikalar, 1168–1169.

declaring new elections scheduled for December 1919. With only candidates endorsed by the ADR allowed to run, the elections unsurprisingly culminated in a decisive victory for the resistance movement.

THE LAST ASSEMBLY OF DEPUTIES AND THE NEW ASSEMBLY IN ANKARA

The last Assembly of Deputies that was in session from 12 January to 18 March 1920 passed the National Pact (*Misak-ı Milli*), which approved the objectives and principles of the resistance movement, including the new "national" borders outlined in the declarations of Erzurum and Sivas, and made them official state policy.[114] In addition to this, it called for complete independence within these borders and demanded the fate of occupied territories be determined through a plebiscite. The Assembly also discussed the possibility of relocating government in case of an occupation of the capital or the dissolving of parliament, which ultimately took place in March 1920.[115] The presence of a parliament dominated by resistance leaders and the dissemination of anti-Entente and pro-resistance propaganda apparently became too much for the Entente powers. As a result, British soldiers entered the Ottoman Parliament, arresting some of the prominent figures of the resistance.[116] In protest, the remaining MPs prorogued the Assembly of Deputies[117] In these events the movement found a significant opportunity and called for new elections to a Grand National Assembly (GNA) to convene in Ankara, which became a crucial step in the political development.

An important connection to the previous assembly was established by incorporating members of the dissolved Assembly of Deputies as members of the GNA. Furthermore, the president of the Assembly of Deputies was elected as its Vice-President, while Mustafa Kemal was chosen as its President. In addition to the members of the Assembly of Deputies, new

---

[114] For the text of the National Pact see Shaw, *Studies*, 347–348. See also MM ZC, D: 4, S: 1, Cilt 1, 17 Şubat 1336 (17 February 1920), 144–145.

[115] MM ZC, D: 4, S: 1, Cilt 1, 22 Kanunusani 1336 (22 January 1920), 6–11.

[116] MM ZC, D: 4, S: 1, Cilt 1, 18 Mart 1336 (18 March 1920), 496.

[117] Ibid, 496–497.

members were also elected. Comprised of only Muslims, Islamic influences dominated the symbols and ceremonies during the opening of the GNA.[118]

It was proposed that this be a constituent assembly, which however was rejected due to objections from prominent leaders such as Karabekir, who argued that the goal of the ADR was not a new political formation or establish a new state, but to preserve the Ottoman lands and throne.[119] At this point, the resistance movement still refrained from direct public confrontation with the sultan. However, this changed dramatically a few months later when the government in Istanbul signed the Treaty of Sèvres (10 August 1920),[120] which, contrary to the principles laid down in the National Pact, entailed significant territorial losses in Anatolia.[121] In the following months, as the state of war escalated, against Armenia on the eastern front and Greece on the western respectively, ties were definitively broken and Ankara began openly accusing the government and the sultan of treason. In response, the government declared the resistance leaders as rebels and convicted them in absentia, even sending loyalist troops, the so-called "Army of the Caliphate" (*Hilafet Ordusu*) to combat the ADR.[122]

These events, coupled with the new parliament representing an alternative centre of governmental power in Ankara, had a crucial effect on the development of the concepts related to nation and nationality. Importantly, after the opening of the Grand National Assembly, the emphasis

---

[118] The original date of opening was 22 April 1920, which was a Thursday. In order to mark the sacredness of the occasion, it was moved to the following day, a Friday, whereby the opening ceremony was integrated into the Muslim Friday rituals, beginning in effect with the Friday prayer at the historic Hacı Bayram Mosque. Prayers were offered for the sultan as well.

[119] Karabekir, *Istiklal Harbimizin Esasları*, 231; Atatürk, *Nutuk*, I, 562.

[120] Helmreich, *From Paris to Sèvres*, 320–321.

[121] Among the treaty provisions, the Ottoman capital, Istanbul, was to be placed under international administration, while large portions of Anatolia were to be ceded to the Entente powers. Additionally, Greece was to receive Izmir and its surroundings, and the treaty envisaged the creation of an independent Armenian state in parts of eastern Anatolia. Although signed by the Ottoman Government in Istanbul, the treaty never entered into force, and was replaced by the 1923 Treaty of Lausanne. For the full text of the Treaty of Sèvres, see Martin, *The Treaties of Peace, 1919–1923*, vol. II, 794–796.

[122] Zürcher, *Unionist Factor*, 116; Şimşir, *Ingiliz Belgelerinde Atatürk*, I, 371–375; Selek, *Anadolu Ihtilali*, I, 371–376.

on "rights" (*hukuk*), which hitherto had dominated the rhetoric of the resistance movement, changed to "sovereignty" (*hakimiyet*), while at the same time, the narrative shifted from a weaker to a stronger position. In the former case, the resistance movement was initially facing serious legitimacy issues, relying on the goodwill of others, and appealing to Entente powers for the recognition of national rights *and* those fighting for them. Then the movement transformed itself into a parliament, established an alternative government, and reorganized the regular army, leading to a position where it could seek independence through its own governmental and military power. This led to the prioritization of the idea of sovereignty of the "nation", or "the people" (*halk*), a term that likewise began gaining ground in the political vocabulary. While self-determination remained central, it now incorporated other elements of nationalism, as the focus shifted to the governmental aspects, such as legitimacy, through representation of the popular will, legality (constitutionality), and viability as a political entity.

Furthermore, during and beyond the Armistice period, the concept of a national "will" underwent a significant transformation. From *irade-i milliye* (national will) at the Erzurum Congress, to *hakimiyet-i milliye* (national sovereignty) with the establishment of the Grand National Assembly. This concept ultimately evolved to include elements of the Kemalist principles of "populism" (*halkçılık*), "nationalism" (*milliyetçilik*), and "republicanism" (*cumhuriyetçilik*) in the early years of the Republic.[123] The two components of the concept, *hakimiyet* (sovereignty or hegemony) and *milliye* (national), served the needs and goals of the resistance movement at the time, as the new regime sought to legitimize its shift in power from the constitutional government in Istanbul and the sultan-caliph to the Grand National Assembly in Ankara.

---

[123] *Hakimiyet-i milliye* was not a new concept at the time of the Armistice, however. The CUP had previously used it for legitimization purposes during another power shift through military intervention. After the constitutional revolution, the CUP utilized this concept to legitimize the revolution and their subsequent takeover of government as the will of the "nation", while describing the suppression of the counterrevolution attempt in 1909 as an expression of the *hakimiyet-i milliye* firmly asserting itself. A few months after putting down the counterrevolution attempt, the CUP Istanbul branch issued a declaration claiming that the *hakimiyet-i milliye* had now fully asserted itself. In this case, the "nation" was defined as "all Ottoman citizens" and declared that this was an expression of Ottoman unity, justice, equality, and liberty for all citizens. *Tasvir-i Efkar*, 10 Temmuz 1325 [23 July 1909].

To attain its objectives, the ADR claimed that it was not a military-bureaucratic or Unionist undertaking, but rather a movement stemming from the nation. However, the definition of this "nation" remained a contentious matter. The parliament served as an important negotiation ground for the components of the resistance movement while revealing at the same time the fault lines of future disagreements and conflict.

OTTOMAN TO TURK OR OTTOMAN AS TURK?

At this point, several important questions arose. First, what were the characteristics of the government in Ankara? The new parliament adopted the name *Büyük Millet Meclisi* (The Grand National Assembly), which was a variation of the names given to the Ottoman Parliament, constitutionally called *Meclis-i Umumi* (The General Assembly), and commonly referred to as *Meclis-i Milli* and *Millet Meclisi* (The National Assembly).[124] However, was this still the Ottoman parliament? According to one MP: "as there aren't any non-Muslims in this Assembly, are we not the representatives of the whole Muslim world? If we are not, we should call this Assembly 'Ottoman National Assembly' or 'National Assembly of Turkey'" (*Türkiye veyahut Osmanlı milleti Meclisi*). The contraction used in this context, *Türkiye milleti* (lit. the nation of Turkey), was quite unusual as *Türk milleti* (the Turkish nation) arguably would have been the more obvious adjective. Moreover, the MP continued to produce interesting verbal variations: "if it otherwise is an assembly pertaining to Ottoman Turkey, then it should be renamed 'The Grand National Assembly of Ottoman Turkey'" (*Osmanlı Türkiyesi Büyük Millet Meclisi*).[125]

The Law on Fundamental Organization brought some clarification on the issue, when the GNA finally adopted "Turkey" as the name of state—whether this was a new state or the Ottoman state changing name was far from clear, however.[126] A declaration attached to the law, for instance, announced that the GNA pledged to save the "sultanate-caliphate institution". Furthermore, this law itself contributed to the

---

[124] MM ZC, D: 4, S: 1, Cilt 1, 17 Şubat 1336 (17 February 1920), 44. See also Kırzıoğlu, *Erzurum*, II, 175, 240–241, 250, 252.

[125] TBMM ZC, D: 1, Cilt 3, 21 August 1920, 387.

[126] *Teşkilatı Esasiye Kanunu* (The Law on Fundamental Organization) adopted January 20, 1921. *Düstur*, 3. Tertip, vol. I, 196–199.

uncertainty. Although often referred to as the 1921-constitution, in fact it represented a balancing act by the new Parliament, as a creation of something in-between. Hence, while the Ottoman constitution of 1876 officially still in effect[127], the GNA, instead of abolishing or making changes directly to the said constitution, adopted the new law as a provisional constitution, designed, as Tevfik Rüştü Bey pointed out, to make the government in Ankara constitutionally grounded and its administration legal and workable.[128] When debating the need for constitutional amendments another MP, Müfit Efendi, stated:

> Currently, the esteemed members of the Grand National Assembly present here represent the Ottoman nation. Hence, they are the entire Ottoman nation. This means that the nation has thus given the right to legislation to the Grand National Assembly, and also given to it the executive power, as there is no ruler present, saying 'until the ruler's return, I will not bestow it on another individual'. (...) As stated in the seventh article of our Constitution [i.e. the Ottoman Constitution of 1876], there are certain tasks that can only be performed by our ruler. In his absence, the Grand National Assembly shall assume the responsibility and authority to perform those tasks.[129]

Although the Law on Fundamental Organization defined the state and its territory as "Turkey", no reference was made to nationality. In an introductory declaration about the law, the GNA spoke simply of the "people of Turkey". The introduction of "people" (*halk*) correlated closely with the Soviet Russian aid, however, which began to flow into the GNA's war effort[130], an additional indication of the importance of

---

[127] As is shown by its proceedings, the GNA initially tried to function within the Ottoman Constitution of 1876. See for instance: TBMM ZC, D: 1, Cilt 2, 24 July 1920, 378; TBMM ZC, D: 1, Cilt 3, 2 August 1920, 69; TBMM ZC, D: 1, Cilt 3, 18 August 1920, 317–318.

[128] TBMM ZC, D: 1, Cilt 3, 18 August 1920, 323.

[129] Ibid, 322.

[130] The Soviet Russian assistance, comprising of financial and military aid between August 1920 and May 1922, was crucial for the GNA government and its military. Yerasimos states that, aside from various types of military equipment, the total sum received by the GNA in this period, which was 11 million rubles and 100,000 Ottoman liras in gold, equated to GNA's entire national defense budget, 1920–1921. Yerasimos, *Türk-Sovyet İlişkileri*, 614. See also Karabekir, *İstiklal Harbimiz*, I, 342.

the external factors vis-a-vis the development of nationalist vocabulary. GNA's declaration stated that:

> The Grand National Assembly of Turkey has been established with the purpose of ensuring the life and independence of the majority of Muslims within the national boundaries, and to save the position of the sultanate-caliphate. Therefore, it [GNA] is convinced that the ultimate and sacred goal, which is to save the people of Turkey from the domination and oppression of imperialism and capitalism, will only be realized by making it [i.e. the 'people of Turkey'] the owner of its own will and sovereignty.[131]

Interestingly, the Law on Fundamental Organization did not mention the term "Ottoman" either, coincided with the GNA distancing itself from the government in Istanbul that had signed the Treaty of Sevres. This development created a dichotomy between Istanbul and Ankara, with an increasingly open hostility, which gradually turned against the sultan as an individual (although this was not explicitly expressed as hostility against the Ottoman sultanate-caliphate throne as an institution). As a result, the use of the term "Ottoman" became increasingly problematic. In conjunction with this, the parliamentary debates in both the Assembly of Deputies and the GNA reveal a marked trend in which the term "Turk" was used and debated more frequently. Furthermore, there were attempts to establish this particular term as a new general marker of identity, capable of serving as a substitute for "Ottoman" in various contexts.[132]

At this juncture, the historical evolution of the concept of "Turk" played a crucial role in facilitating such attempts. With its meaning highly blurred and boundaries fluid, the concept could vary depending on context, region, actors, and groups. Similar to the flexibility of the term "Ottoman", "Turk" could be employed in various forms, serving multiple purposes within the tripartite framework of Ottoman, Muslim, and Turk. This allowed it to convey a similar meaning as "Ottoman" and operate in a comparable manner, encompassing Muslims, Ottoman Muslims, Turkish-speaking Ottoman Muslims, and individuals affiliated with the Ottoman state or loyal to the sultanate-caliphate.

However, while "Ottoman" did not evoke protests, "Turk" often did, particularly when it was perceived as an ethnolinguistic reference, in which

---

[131] TBMM ZC, D: 1, Cilt 5, 18 November 1920, 416.
[132] TBMM ZC, D: 1, Cilt 5, 18 November 1920, 410.

case caused heated debates primarily driven by dissatisfaction from non-Turk members who demanded clarification of the concept. One of the most noteworthy debates in this regard occurred during the discussions on the National Pact, one of the fundamental documents of the resistance movement. Protests erupted when the debate led to questions about the nation and its relationship to the concept of "Turk". The excerpt below from the parliamentary session on 19 February 1920 constitutes one of the clearest indications of the nature of the discussion, what was at stake, and what caused the most resistance:

> **Abdulaziz Mecdi Efendi:** In our recent discussions, some important concepts have been uttered to which this parliamentary Assembly must direct its attention. When a statement like "the nation to itself" is made, one word to consider is the word "nation" [*millet*]. Another such word is "Anatolia". I do not want to go into detail regarding the borders of Anatolia as it appears in our and the European geography books. Rather I want to speak in terms of the general concepts and understanding of the majority of the population and the common people. Upon hearing the word Anatolia, one of our esteemed colleagues protested, asking, "What about the Turks in Rumelia?" In fact, he was right in his protest. At this point, as a reaction to the word "Turk", one of our companions, who did not take an active part in the discussion, added, "Then what about provinces like Diyarbekir and Erzurum?" Further, the same person found many different meanings in the word "Turk". I want to draw the attention of this High Assembly to this aspect, with your permission, and ask you kindly to provide a definition of the word "Turk" ["*Türk' kelimesine mana verilmesi*" can also mean "to make sense of the word 'Turk'"].
>
> In my understanding, whenever there has been a mention of Turkish history here, what was meant was the different Islamic elements [*anasır-ı muhtelife-i islamiyye*] like Turk, Kurd, Laz, and Circassian. Isn't that so? (Voices saying, "Yes, indeed, it is so"; applause.) If the meaning of "Turk" is not so, then I kindly ask you to say "the Islamic element" instead of "Turkish". But, if the word "Turk" indeed means what I have presented here, and you as members of this High Assembly understand it as such, then there is no harm in it.
>
> **Riza Nur Bey (Sinop):** It is so!
>
> **Hüseyin Bey (Erzurum):** In fact, even the Jews are included!
>
> **Abdulaziz Mecdi Efendi (continues):** When the Assembly interprets and defines the word Turk in this way and proclaims to the general public as such, then people defining themselves as Kurd will not see any problem

in its use; therefore, to prevent suspicions of political ill intent let us use concepts like Turk, Kurd, Laz, Circassian, or the Islamic element.

Tunalı Hilmi Bey (Bolu): Muslim Ottomans!

Abdulaziz Mecdi Efendi (continues): At this juncture, instead of "nation" it is more suitable to say "peoples living inside the Ottoman Domains" [*Memaliki Osmaniyyede sakin olan akvam*]. Further, instead of "to the nation itself", let us say, the "Ottoman nation" [*millet-i Osmaniyye*]. Let us not speak under the impact of the current state of confusion and turmoil. In the future peace the Christian elements living in this country are likewise included in this concept [i.e., the Ottoman nation]. Among the final stage electors there are some Christians, and even among those who have signed our election papers. (Voices saying, "They are participants in all that.")

Seeing that they take part in all that, we have to state these facts very clearly. These are words of immense importance for the future peace. Let us not give in to the current situation of turmoil. In terms of "the Ottoman nation", what I call political suspicions will be lifted, and in this regard I have to make a kind request: the concept "Anatolia" leads to some misunderstandings; instead let us use "the Ottoman domains". Further, instead of "nation" [*millet*], let us say "the Ottoman nation" [*milleti osmaniyye*]. (Voices shouting, "The nation means the Ottoman nation.").[133]

Similar debates transpired in the GNA. For instance, when Yusuf Kemal Bey made frequent references to "Turk" and "Turkishness" in a speech, a debate on health policies turned into a discussion on the nation, while a clearly annoyed Emir Pasha, asking why he only referred to health services for Turks, explained why this constituted a problem:

Yusuf Kemal Bey (Kastamonu): I believe every Turk [*Türk*] will say that the health affair is the first thing that must be done in our country. Because without health, there will be no Turkishness [*Türklük*], and so no Turk to serve. Neither internal nor military affairs will remain. To protect the Turks, first, the health should be protected (applause). (...) If we do not quickly eliminate diseases that threaten Turkishness [*Türklüğü bitiren*], if we do not find the means to ensure the well-being of the Turkish family [*Türk ailesinin*] and the individual Turk [*Türk ferdinin*], it will all be in vain, no matter what we do, it will all be in vain.

---

[133] MM ZC, D: 4, Cilt 1, 19 February 1920, 170–171.

> **Emir Pasha (Sivas):** I object to the fact that Yusuf Kemal Bey in his speech only expresses the need to protect the health of the Turks. (Voices shouting: it meant Muslims. Do not play with words). Please allow me ... I request that we not use the term Turkishness [*Türklük*] separately. Because we did not come here in the name of Turkishness. [*Türklük namına biz buraya cemolmadık*] (Noises). Please, do not just say 'Turks'. It is enough to say 'Muslims', 'Ottomans' even (Voices shouting: it was said Muslims). In this homeland, there are Circassians, Chechens, Kurds, Laz and some other Muslim tribes [*Bu vatanda Çerkeş, Çeçen, Kürd, Lâz ve daha birtakım kabaili Islamiye vardır*]. Let us not use words that may create division and exclusion towards those. (Noises).[134]

This led Mustafa Kemal Pasha to intervene to ease the tensions, by emphasizing what an otherwise very outspoken and critical Assembly broadly could agree upon:

> **Mustafa Kemal Pasha:** Gentlemen, I would like to make a point or two with the request that the issue will not be repeated. The members of this assembly, which constitute the Supreme Assembly, are not only Turkish, not only Circassian, not only Kurdish, not only Laz. But together they all constitute the Muslim element, which is a sincere assembly [*mecmua*]. (...) Our national border runs from the south of Iskenderun to the east, encompassing Mosul, Sulaymaniyah and Kirkuk. We have said, 'this is our national borders'! But there are both Turks and Kurds in the north of Kirkuk. We did not separate them.
>
> Therefore, the nation we are concerned with protecting and defending is not made up of only one element. It is made up of different Muslim elements. Each Muslim element that makes up this assembly [*mecmua*], is our brother and our fellow citizen sharing the same interests. As we also have accepted and confirmed here in the first lines of our fundamental principles: these various Muslim elements are citizens who fully and always respect each other's rights, be they ethnic, social or geographical. Hence, we have common interests. The unity we strive for is not only that of Turks, or Circassians, but the amalgamation of them all; one Muslim element. I therefore ask you, that it should be understood thus, and not be given any room for suspicions.[135]

---

[134] TBMM ZC, D:1, Cilt 1, 1 May 1920, 164–165.
[135] Ibid, 165.

Hence, when the discussions intensified, and the unity of the ADR coalition seemed questioned by inter-ethnic strife and divisions, Muslimness came to the rescue serving as a safe position to fall back on.[136] Another safe point was provided by the conceptual fluidity of terms, for example, the argument that "Turk" fundamentally meant "Ottoman" and "Muslim". However, the very identification of various ethnic groups as constituting the resistance movement, not as a single Muslim entity but as distinct Muslim elements with specific "ethnic, social, or geographical rights" and united by "mutual interests", indicated the recognition within the movement of differences at multiple levels. This highlighted the preconditions for maintaining unity, but also the potential for fragmentation and the difficulties facing the GNA as the Armistice period drew to a close and the final war victory against Greece was achieved in August–September 1922. At the same time, a recurring friction was taking shape between what was deemed a "modern" conceptualization of the nation and the predominantly Muslim nationalism of the resistance movement. While Muslim national identity strengthened, the GNA regime in Ankara faced a serious decision, not the least concerning the template "Ottoman", "Muslim", "Turk", and their connotations.

---

[136] For a further discussion on this particular debate, see Eissenstat, "Metaphors of Race and Discourse of Nation," 246–247.

CHAPTER 7

Reframing the Nation

> Previously, every individual who embraced the Islamic religion, in other words, converted to Islam, would suddenly become a Turk. However, this is no longer the case and cannot be so. Now, in order for Turkishness to emerge and be a fundamental part of one's soul and existence, the main elements that constitute the nation must be there.[1]
>
> Religion: 3. Belief in and strong attachment to an idea or ideal. *Kemalism is the religion of the Turk.*[2]

With victory on the battlefield for the GNA forces in August–September 1922, a new armistice agreement was signed in Mudanya (11 October 1922), marking the cessation of hostilities and laying the grounds for subsequent peace negotiations. With peace on the horizon and the new regime in Ankara dominating the scene, and at a position to decide the fate of country and state, attention naturally turned towards addressing critical issues within the political system, most pressing of which was

---

[1] *Eskiden İslâm dinini kabul eden, yani İslamlığa geçen her birey Türk oluverirdi. Şimdi ise öyle değildir ve olamaz. Şimdi Türklüğün ruhunda ve varlığında belirip temel olması için, ulusu oluşturan başlıca etkenlerin bulunması gerekir.* Tekin Alp (1928), *Türkleştirme*, 37.

[2] (*Din: 3. inanılıp çok bağlanılan fikir veya ülkü. Kemalizm Türkün dinidir*) Türk Dil Kurumu (1945). *Türkçe Sözlük*. Istanbul: Cumhuriyet Basımevi, 153. The emphasis is from the original text.

the question how to deal with the coexistence of two governments and parallel constitutions.[3] In the meantime, the relations between the two governments had deteriorated beyond repair. Dominated by the anti-CUP party, Istanbul had adopted a hostile attitude against not only the leaders in Ankara, whom it saw as the mere continuation of the Unionist cadres, but also the resistance itself. The GNA in turn used this anti-resistance stance to present both the sultan (Mehmed VI Vahideddin) and his government as collaborators and traitors. The moment of reckoning came when the Great Powers invited both Ankara and Istanbul to the peace talks, to which the GNA responded by passing two new decrees, amidst intense debates, which declared the final demise of the Ottoman Empire and its replacement by the GNA government within its "national borders".

While Decree 307 stated that sovereignty belonged to the nation, solely embodied in the GNA,[4] it was followed up by Decree 308, which declared the separation of the caliphate from the sultanate, which the GNA just before had abolished by the relatively simple act of raising hands. Additionally, the GNA appointed Abdulmecid Efendi, the Ottoman heir to the throne, as caliph, rewarding him for supporting the resistance during the National Struggle.[5] In theory, at least, this detachment separated the spiritual authority of the Ottoman throne from its political.

Notably, with the proclamation of the Republic in October 1923, Turkey functioned as a republican caliphate until March 1924. During this period, the country had a president as the head of state and an

---

[3] These were the Ottoman constitution of 1876 (*Kanun-i Esasi*) and the constitution of 1921 (*Teşkilatı Esasiye Kanunu*) respectively. Originally created by the GNA in Ankara as a temporary arrangement, with a limited number of provisions, the 1921 constitution was intended to enable the GNA to function with a degree of legality and legitimacy, while keeping the Ottoman constitution of 1876 officially intact and untouched. See in that regard Tanör, *Osmanlı-Türk Anayasal Gelişmeleri*, 268.

[4] The pparliamentary Decree 307, dated 30 October 1922 further stated: "It is decided that The Ottoman Empire has now ended and replaced by the Grand National Assembly Government. The new Government of Turkey is the successor of the Ottoman Empire within the national boundaries. With the Law on Fundamental Organisation the sovereignty of the nation has been transferred to the Grand National Assembly Government, rendering the sultanate in Istanbul null and void and relegated to history. *Düstur*, 3. Tertip, vol. III, 149, 30 Teşrinievvel 1338 (30 October 1922).

[5] Zürcher, *Unionist Factor*, 137.

Ottoman caliph as the spiritual leader of the "nation". Whether the latter was restricted only to Muslims in Turkey, or included Muslims as a whole was still unclear. The arrangement made the new regime highly uneasy, however, and put the caliph in a vulnerable position. Being an iconic institution in the country, symbolizing both Ottomanness and the imperial past, and occupied by a member of the royal house of Osman, the caliphate became a point of contention for Mustafa Kemal (Atatürk) and his government from the beginning.[6] They immediately problematized the existence of the caliphate since it represented an important reminder of the Ottoman throne and as such a potential power base and rallying point for various opposition forces wanting to challenge the new regime of Mustafa Kemal's authority.[7] With the onset of the political process, thus began the problematization of everything "Ottoman".

A (Partial) Farewell to Ottomanness?

While the new armistice brought about a wide range of potential paths and critically important decisions, including the future of the state and the new regime under Atatürk's leadership, this process also saw a significant overlap between issues related to demography, territory, hegemony, and security. This above all meant redefining boundaries, not least the physical and psychological, revolving around questions such as how to reconceptualize national identity and unity in a post-Ottoman framework, the place of non-Muslims within the nation, where to draw the line when translating Ottoman Muslimness into Turkishness, and not least how to reconcile ethnic differences within the Muslim population.

Tunalı Hilmi (1863–1928), a well-known politician and writer, was another political figure attempting to make sense of the new realities and the effects of the momentous events taking place before his very eyes, especially those which had a profound impact on his Ottoman identity and Ottomanist ideal. Although often portrayed as a "passionate Turkist",[8] Tunalı's own statements point to an individual with a highly complex intellectual and ideological development not easily defined in

---

[6] A considerable part of Mustaf Kemal's press meeting in 16/17 January 1923 revolved around the caliphate issue. Atatürk, *Eskişehir-İzmit*, 124–146.

[7] Orbay, *Cehennem Değirmeni*; Tunçay, *Tek-Parti*, 70–74.

[8] Gövsa, *Türk Meşhurları Ansiklopedisi*, 175.

fixed categories. From the parliamentary floor of the first Grand National Assembly (1920–1923), Tunalı repeatedly identified himself as a representative of "Ottomans" and "Ottoman Muslims". However, in two of his works, published in 1921 and 1922 respectively, he acknowledged a profound transformation occurring within him.[9] This change, he described as a disappointment, a sense of separation, and loss in the face of the disintegration of the Ottoman Empire, because some of the Ottoman population "elements" refused to support its defence, while certain groups even rebelled against it, to which he gave the Arab revolt as an example.[10] "My soul gave up", Tunalı said, "split in two, finally letting go of the other half".[11]

Sadly, Tunalı did not specify precisely what he was letting go. Only implicitly did he indicate that it was about a final acceptance of the loss of the Empire and its vast territories and peoples. And with this acceptance, he began rethinking his Ottoman identity and his Ottomanist ideology. In search of answers, he began analysing what Ottomanism had meant for him in the past and what it would mean in the future. He described, how "wholeheartedly" he had believed in Ottomanism and had wanted to see it succeed. So much so that, "not even my father in spirit, Namık Kemal, had been as devoted as I to the ideal of a comprehensive and flourishing Ottomanness".[12] The main elements of his identity, Tunalı identified as "Ottoman, Muslim, Turk, human being", thus adding a fourth category to the familiar template proposed by Yusuf Akcura almost two decades earlier. Tunalı described this composite identity with an analogy of the human organism. "Turkishnes", he said, "I saw as my life essence and blood, my Ottomanness the body, my Muslimness its life energy, my humanity a crown and a mark of honour". Of the four, Tunalı highlighted Ottomanness as the most important, functioning as the organizing

---

[9] Tunalı, *Mebuslar Meclisi*.

[10] Here Tunalı was referring to the revolt in the Arabian Peninsula against the Ottoman Government in 1916. Led by the Grand Sharif of Mecca and the Hijaz, Husayn b. Ali, who belonged to the Hashemite family and was a descendant of Prophet Muhammad. In this context, Tunalı's accusation of "treachery" seems directed against the "descendants of the Prophet" rather than Arabs in general. Although the revolt was limited in scope and effect, it held considerable symbolic significance, laying the foundations for a later narrative in Turkey of an Arab betrayal against the Turks with British support. *Tarih IV*.

[11] Hilmi, Istanbul'da mebuslar meclisi, 12–14.

[12] Tunalı, *Mebuslar Meclisi*, 13.

principle, the general well-being of which "would determine the health condition of the rest".[13]

While admitting his Ottomanist ideal had ended in disappointment, Tunalı nevertheless pointed out that some of its underlying principles would continue to shape his thoughts and ideas. "I was not an Ottoman in mere sentiment", he noted, "To me Ottomanness represented a pot standing on three legs; language, administration, and representation". These, he pointed out, stood for decentralized rule, respect for local languages, local administration and representation. "Unfortunately", he said, "this did not materialize, hence our present misfortunes". These elements of his "Ottomanism", Tunalı noted, would become highly relevant in the future, because, as long as differences existed, the significance of the underlying principles of Ottomanism would likewise persist. Interestingly, this brings to mind Gellner's concept of minority-haunted states, with "self-defeating" nationalisms, that inherit the same problems of the larger states they replaced.[14] Considering the Ottomans' enduring problem of how to integrate differences into a cohesive sociopolitical framework was inherited by Turkey as well, and Anatolia still containing differences of various kinds, including ethnic and religious, Tunalı pointed out, past Ottoman(ist) experiences would provide valuable insights for the future. Notably, the aspects of Ottomanism highlighted by Tunalı as remedies, such as decentralized rule and local administration, as well as representation of local interests and groups within the central government, continued to find expression in various forms, including within political parties, in the Kemalist Republic. Nevertheless, both the principles and the parties were often pushed into a position of opposition, a fate that did not significantly differ from their experience during the second constitutional period.

---

[13] Tunalı, *Mebuslar Meclisi*, 13.

[14] Gellner wrote: "Plural empires collapse, and with them the entire dynastic-religious style of political legitimation, and it is replaced by nationalism as the main effective principle. A set of smaller states emerge, purporting to fulfil the national destiny of the ethnic group with which they are identified. This condition is self-defeating, in so far as these new units are just as minority-haunted as the larger ones which had preceded them. The new units are haunted by all the weaknesses of their precursors, plus some additional ones of their own." Gellner, *The Coming of Nationalism*, 111–112.

"National" Territory and Its "Nation"

As the National Struggle neared its conclusion in late 1922 and early 1923, with the signing of the Armistice of Mudanya and the commencement of the Lausanne peace talks marking the end of its military phase, one obvious boundary to draw was regarding the new territory as separate from the rest of the previously Ottoman domains, which only a few years earlier had constituted the "homeland" (*vatan*) and defended in war by the same political and military-bureaucratic elite now sitting in the Grand National Assembly. In that regard, the president of the Assembly and commander-in-chief, Mustafa Kemal (Atatürk), delivered a striking account in an attempt to evaluate the recent past, characterized by devastating wars, end of the empire, loss of territory and population, and new possibilities for reconstruction. In January 1923, during an extensive press conference in Izmit,[15] he addressed the members of the Istanbul press:

> Indeed, the demographic situation of the country is at a distressing level. I believe that the entire Anatolian population does not exceed eight million.[16] However, instead of creating a state for the eight million in Anatolia, we aspired to establish great empires and carried out conquests. Wherever we conquered, we took the Anatolian people with us and caused them to be killed. As an example, you recall that despite forty-five years since the opening of the Suez Canal, the number of Anatolian youths who went to Yemen and died during this period is, I believe, around one and a half million. Therefore, if we consider the number of Turks we have caused to be killed to preserve Syria, Iraq, and Africa, the total would reach millions. Now, we want to make up for this [loss]. (...) it is necessary to bring population elements of the same ethnicity and culture (*aynı ırk ve aynı harstan olan*) that are now outside our national borders in order to increase our population by enabling them to live prosperous lives. This will be pursued as well. However, in my opinion, it is necessary to transfer

---

[15] For a complete transcript, provided in both Latin and Ottoman scripts, of Atatürk's Izmit press conference held on 16–17 January 1923, refer to Atatürk, *Eskişehir-İzmit*, 81–171. For a complete but simplified Turkish version, see also Atatürk, *Atatürk'ün Bütün Eserleri*, vol. 14, 263–306. An earlier censored version is provided by Arar in his *Atatürk'ün İzmit Basın Toplantısı* (1969).

[16] The first census of the republic implemented in 1927, showed the population of Turkey as 13,649,945 (T.C. Başvekalet (1927). *Umumi Nüfus Tahriri*. Ankara).

all Turks from Macedonia and Western Thrace here, and we should not consider undertaking another campaign to Europe.[17]

Although highly critical of those, he identified as "we", who conducted imperial wars of conquest, at the expense of Anatolian lives, for the defence of countries "outside national borders", instead of being contended with creating a state in Anatolia alone, Kemal did not clarify to whom this "we" referred. If the Ottoman state elite, went to war and "took the Anatolian people" with them, Mustafa Kemal would have been a leading member thereof. He had fought on the battlefields of "Syria, Iraq, and Africa", to defend the Empire. Unfortunately, though, Kemal did not provide a further discussion on why exactly he and the "we" he identified with had done just that.

Given the considerable reduction of the "national borders" and the population within so drastically and fast, the MPs found it often too overwhelming to be able to define the outcome in clear terms, not least in relation to the reconceptualization of the territory and population at hand as the new "national". On several occasions, when discussing practical matters, the Assembly often found itself in heated debates on the grand issues pertaining to defining the nation and deciding whom to allow access to the "homeland".

Such a debate erupted in connection with a law proposal concerning the termination of office of those military personnel whose places of origin were now outside the "national borders" and who had not participated in the national struggle.[18] General Kazım (Özalp), the minister of defence, tasked with answering questions on the issue, tried first to lay it to rest stating that this was not the right time to launch such a purge within the military. Due to the complexity of the matter, it was better to postpone it until an overall picture of the situation of the army could be gained. However, to an ardent discussant such as Mustafa Bey (MP for Çorum), this was not a satisfactory answer, which led him to delve deeper into the matter, laying bare some of the unspoken realities. In his opinion the question was not about military officers whose "home countries" (*memleket*) were now outside the "national borders", because the current borders of Turkey were not "national" at all. In fact, they were

---

[17] Atatürk, *Eskişehir-İzmit*, 112–114.

[18] TBMM GZC, 2:1, Cilt 2, 24 Eylül 1339 (24 September 1923), 233; TBMM GCZ, 2:1, Cilt 4, 24 Eylül 1339 (24 September 1923), 306–310.

political, meaning they comprised areas under the de facto control of the army of the Ankara government. Yet this line of thinking led him up some hostile avenues towards those he deemed outsiders:

> The population of countries now outside our political borders are different in kind. Those who are Turks, but have found themselves outside these political borders are part of this [country], so we will not expel them. However, those whose home countries now are outside these borders, and whose national element has formed a separate political entity [i.e. they have created their own state], leave. So, let Arabs and Albanians leave.

To make the matter even more complicated, Muhtar Bey posed the question:

> What do we do with a person who belongs to a fundamental element of a country now outside national borders, and has never served the national cause [i.e. participated in the national struggle for independence], but lives in Istanbul? (Cries of 'That part of the discussion is over!')

Ali Cenani gave an implicit answer with an economic twist:

> In Syria, Damascus, and Aleppo, they have left not one single Turkish official. They expelled them all with a stick in their hands. We, on the other hand, still try to shelter them. The moment we stop paying them their salaries, they will immediately leave for their own countries, and find work there. Thus, the soul of the matter is economy (*meselenin asıl ruhu iktisadidir*). A small country cannot feed the wreckage left behind by the old Ottoman Empire.

This was a clear indication that the understanding was established among the deputies that the Ottoman reality had ceased to exist, and a "small country" had taken its place, and this "small country" had limited resources that some of the political leaders wanted to reserve for those who were deemed one of "us".

Another complicated issue in relation to national belonging was how to decide the nationality of those Ottomans who, now that the war had ended, found themselves, for different reasons, cut out from the "homeland", and might want to be repatriated. This became a pressing matter when the GNA began considering the situation of Ottoman military personnel who had served in Yemen but, owing to circumstances including the WWI and their distance from Anatolia, had become stranded.[19] They now wanted to return "home", but did not have the material means to do so, and, as it was to turn out, might not even be entitled to. For, as former Ottoman citizens, what exactly made them Turkish? Turkey had declared itself the successor of the Ottoman state, for instance, pledging to pay off some of the Ottoman state's foreign debt. However, would it suffice to be "Ottoman" to claim entrance and belonging to Turkey and Turkish nationality?

This was a moment of reckoning for the GNA. The physical extent of the "national borders" (*hudud-i milli*) were more or less demarcated, in spite of disagreements such as that over the Mosul issue; however, establishing the borders in the minds and sentiments of the members of parliament and the resistance movement posed a much graver challenge. As such, it reflected an important exemplar of the problems pertaining to defining the nation on the basis of complex inclusion and exclusion processes. Kazım (Özalp) Pasha, minister of defence, again found himself at the forefront of these debates. He stated that among those stranded in Yemen there were "Albanians", "Arabs", and "those from Syria" (*Suriyeliler*). Thus, he said, "There are people among them belonging to other nations. We want to limit the issue to those who belong within our national borders that is those who are from Turkey. Those outside our national borders can go to their own countries".

Another MP, Vehbi Bey (Karesi), outlined the practical problem confronting the parliament, pointing out that the Ottoman Empire had been an "international empire" (*Beynelmilel Imparatorluk*). Therefore, he warned, if the parliament were not careful in defining the borders of the current nation, the law on repatriation could open the doors to people from all over its previously vast territories seeking a place in the homeland, settlement, work, and a share in the limited resources of the country. Then, he said, "they will become government servants, even ministers … and later still claim pensions from us". He demanded a thorough investigation in order to determine unequivocally whether the military personnel in question really were "from Turkey" (*Türkiyeli*).[20] Another

---

[19] Eissenstat, "Metaphors of Race and Discourse of Nation," 249.

[20] TBMM GCZ, 2:3, vol. 4, 22 Eylül 1339 (22 September 1923), 262–263.

delegate expressed confusion on the issue. Who, exactly, were the individuals concerned? "Are they", he asked, "men from Turkey, who went there [to fight]? Or do they belong to local populations in those areas, who have served in our army, and remained there? Furthermore, is it even right to make a distinction between these two?" As "our" army, in this case, meant "Ottoman", the question was further extended to establishing the exact connection between Turkishness and Ottomanness, and whether the service to the Ottoman state would entitle someone to special treatment in this regard.

Ultimately, though, as Kazım Pasha's recurrent answers illustrated, defining the "Turk" in exact terms presented too complicated an issue, the attempts often ended in circular descriptions, that the designation *Türkiyeli*, which meant from or belonging to, as a general marker of national identity, referred to those who were "from Turkey". Anyone requiring a better definition, Kazım Pasha said, should consult the statutes of the People's Party. Unfortunately, though, as one who consulted the said statutes of 1923 would find out, these were equally vague on the issue, article three, for instance, defining Turks as "everyone who accept Turkish nationality and culture". The closest thing to consensus, it seemed, was to stick to the highly ambiguous term, *Türkiyeli*—for the time being at least—which appeared in the final wording of the law that listed the conditions governing the right to repatriation. The fact that the delegates settled on a vague but flexible, and therefore more widely acceptable, concept like *Türkiyeli*, thereby evading ethnic definitions, clearly illustrated the Assembly's reluctance to open up the issue for in-depth discussions, negotiations, and disputes.[21] Aware of the difficulty involved, the delegates tacitly decided that it was better to avoid disagreement on the issue by preserving ambiguity, allowing realpolitik to lead the way as it had done throughout the Young Turk period. Postponing the negotiations did not bring greater calm, however, as similar unease would surface repeatedly in subsequent years.

---

[21] Interestingly, this word has been revived during the AKP government, who launched it as an "upper" corporate political identity (*üst kimlik*) for Turkey's population as a whole, thereby above all hoping to curb Kurdish nationalism.

NON-MUSLIMS AND THE NATION

Although Tunalı did not specify what he exactly meant by "insights" from the Ottoman past, his emphasis on reconciling differences in the future society of Turkey, was especially relevant for the Ottoman non-Muslim population, the *Rum*s and Armenians in particular, who during the National Struggle, as the Ottoman Muslim nation's other. Very early on, however, the GNA government made clear its stance on the non-Muslim presence on Anatolian soil, especially if it was a non-Muslim population amounting to over a million individuals. As such the understanding of defining a nation in terms of religious affiliation, in itself a highly persistent Ottoman legacy, continued unabated. Moreover, as evidenced by the Lausanne Treaty, this belief was shared by other states as well, most strikingly illustrated by the population exchange between Turkey and Greece. According to the agreement, around 1.2 million "Greeks" would be expelled from Turkey to Greece, while approximately 400,000 "Turks" the other way.[22]

As scholars have noted, a crucial aspect of the agreement was the criteria used to identify the deportees. The first article stated that the compulsory exchange, beginning on 1st May 1923, would include "Turkish nationals of the Greek Orthodox religion established in Turkish territory, and of Greek nationals of the Moslem religion established in Greek territory".[23] As such, the criterion of deportation was purely religious affiliation. In this logic, "Turks" referred to Muslims residing in Greece, while "Greeks" denoted Greek Orthodox Christians in Turkey. However, separating the population, turned "nationals", of the two countries based on religion implicitly acknowledged the immense challenge in defining what the Ottomans had called the "elements" (*anasır*) along viable and distinct ethnic lines. This was a difficulty various Ottoman parliamentary assemblies had grappled with during intense debates on Ottomanness and ethnic identities, in the face of which MPs often had emphasized the importance of commonality based on an inclusive marker of general identity.

---

[22] Hirschon, *Crossing the Aegean*, 100–101.

[23] "Convention Concerning the Exchange of Greek and Turkish Populations, Signed January 30, 1923" in Martin, Lawrence (ed.) (1924). The Treaties of Peace 1919–1923. New York: Carnegie endowment for International Peace, 1036.

However, for those highly diminished number of non-Muslims still residing in Turkey, the Lausanne Treaty contained a wide range of provisions to safeguard their minority rights. This was followed by legal measures granting them equal political and citizenship rights. There was a general reluctance within the Grand National Assembly, however, to grant such rights. When unavoidable to do so because of the treaty provisions, the MPs resorted to highly creative methods of formulating laws that aligned more closely with their own understanding and interests, while still outwardly appearing to abide by the said provisions. Especially when it came to defining nationality in relation to equal citizenship rights to non-Muslims, the MPs had a hard time reconciling the idea of non-Muslims as "Turks" belonging to one nation. According to this perspective, being a Muslim was intrinsic to being a Turk, thus virtually excluding the non-Muslims.

Some members of parliament openly admitted this regarding a proposed law on the offsetting of Ottoman Turkish public debt, which had accumulated during WWI. In order to finance the war, the Ottoman state had resorted, among other things, to contracting debt through domestic borrowing. The question posed by some members of the Assembly was whether to offset those debt contracts issued to non-Muslims, meaning if the state was obliged to pay its debt to certain "groups" and organizations who had acted reprehensibly during the WWI and the War of Independence. This question was also related to the property rights of non-Muslims, especially those that had been forced out or emigrated from Turkey. Although the language of the Law on General Offsetting was on the whole quite neutral, it had, especially with its much debated Article Two, the potential to cause dire consequences for non-Muslims:

> Those individuals from regions separated from Turkey, who are not Turkish citizens, and those who, as members of political groups and organizations, have worked for the separation from the homeland some of its territorial parts, cannot benefit from this law regarding their receivables from the treasury.[24]

---

[24] TBMM GCZ, 2:2, vol. 4, 3 Nisan 1340 (3 April 1924), 428.

7 REFRAMING THE NATION 177

This meant that, if passed, the Turkish state would refrain from paying out on the debt contracts held by the abovementioned category of non-Muslims: those who were no longer Turkish citizens or those who had engaged in separatist activities. The explanation offered by Hasan Fehmi Bey (Minister of Finance and the architect of the proposal) of the real intent behind the law proposal, and the specific wording of it, is rather astonishing. In his words:

> The intent behind this article [i.e. Article 2] is to avoid offsetting those debt contracts – issued as part of national and military obligations – held by *Rum*s and Armenians who have been deported or have disappeared. As a result [of their actions], both during the Great War and the War of Independence, the Armenians have caused the ruin of Eastern Anatolia, while the *Rum*s caused the ruin of Western Anatolia and made the War of Independence all the more difficult for us and so devastating to this country. With this law, we are dealing with the devastating effects of these wars. Therefore, we have devised a solution in order to prevent the *Rum*s and the Armenians from benefiting from payment of the national obligations contracts. But of course, we could not say this to the *Rum*s and Armenians openly [i.e. that the law is targeting them directly]. Various formulations and methods have been considered. Different formulations have been tried out. Eventually, we came to this least objectionable or non-objectionable formulation.
>
> As you will remember, a derelict property law has been issued stating that those who have deserted/fled (*firar edenler*) will have their property confiscated by the government. Now I ask you, gentlemen, and Musa Kazım Efendi in particular: Which government and which public servant has ever confiscated one single Muslim's property?
>
> The intent was to hide these two elements behind the political group category. Of course, it was stated that it was the derelict property of those precise individuals [*Rum* and Armenian] "who fled and disappeared" that was meant by the law. It was natural to confiscate their property. In fact, it is written in the minutes of the closed sessions of the Assembly, after the passing of this law, this honourable Assembly had asked the Minister of Finance at the time: "Will you make sure, by a secret decree, that this article of the law doesn't include Muslims who fled or disappeared?" He answered: "Yes". After receiving and recording this reassurance the Assembly proclaimed this article to the outside world.
>
> We have to do the same with this article here. Now, in Istanbul in particular, 2/3 of the military obligations [debt contracts] from the Great War

are, I believe, owned by the *Rum*s and the Armenians. Before the Great War, and even during the early years of the Great War, Muslims had not yet gone into business. There existed only a very limited number of Muslim stores. In some of the great cities there existed but a few of them. Therefore, the war obligations [debt contracts] were acquired by them [*Rum*s and Armenians], and they are in possession of those contracts. If we now, just like that, wish to make the *Rum*s benefit from this, then we will face [payments amounting to] a great many millions. However, some of the *Rum*s still remaining in Istanbul are included in the provisions of the population exchange agreement. As to the Armenians, there are still some in our country. In Ankara only, according to my estimates, there are perhaps no less than 4-500,000 liras worth [of contracts] in the hands of non-Muslims. Hitherto none of these has been paid, nor offset. If we now remove this article it would enable them to benefit from this right [given by the Law on General Offsetting] in the same way as tradesman Mehmet Efendi and Ahmet Efendi.

ZEKÎ BEY (Gümüşhane): God willing, it will not end up in others' hands.

HASAN FEHMİ BEY (Devamla): It depends on the name in which it is registered; thus, even if it is bought by others, the contract will still belong to Kostis and Serkis.

ZEKÎ BEY: Thank God.[25]

What is most striking about Hasan Fehmi's speech, besides the shocking reasoning of the government, is the reference to broader socioeconomic aspects of the matter, thereby taking the issue far deeper than the outward conflict between Muslims and non-Muslims, to the century-old accumulated socioeconomic conditions. As Hasan Fehmi openly admitted, what was at stake was much more complex than the mere Muslim/Non-Muslim divide. It was, rather, an economic and social conflict, which happened to have religious affiliations as lines of demarcation. Since the Ottoman economy had opened up to the global economy during the nineteenth century, the particular winners in the process had been the non-Muslim segments of society, placing some Muslim groups/classes on the losing side in economic terms.

During the WWI years, however, the political elite of the empire had very actively sought to turn the tide: seizing the property of non-Muslims

---

[25] TBMM GCZ, 2:2, vol. 4, 3 Nisan 1340 (3 April 1924), 429–430.

by a wide range of means and transferring it to Muslims, with the goal of creating a Muslim middle class. As Hasan Fehmi bluntly admitted, the Muslims had not "gone into business yet", "only a few Islamic firms existed" by the time of WWI. Subsequently, the majority of businesses owned by non-Muslims "were taken from them" and placed into the hands of "the merchants Mehmet Efendi and Ahmet Efendi". As clearly illustrated by this debate, now the newly formed Muslim middle class wanted to retain its recently acquired possessions, which meant barring the former owners from claiming compensation. If the *Rum* population was allowed to benefit from the provisions of the treaty, Hasan Fehmi pointed out, "we would have to pay up countless millions".[26]

Thus, the primary objective of the Law on General Offsetting (*Mahsubu Umumi Kanunu*), Hasan Fehmi further added, was to devise a method to hinder Greeks and Armenians from capitalizing on the treaty provisions. However, as it would have violated the Lausanne Treaty to explicitly mention "Greeks and Armenians", the proposal was formulated differently. This was not deemed sufficient, however, as Jews were targeted as well. Zeki Bey, for instance, who accused the Jews of "sucking the country dry like leeches" (*Memleketi sülük gibi emen yahudilerdir*), was aided by Refik Bey (Konya), who accused the Jews of collaboration with the enemy—in this case Venizelos.[27] According to Refik Bey: "the nation has no money to give to those like Kiryako, Petro, children of Beşiktaş, who shouted 'Zito Venizelos' in order to destroy all that is sacred to us".[28]

Hacim Muhiddin Bey continued from where the former two left off, claiming that there was now a dangerous element in Izmir. His speech was interrupted by shouting of "Mishon" (*Mişon*, anti-Semitic epithet) from some delegates. Hacim Muhiddin added that this "element" had at the time of the "occupation" (*isgal*) collaborated with the Greeks, and

---

[26] *Rumları müstefit ettirmek istersek gayet azim milyonlarla karşılaşacağız.* TBMM GCZ, 2:2, vol. 4, 3 Nisan 1340 (3 April 1924), 429.

[27] Eleftherios Venizelos (1864–1936) was the main political figure in Greece at the time and played a crucial role in Greek-Ottoman relations, not the least during the wars between 1912–1922.

[28] *Mukaddesatımızı mahvetmek için Zito Venizelos diye bağıran Kiryako, Petro'ya Beşiktaşın çocuğuna ordular teşkil eden heriflere milletin verecek bir parası yoktur.* TBMM GCZ, 2:2, vol. 4, 3 Nisan 1340 (3 April 1924), 430.

"done more damage to the Turks than did the Greeks".[29] Today, he said, "they are sucking dry the commercial veins of Izmir and its vicinity, and of Istanbul even, and they occupy the most important positions. (Cries of "Who are they?") The Jews".[30] When drafting the proposal for the law, Hasan Fehmi Bey said, the commission had only thought of the *Rum*s and the Armenians, because those "had been the cause of the disaster that befell Anatolia". "But as it turns out", he continued, "there is also a need to include in the scope of the law the Jews". That the non-Muslims would hardly be accepted in the new Turkish state was made clear by Mustafa Kemal during his meeting with the Istanbul press in January 1923. Asked whether Armenians would be allowed in the country, Mustafa Kemal answered:

> We cannot prevent individuals from entering the country. It is not only Armenians but also the Chaldeans and Assyrians who desire this homeland. If we have to provide a homeland for all of them, there won't be any homeland left for us. They are demanding so much homeland from us.[31]

Regarding minorities, population exchange, and the Patriarchate, Kemal stated:

> In the question of minorities, population exchange has been accepted as the basis for the state of affairs. However, we could not remove the Istanbul *Rum*s and the Patriarchate. We only insisted that the Patriarchate does not engage in political matters. They wanted to turn the issue of the Patriarchate into a matter of Christianity. We did not insist too much on this point.[32]

---

[29] ... *bu unsur işgal zamanında Yunanlılarla beraber bulunmuştur ve Türk unsuruna Yunanlılardan daha ziyade zarar ika etmişlerdir.*

[30] ... *Bugün İzmir ve havalisinin ve hatta İstanbulun iktisat damarlarını emiyorlar ve en mühim mevkilere geçiyorlar. [Kimler onlar sesleri.] Yahudiler.*

[31] Atatürk, *Eskişehir-İzmit*, 114.

[32] Atatürk, *Eskişehir-İzmit*, 92.

Mosul or the "Homeland"?

Another instance of defining the "national" territory, while realigning expectations with realities, emerged in relation to the peace negotiations in early 1923. The fate of Mosul was a highly delicate matter, as it involved the question of relinquishing territory, an all too well-known and dreaded topic in the late Ottoman context. The issue was complicated even further by the fact that the region was inhabited by a Kurdish majority, presenting the ensuing debates in parliament as a stress test on Muslim unity.[33] As will be remembered, during the National struggle, in its early phases in particular, where it became vital for the resistance movement to gain the support of Kurds for the national cause, the territory to be fought for and saved was demarcated to include Ottoman Anatolia and Kurdistan. In his public speeches on the issue, Mustafa Kemal himself had provided clear delineations of Turkey's future borders to the South-East, which included Mosul. Indeed, in an interview in January 1923, Mustafa Kemal repeated this delineation, saying:

> The Mosul province is within our national borders. I came up with the term "national border" myself. It was necessary to have a border that would be the basis for the armistice. What could this border be? Then I thought of making the border the places where our bayonets were present. Then, inspired by the Wilson principles, I called the border starting from İskenderun and including Mosul within our territory the national border. Indeed, at that time, we had an army south of Mosul. However, shortly after, a British commander came, deceived İhsan Pasha, and positioned himself there. Mosul is very valuable to us; firstly, it has endless wealth in the form of oil resources in its vicinity. Secondly, just as important as the first, is the Kurdish issue.[34]

During the same interview, however, Kemal emphasized that Mosul was no mere territory with valuable resources:

> Curzon says: "Mosul is an integral and inseparable part of Iraq. Mosul is vital for Iraq. We cannot give it away, but if you wish, we can involve you in the oil resources." But for us, the Mosul province is not about oil; it is an issue of home country (*memleket meselesidir*). The bottom line is that it

---

[33] Eissenstat, "Metaphors of Race and Discourse of Nation," 248.
[34] Atatürk, *Eskişehir-İzmit*, 94.

was decided the issue of Mosul would be resolved in conjunction with the matter of the Straits and the Islands, whereupon the negotiations came to a halt at that stage.[35]

However, in the face of staunch resistance from the British government to relinquish its predominance in such an area as Mosul, the GNA government was confronted with a dilemma; a quickened peace process, leaving out Mosul, or resuming the war because of the Mosul question. Mustafa Kemal hinted at this in his interview, as he posed the question: "However, if we don't take Mosul, are we going to continue the war? I even ask you: Is it reasonable to continue the war for Mosul when everything seems to be settled?"[36] Favouring the first option, peace, without Mosul if necessary, the government began showing signs of softening on the issue.

In the prospect of losing a region predominantly populated by Kurdish speakers, the government met intense criticism from the opposition, particularly MPs from the Eastern regions of Anatolia. Another case echoing Namık Kemal's old question, is whether Silistra was merely the city of Silistra, or the "homeland". According to many MPs, the answer was clear when applied to the Mosul question. According to Huseyin Avni (Ulaş), for instance, the government was preparing to sacrifice a part of the homeland (*memleket*):

> Let us not be fooled, gentlemen. Mosul will remain in a state of anticipation for a year. It is a mockery to this nation. Did you take Egypt from the English? Did you take Cyprus? If they do not give Mosul to you today, why would they give it to you tomorrow? Isn't their goal to establish a Kurdish government there, to divide your country, and ultimately to create an Armenia? Kurdistan, I tell you, cannot form a government. Kurds have no language. They have no literature, no alphabet. Tomorrow, Armenians will dominate those lands. Armenian culture will prevail. Tomorrow, Armenians will establish a government there. (Cheers, applause). (...) As a result, I fear that, with British deception, this will spread as far as my own place of origin, Malatya, where the intellectuals will be slain and the helpless people left to become slaves. I fear this threat. Ultimately, an Armenian state will

---

[35] Atatürk, *Eskişehir-İzmit*, 92.
[36] Atatürk, *Eskişehir-İzmit*, 94–96.

come into existence, gentlemen. I fear the Armenian ideal. We have to fear that when facing it. May God make us see the Turkish ideal also.[37]

According to Hüseyin Avni, the English and the French would always stick together and never be friends of the Turk. But, the real danger, he argued, was the Armenians and the alarming prospects of living under Armenian "culture" (*hars*). It is of considerable interest to note that the protests against the surrender of Mosul came from the Second Group, comprising people originally from Anatolia, and were directed against Mustafa Kemal's First Group, who was born and raised in the Ottoman Balkans. Hüseyin Avni further claimed that, in time, if Mosul was lost, the Kurds would be "poisoned" against each other, and the situation would get out of control, whereupon some deputies shouted that he should be more precise about what he meant:

> **Hüseyin Avni**: Gentlemen! If it is necessary to sacrifice Mosul, [when you do so] do not present it to people as if it is not a fake peace, a half peace. I tell you this. To put off the fate of Mosul to the following year[38] is to deceive people. You are giving it away, while claiming the contrary. (...) Gentlemen! If you are giving away Mosul, tell the people, "We have temporarily given it to the English. (...) Do not deceive people by saying that if the League of Nations does not grant us Mosul, then we'll go to war. (...)
>
> **Hulusi Bey (Erzincan)**: No, no one is giving it away.
>
> **Hüseyin Avni**: The English are giving it away. The Kurds do not think in this way. Kurds are brought up with Turkish culture. They are nothing but Turks, gentlemen. Today, in order to make peace, the cabinet wants us to make a concession to the English. If a concession is necessary, it may be given, as a parliamentary decision, for [the sake of] peace. Our claim on Mosul is definitively being given up in order to resume peace talks. I cannot lie to the people. From this very pulpit I will cry out that you have sold out Mosul. How else will you put this? I will tell people they are being deceived. For you cannot claim otherwise. There are Egypt and Cyprus standing before us as clear examples. You could not take those back then, and you cannot take back [Mosul] now. You will give it up, but at

---

[37] TBMM GCZ, 1:3, vol. 4, 4 Mart 1339 (4 March 1923), 93.

[38] I.e., by leaving Mosul out of the peace talks, to be decided upon by the League of Nations.

least don't give it for free, make it more expensive. But we sell the peace too cheap.

Nuri Efendi (Bolu): What shall we do then to sell it expensively; sacrifice the lives of 100,000 more Anatolians?

Hüseyin Avni Bey (continues): Gentlemen! I am a Turk too. We did not make a distinction between Turks and Kurds when we drew up the National Pact (loud noises).[39]

It is interesting to see Hüseyin Avni referring to his own *memleket* as being in acute danger of falling under Armenian rule. Apparently, delegates originating from the border regions of Anatolia had a more sensitive approach to surrendering territory, although delegates from Thrace were also apprehensive about the issue. Şeref Bey from Edirne, for instance, joined the discussion stating that he could not understand why the area stretching from Mesto Karasu to Usturma was defined as being outside the borders of Thrace. Ceding this area was, in Şeref Bey's opinion, the "greatest disaster" (*felaketin en büyüğü*). Yet, rather than being an emotional appeal—as one could expect as this was a part of his *memleket*—Şeref Bey presented a primarily rational argument as to why it had been the wrong decision. In his opinion, the region now relinquished constituted the most fertile of lands, bringing in immeasurable wealth. Only then was the economic aspect supported by the emotional, as he claimed that "this area is purely Turkish [*Türk oğlu Türk'dür*], from top to bottom, with no single acre of land containing Christians".[40] Deputies of Kurdish origin expressed the most pronounced unease about the prospect of ceding Mosul. According to Yusuf Ziya Bey:

> I hope that Mosul will be defined as a part of Turkey, for it is a part of Turkey, inhabited by Kurds and Turks. The majority of its inhabitants are Kurds. Mosul has an important place in the history of the Kurds. If it had been another place, I would probably not have been this worried. ... Friends, as it is impossible to partition one human being into two, or separate its parts from one another, is it also impossible to separate Mosul from Turkey. With your permission, I would like to express my intent more openly, for history is listening to my voice.

---

[39] TBMM GCZ, 1:3, vol. 4, 4 Mart 1339 (4 March 1923), 92–95.
[40] Ibid, 101.

Durak Bey (Erzurum) interrupted by saying that no problems existed between Turks and Kurds (*Türk Kürt meselesi yoktur*), but Yusuf Ziya Bey continued regardless. In his opinion, Turks and Kurds had to combine to form a unity of purpose and work together. If not, they would not have a future. This was a simple fact proved by the current circumstances. However, he warned, "if one of them betrays the other, there is no future for either of them" (*herhangisi herhangisine ihanet ederlerse ikisi içinde akibet yoktur*). Although he did not clarify what he meant by "betrayal" (*ihanet*), or common future, when read in context it is clear that this meant that he saw the surrender of Mosul as a betrayal of the Kurds, thus making a clear distinction between Turks and Kurds, and the uneasy partnership between them. If his fears came true, and Mosul was lost, he said, then a worst-case scenario would play itself out, while the Kurds of the region were unaware of what actually was going on beyond the two sides of the newly created borders through Kurdistan:

> But soon they will see clearly, and the curtain of the Karagöz shadow theatre play will be lifted, making visible the other side. What will happen then? I will tell you, members of this high assembly, those who are Turkified like myself [*benim gibi Türkleşmiş olanlar*] will draw back to this side. Then, the Kurds will begin fighting each other. A great struggle will ensue. The unity of the Kurds and their loyalty cannot be obtained by the separation of the Kurds, but is dependent on them being governed as a whole. The soul of the Kurds is not yet poisoned. It is not poisoned by politics. [*Kürd'ün ruhuna zehir aşılanmamıştır. Siyaset zehiri aşılanmamıştır*] I beg you, do not inject this poison.[41]

Although Yusuf Ziya Bey's speech contains many layers of meaning which are of crucial relevance to the development of Kurdish sentiments in the subsequent years, of particular importance here is his stress on the loyalty of the Kurds as being conditional, and his comment that the Kurds were not yet "poisoned by politics". While its precise meaning remains an open question, the resemblance here with Babanzade Ahmed Naim, who in 1916 claimed that the Turks had already contracted the poisonous disease of nationalism, the Arabs were probably beginning to get it, but the Kurds were not yet showing any signs of the "illness".[42] In that case, Yusuf Ziya

---

[41] TBMM GCZ, 1:3, vol. 4, 6 Mart 1339 (6 March 1923), 163.

[42] Babanzade Ahmed Naim. (1332 [1916]). *Islamda Dava-i Kavmiyyet*, 6.

Bey's statements may be read as referencing the probability of awakening nationalism among the Kurds by the partitioning of Kurdistan between the new states in the Middle East, giving rise to feelings of separation and longing for (re)unification of people and territory that once formed a whole.

Also, of crucial importance was the fate of promises given and deals struck between Kurdish elites and the resistance leadership, who publicly emphasized the Turkish-Kurdish solidarity and their shared goals and interests. Some of the most striking of these explicit utterances were made by Mustafa Kemal himself, as head of parliament and government at the time, as late as 1922, when he claimed that the government acknowledged the Kurds' right to form a Kurdish autonomous region. As the "whole world" was now following the principle of national self-determination, he said, "and we also accept this principle", the Kurds would decide for themselves:

> In regions inhabited by Kurds we support the gradual establishment of local government (...). The right of nations to determine their own destiny is a well-accepted principle in the entire world. We also accept this principle. As may be realized, though, Kurds having thus far completed the organizational requirements concerning local government, and we having gained the support of their leaders and notables in this concern, when casting their votes, they thereby have made clear that they already are in control of their destiny, and that they wish to live under the government of the Grand National Assembly of Turkey.[43]

In a similar wording, Mustafa Kemal repeated this statement in January 1923 during a country tour through Western Anatolia, once again publicly acknowledging the Kurds' right to autonomy. Asked by a journalist about the "Kurdish issue" (*Kürt meselesi*), Kemal explained:

> as you may know, Kurdish elements within our national borders are settled in such a way that they have limited concentrations in specific areas. However, over time, as they gradually lost their demographic concentration, they simultaneously mixed into the Turkish elements creating such borders that drawing a border in the name of Kurdishness would require destroying Turkishness and Turkey. For instance, it would be necessary

---

[43] TBMM GCZ, 1:3, vol. 3, 22 Temmuz 1338 (22 July 1922), 551.

to draw a border that extends to Erzurum, reaching Erzincan, Sivas, and Harput. One can even consider the Kurdish tribes in the deserts of Konya.

Therefore, rather than imagining (*tasavvur*) a separate Kurdishness, local autonomies will in any case be established in accordance with the provisions of the Fundamental Law on Organization. Then, the residents of those provinces that are Kurdish will govern themselves autonomously. In addition, when speaking of the people of Turkey (*Türkiye halkı*), they [i.e. the Kurds] must be included therein too. If they are not mentioned together, they will likely make up issues of their own. Now, the Grand National Assembly of Turkey consists of representatives with authority from both Kurds and Turks, and these two groups have united their interests and destinies. They understand that this is a joint matter. Attempting to draw a separate border would not be correct.[44]

Admittedly, Mustafa Kemal's acknowledgement of Kurdish autonomy is quite striking, and even more so that he envisioned such "autonomies" based on the 1921 provisional constitution, the Fundamental Law on Organisation (which was to be replaced by the Turkish constitution under the same name but with radically new content). However, when we look at the two statements above more closely, it becomes obvious that the message therein contains several layers of meaning. Kemal's reasoning suggests that the Kurds had the right and would be granted local autonomy, but that they somehow willingly had relinquished their right to self-government, or independence, when they threw in their lot with the Turks. By coming to Ankara, and entering the Grand National Assembly as representatives of their localities, they had demonstrated the popular will and were already governing themselves through the parliament and government in Ankara.

THE HALKISTS AND THE TURKISTS—POWER POLITICS AND NATIONALISM

As discussed in the previous chapter, during the National Struggle two concepts in particular gained prominence, "national rights" and "national sovereignty". In the post-war period and the early republic of the 1920s these were superseded by new concepts in accordance with the changing political realities. Among these was the so-called "populism" (*halkçılık*),

---

[44] Atatürk, *Eskişehir-İzmit*, 104.

which has often been characterized as an early expression of Turkish nationalism of the Kemalist regime. Stanford J. and Ezel K. Shaw, for instance, wrote in their influential *History of the Ottoman Empire and Modern Turkey:*

> Closely connected with Turkish nationalism was the Kemalist doctrine of Populism, a corollary to Republicanism, that government was of the people, not the Ruling Class. This idea had various manifestations. One was that all citizens of the Republic were equal regardless of class, rank, religion, or occupation. (...) Citizens therefore could no longer be given different rights and positions according to their *millets*.[45]

Before delving further into the various aspects of this multi-layered concept, it is important to note that translating *halkçılık* as "populism" is laden with serious problems, not least because it bore different meanings for different actors and it underwent radical changes during the Atatürk era. Tunalı Hilmi, for example, presented a variation of the concepts as part of his socioeconomic and political critique of the Ottoman Empire and Turkey, as well as a solution model. In his coinage the term *halk* received the unusual suffixes "lık" ("of" or "from") and "lılık", ("of" or "from" plus "–ness"), that is "of the people" and "of the peopleness" respectively. In Mustafa Kemal's usage the term became *halkçılık* that is "people"- "ism", or *halk*ism. As discussed in the previous chapter the concept gained increased usage after the opening of the Grand National Assembly, finally supplanting the concept *hakimiyet-i milliye* (lit. sovereignty of the nation). Then in 1923 "halkism" was closely tied to the republican regime and its legitimation. In Tunalı's usage, it meant government of and by the people. In Mustafa Kemal's early usage, it likewise meant that the "people" was the sole source of legitimacy of government. As such, it meant that power belonged to the "people", and not the Ottoman monarch or his divinely legitimized throne.

Tunalı gave the concept a distinctively class struggle aspect, between the elites and the common people, the city and the village, and the oppressors and the oppressed respectively, while in the Kemalist rhetoric halkism was the very rejection of class divisions and interests. Just because the Empire ended, Tunalı wrote, it did not necessarily mean the end of the ills and shortcomings experienced under Ottoman rule.

---

[45] Shaw, *History*, II, 378.

These ills, he identified as political and social "despotism" (*istibdat*). The Unionist regime he criticized for "a deceitful constitutionalism", "despotic freedom", and "broken equality".[46] Now, he said, political despotism had been torn down, next is to tear down "social despotism" (*içtimai istibdat*) of the "aghas", "headmen" and "notables" (*ağacılık, başcılık, bey*), to bring an end to their "plunder" (*talancılık*), injustice (*zulüm*), "oppression" (*ezdiler*), exploitation and neglect.[47] The solution to these problems, he noted, was democracy and a democratic mindset (*demokrasi ve demokratlık*), meaning government "for and by the people" (*halklı, halklılık*),[48] which he ascribed to his Ottomanist ideals that he emphasized he had defended and would continue to defend.

In his *Mebuslar Meclisi*, published in 1921, Tunalı was hopeful for the future. Although he in mournful terms described the "split" in his soul, he praised at the same time the Grand National Assembly for realizing some of the ideals of Ottomanism. As a sign, he cited the direction laid down by the GNA in terms of local representation and decentralized rule, which he prayed would continue, and "people finally find happiness".[49] In his *Millet Meclisi*, released the following year (1922), however, Tunalı Hilmi turned to staunch criticism, disappointed with the MPs for rejecting his bill on furthering decentralized rule and local representation. Accusing the MPs of being afraid of democracy and the people, he expressed concern that the GNA government would mirror its Ottoman predecessor, which ended up "oppressing everyone" (*herkesi ezerse*).[50] Tunalı further criticized the elitist nature of the GNA, noting the absence of the rural population in parliament despite them being the "backbone of the country". He found this similarity with the Ottoman parliament ironic, considering that the GNA government was led by those who called themselves "halkists".[51] Not believing this to be the case, Tunalı argued that the GNA was predominantly influenced by urban dwellers (*şehirliler*) primarily focused on advancing their own interests while aligning itself

---

[46] Tunalı, *Millet Meclisi*, 4.
[47] Tunalı, *Millet Meclisi*, 8; Tunalı, *Mebuslar Meclisi*, 3, 9, 12.
[48] Tunalı, *Mebuslar Meclisi*, 4; Tunalı, *Millet Meclisi*, 8.
[49] Tunalı, *Mebuslar Meclisi*, 12–14.
[50] Tunalı, *Millet Meclisi*, 21.
[51] Tunalı, *Millet Meclisi*, 42; Tunalı, *Mebuslar Meclisi*, 9.

with those who exploited the rural population that made up the vast majority of the "people".[52]

Furthermore, the interpretation of halkism as an expression of Turkish nationalism in the hands of Mustafa Kemal and his followers,[53] the halkists (*halkçılar*), often overlooks important points. The observations of one of the main figures of Turkish nationalism and the chief ideologue of the CUP, Ziya Gökalp, provides striking nuances in that regard. In his famous *Principles of Turkism*, wherein Gökalp analysed the historical development of Turkish nationalism, or "Turkism" (*Türkçülük*) which was the usual term for it at the time. When situating Turkism in the Armistice Period, Gökalp spoke of two separate groups, the halkists and Turkists. Halkism was a political program, Gökalp argued, and, while implementing this program, the halkists "unintentionally" (*bilmeden*) achieved goals that were in line with Turkism. The halkists focused solely on taking over the reins of government, and they claimed to do so on behalf of the people, hence their name. According to Gökalp, this sequence of events was already in line with the path followed by Turkists, and they supported the halkists.[54]

If true, Gökalp's observation sheds important light on the nationalism of the early Kemalist leadership. The significance of his claim lies in the assumption that the leaders of the resistance movement were not driven by ideological concerns, but rather their direction was in line with the Turkists. This reading of events and policies has significant implications for the understanding of developments leading to the National Struggle as well. As we have seen in previous chapters, the CUP was led by the activist wing. In the Unionist mindset, the preservation of the state held paramount importance, coupled with the determination of the CUP to retain its power, while the ideological aspects could be pragmatically tailored toward that end. This time, their actions and interests favoured

---

[52] Tunalı, *Millet Meclisi*, 52. TBMM ZC, D: 1, Cilt 3, 19 August 1920, 344; TBMM ZC, D: 1, Cilt 3, 22 August 1920, 426.

[53] Shaw, *History*, II, 378.

[54] However, what Gökalp seems to have forgotten is that just ten years prior, the same Unionists were propagating the concept of "rule of the people" (*hakimiyet-i milliye*) as a foundation of Ottoman unity. During that time, the "millet" was claimed to be the "Ottoman nation." Thus, the use of the concept *hakimiyet-i milliye* to legitimize political takeovers was not new. However, the changing content of the concept is important. The question arises: sovereignty of which "nation"?

a direction aligned with ideas nurtured by the Turkists. Being the case, the Turkists followed suit and assisted them, acting as an intellectual and ideological unit that provided an explanation of rationalization in retrospect. In addition, while providing an explanation for how the activist character of the resistance movement intersected with ideology, Gökalp's reading at the same time drew a picture of the role of intellectuals and ideologues as important only as far as they aligned themselves with the course laid by the political leadership.

In the following years, the references to the "people" (*halk*) became the core term of the Kemalist political rhetoric, arguably even more prevalent than "nation" (*millet*). So much so that when Atatürk turned his First Group in the Grand National Assembly, by virtually monopolizing the organizational structure of the resistance movement, into a political party in 1923, he named it the "people's" party.[55] Only later, in 1924, did the People's Party (*Halk Fırkası*) add to its name the term "Republican", as a reaction to the newly founded opposition, the Progressive Republican Party (*Terakkiperver Cumhuriyet Fırkası*).

As such the "halkism" (*halkçılık*) predated the "republican" (*cumhuriyetçi*) in name and the "nationalist" (*milliyetçi*) in principle.[56] Thus, the 1923 People's Party statutes (*nizamname*)[57] only mentioned "halkism" as its fundamental principle.[58] This would later change to "republican", "halkist" and "nationalist" in 1927,[59] and, in 1931, find its final form as the so-called Six Arrows (*Altı Ok*), which defined the RPP as "republican", "nationalist", "halkist", "statist" (*devletci*), "secular" (*layik*), and "reformist" (*inkilapçı*).[60] Listed in that specific order in

---

[55] Atatürk, *Eskişehir-İzmit*, 158; Tunçay, *Tek-Parti*, 366–368.

[56] Although Erik Zürcher points out that The Republican People's Party adopted "nationalism" as basic principle and part of the Six Arrows in 1931 party program, it is important to mention that "nationalism" was added as party principle, stated in RPP party statutes functioning as party program until 1931, already in 1927. BCA 490.01/212.840.2. See also Zürcher, *The Young Turk Legacy*, 232.

[57] Until 1931 The People's Party did not have an official party program, named as such, but the party statutes contained much of the elements later adopted as party program. Hence, the basic principles of the party previously stated in the statutes were later transferred into the 1931 party program.

[58] *Halk Fırkası Nizamnamesi*, 1339–1342 [1923-1926]. BCA 490.01 / 212.840.2.

[59] *Cumhuriyet Halk Fırkası Nizamnamesi*, 1927. BCA 490.01/212.840.2.

[60] *CHF Programı*, 1931, BCA 490.01/212.840.2.

the original documents, the importance ascribed to these terms seems to have moved accordingly as years passed in the early republic. Under "general principles" (*umumi esaslar*), the statutes defined the purpose of the People's Party as:

> Article 1—The People's Party is a political organisation established in accordance with the Law on Associations. Its purpose is to provide guidance for the execution of national sovereignty of and by the people, to elevate Turkey into a modern state, and to strive to establish the supremacy of law above all powers in Turkey.
>
> (Article 2)—In the perspective of the People's Party, the concept of the people is not exclusive to any particular class. All individuals who do not claim any privileges and generally accept absolute equality under the law are considered part of the people. Halkists are individuals who do not accept the privileges of any family, class, community, or individual and recognize the absolute freedom and independence in making laws.
>
> (Article 3)—Every Turk and any person coming from outside who embraces Turkish nationality and culture, can be a member of the People's Party.[61]

The reference to the Law on Associations is noteworthy here, as it is the same law adopted by the Ottoman Assembly of Deputies in 1909 discussed in Chapter 5. As will be remembered especially Article 3 of this law, making it illegal to form political organizations based on "ethnicity or race" had aroused disputes in the Ottoman parliament. In accordance with Article 3, it would have been in fact against the law for RPP to adopt "Turkish", meaning "ethnicity or race", nationalism as a basic principle. The direct reference to "Turks" as members, however, would constitute a problem in that regard.

Second, the specific usage of "the people" (*halk*) in close affinity with "Turk", "Turkish nationality", and "Turkish culture", presents it here as a reframing of, and a careful alternative to, the "nation" (*millet*). In this case, however, the *halk* included, "everyone who do not claim any privileges and generally accept absolute equality under the law", as well as

---

[61] *Halk Fırkası Nizamnamesi*, 1339–1342 [1923–1926]. BCA 490.01/212.840.2., p. 1.

"Turks" *and* those "from outside" who embrace Turkish "nationality and culture". As the term "nationality" (*tabiiyet*) in this context refers to the old Ottoman term for "citizenship", "embracing" it likely meant acquiring Turkish citizenship. If so, it reflected a civic and voluntarist aspect of nationhood. "Embracing" "Turkish culture" on the other hand pointed in another direction, which, as Erik Zürcher has pointed out, would prove to be highly exclusive in its membership criteria.

THE POLITICAL PROCESS AND MUSLIM UNITY

As the term "Ottoman" (*osmanlı*) had become problematic during the National Struggle, so became Muslimness as a marker of national identity in the early republic. Although Mustafa Kemal still could declare as late as October 1924 that "In Turkey, there were and still are essentially no reactionaries. There were suspicions, there were doubts",[62] this would change radically in the turmoil of 1925–26, as much so that emphasis on Muslim identity in public political discourse became associated with the image of religious "reaction" (*irtica*) as the main antagonist of the new republican regime. Considering they had acted, fought, and ruled together, knitting along the way a close web of connections and interests the fragmentations within the Muslim coalition forged during the National Struggle was significant and had crucial implications for the stability and cohesion of Turkey, laying the grounds ultimately for the future so-called Kurdish question and the armed conflict in Eastern Anatolia.

Ironically, the Muslim groups' quarrelling among each other happened at a time when an Ottoman Muslim polity within a single territory had become highly realistic,—clear evidence that the "Muslim nation" (*millet-i Islam*) was not so coherent after all and that the loss of the vast majority of the Christian population had a significant impact in that regard. As identity is inevitably dependent on difference, by cleansing the non-Muslim population, the Ottoman Muslim majority clearly lost a pivotal part of its identity and thus "Muslimness" some of its utility. This would pose a considerable challenge to the new state and regime: still in the making and therefore in dire need of legitimacy and identity. The lost reflection of the "other" created a new dynamic in the country now called

---

[62] *Türkiye'de esasen mürteci yoktu ve yoktur. Vehim vardı, vesvese vardı.* Mustafa Kemal's interview in *Vakit*, 31 October 1924. See a reprint of the text in Atatürk, *Söylev ve Demeçleri*, III, 106–108.

Turkey (*Türkiye*), for the Kemalist regime relied on the Muslim population of Anatolia to provide the "national" raw material to carve out a new nation.

At this point, however, a significant discrepancy emerged in relation to the national question, the requirements of the new state formation, and the needs of the Kemalist regime for legitimacy and consolidation. This problem, often overlooked by the scholarship, is partially touched upon by Mete Tunçay.[63] Analysing Kemalist nationalism, Tunçay makes a striking observation in relation to the transition to the republic.[64] He asks, why the Kemalists chose to break with the Muslim nationalist trend, when considering that Anatolia demographically now had become more Muslim than it had ever been because of the policies of the CUP and the GNA government leaving Anatolia almost empty of its non-Muslim population. In addition, Ottoman Muslim nationalism had proven to be highly effective for mass mobilization during the National Struggle and provided the leaders with powerful tools for a nationalist discourse, encompassing political, territorial, cultural, and historical claims for national unity and self-government. It also served as a basis for national identity formation, contributing to the distinction between "us" and "them". Zürcher, in agreement with Tunçay on the issue, provides an answer, ascribing the radical change in policy to Atatürk's modernization project, *inkilap* (lit. revolution or radical reform), with special emphasis on secularism and Western-oriented sociocultural reform. Zürcher writes:

> In 1923 the Anatolian Muslim population had managed, against all odds, to secure the continued existence of a state of their own in Anatolia, but from 1923–4 on the Kemalist leadership of the Republic broke the bonds of solidarity forged during the preceding ten years and opted instead for far-reaching secularization and for Turkish (as opposed to Ottoman-Muslim) nationalism and nation building. More research is needed on the reasons underlying the change, but there can be no doubt that the decision was deliberate to seek a new Turkish national and secular corporate political identity in order to replace the Ottoman-Muslim one. (...) Now that the danger to independence had passed and they could create what

---

[63] Tunçay, *Tek-Parti*, 208–217.
[64] Tunçay, *Tek-Parti*, 215–216.

they considered the ideal circumstances for successful modernization, they opted for secular Turkish nationalism.[65]

The Muslim nationalism of the period before 1923 was a genuine popular movement, which made possible the mobilization of the masses, but it was unsuitable as the glue to hold together a society modernizing itself on the basis of secularism and positivism.[66]

Although Atatürk's reform mindedness and the centrality of modernization within state and society in his political agenda is undeniable, there are several significant nuances often overlooked when discussing the shift in policy and rhetoric in late 1922 and early 1923. It is crucial in this regard to assess the function of *inkilap* within Turkish politics in the aftermath of the abolition of the Ottoman sultanate. Soon after this crucial event, Yunus Nadi (Abalıoğlu), an influential journalist and politician and a member of Mustafa Kemal's governing First Group (*Birinci Grup*) foresaw the coming of a political storm, which he rather provocatively called "the new era of conflict" (*yeni cidal devri*).[67] In Yunus Nadi's opinion, many issues of political and ideological difference hitherto pushed into the background because of concern for the war effort would now surface in full strength and be fought over on the political stage. If so, Yunus Nadi's prediction would mean that the next decisive political confrontation would occur within the ranks of the resistance movement itself, with dire consequences for the political coalition based on Muslim unity.

At this point, the public attention was primarily directed towards the leader of the movement, the president of the GNA and commander-in-chief, Mustafa Kemal and his plans in Turkish politics. When the war ended in late 1922, there was an expectation among many MPs, the opposition in particular, that Mustafa Kemal would step down from active politics. As the argument went, in his capacity as a renowned general, his task had been to win the war and obtain national independence. Now that the war had ended and these goals attained, it was suggested, that the time had come for the general to relinquish power and set the political process free. Kemal was reminded in this regard that he himself had

---

[65] Zürcher, *The Young Turk Legacy*, 231–232.
[66] Ibid, 234.
[67] Yunus Nadi, "Yeni Bir Cidal Devri," *Yenigün*, 26 November 1922.

promised he would return to the "bosom of the people" once the war had ended and independence won. Mustafa Kemal, on the other hand, proclaimed that he would not and could not step down because, although independence had been won, the struggle had not yet ended.[68] The national struggle had to be fought and won on the civilizational level as well. "Our revolution" (*bizim inkılabımız*), he noted, would surpass the "constitutional revolution" (*Meşrutiyet inkılabı*). Comparing it to the French Revolution, evidently a general theme and a frequent point of reference among Atatürk's generation, *inkılap* would be an enduring and unstoppable revolution that would continue for generations to come:

> Gentlemen! We have made a true revolution and we sill continue in our revolution. (...) The French Revolution continued for almost a century. It will be a mistake to assume a fundamental revolution to be completed in three years.[69] (...) The law of the revolution is above existing laws. As long as we are not killed or the thought currents in our minds are not quashed, the progressive revolution we have embarked upon will never cease for a moment. It will always be the same in the generations that come after us![70]

This struggle to "attain the levels of modern civilization" (*muasır medeniyet seviyesine ulaşmak*), he claimed, was an even bigger goal for the nation, one he made the basis of his legitimacy and future vision.[71] The war would continue, this time on the civilizational front, and who more suitable to lead this national cause than the man who had provided his country its independence? This practically set the stage for the political process in the early republic and had crucial implications for national identity construction. For the modern, of which Atatürk declared himself the leading champion, meant "Western" in Kemalist vocabulary, and was to form the cornerstone of his *inkılap*, to be implemented top down in society.

---

[68] Atatürk, *Eskişehir-İzmit*, 160–164.

[69] Interestingly, here Atatürk dated the beginning of his revolution at 1920, presumable taking the opening of the GNA as the dividing line. In his famous Speech (*Nutuk*), however he sat the starting date as 19 May 1919, his landing in Samsun.

[70] Atatürk, *Eskişehir-İzmit*, 162–164.

[71] *Vakit*, d. 31. oktober 1924. See also Atatürk, *Söylev ve Demeçleri*, III, s. 107.

Hence, the "Turkish nation", demographically consisting primarily of the rural population of Anatolia, epitomized by Atatürk's statement that "the villager is the master of the nation" (*köylü milletin efendisidir*), and comprising over 80% of the total population in the 1920s, was going to be "civilized" along Western cultural lines. This idea of civilizing the countryside was nothing new of course, particularly in light of Ottoman(ist) ideas and practices of civilizing the rural areas and the nomadic peoples.[72] Especially the Tanzimat reforms had been criticized by the Young Ottomans for being excessively Western.[73]

Yet, this well-known late Ottoman state ideal of civilizing the masses along the lines of the high culture of the political centre created challenges on both practical and ideological levels. These challenges manifested themselves, particularly as a discrepancy between nation-building and regime-related policies and rhetoric. In the transition from empire to republic, religion was gradually replaced by "culture" (*hars*) as a basic criterion for Turkish national identity. But according to Atatürk's *inkılap*, the culture of modernity was "western" culture, which the (new) Turkish "nation" would aspire to and adopt. While thus implicating the Anatolian population's existing sociocultural inadequacies, the latecomers and outsiders were expected to firmly accept and practice "Turkish culture" as it was, as something distinctively "Turkish" already present.[74]

Confronted with this apparent inconsistency between awakening the ancient nation and a national identity rooted in the "real" essence of the "people", encompassing their traditional, rural, and popular culture, and the aspiration to create a new Turkish citizen culturally western, secular, and modern, Atatürk found some support in Ziya Gökalp's ideas. Gökalp, through his distinction between culture (*hars*) and civilization (*medeniyet*)—originally adopted from Tönnies' concept of *gemeinschaft* and *gesellschaft*—had attempted a kind of reconciliation between the two. Hence, the new Turkish national identity was going to have a popular cultural basis, originating from the "Turkish people", with a western civilizational superstructure. Atatürk never really described in detail how to reconcile these two on the practical, or even theoretical, level—a problem, which has haunted Turkish society and politics ever since.

---

[72] Deringil, *Domains*, 41, 101.
[73] Mardin, *Genesis*, 115.
[74] Zürcher, *The Young Turk Legacy*, 234.

Furthermore, these discrepancies, coupled with the inextricable intertwining of cultural reform with power politics and the legitimation of the new regime, had the effect of highly politicizing the cultural expressions, symbols, and terminology that had been assigned the task of unifying and reshaping the "Turkish" nation. As a result, the unifying principles themselves became an integral part of an ongoing political battle that cut through the diverse layers of society, encompassing its ethnically, socially, economically, culturally, and religiously diverse demography.

A crucial development in that regard was the transition from the first to the second Grand National Assembly, as the former decided (1 April 1923), after three years of intense work, to hold new elections. These resulted in one of the most significant changes in the transition from empire to republic: a general purge of oppositional voices in the first parliament. Partly by intimidation and manipulation of the electorate during the two-tier election system and partly stemming from Mustafa Kemal's strict monopoly over and control of the organizational structure of the resistance movement, only those on his list of candidates, with one exception, found a seat in the second parliament.[75] It was this Assembly (1923–27) that drew up a new constitution, proclaimed the republic, made Ankara capital, abolished the caliphate, witnessed the republic's first Kurdish rebellion, reestablished the Independence Tribunals (*Istiklal Mahkemeleri*) to pass sentence on the political opposition and rebels alike, witnessed the launching of the Atatürk revolution, abolished the fez, introduced the hat as new "national" headgear, and oversaw the population exchanges.

As Atatürk continued emphasizing "unity of powers" (*vahdet-i kuvva*) manifesting itself as the "national will", embodied in the parliament and implemented by the governing party, and his view on political opposition as mere party-politics in the hands of self-seeking politicians trying to further individual or group interests, it became clear that he expected a unified and docile parliament.[76] In Atatürk's words:

---

[75] Karabekir, *Paşaların Kavgası*, 133; Demirel, *Birinci Mecliste Muhalefet*, 598; Tunçay, *Tek-Parti*, 53–57.

[76] This was a shorter version of Atatürk's lengthy explanation in the GNA in December 1921. There, denying the validity of the principle of the separation of powers, Atatürk stated that in nature, reality, and the world there was a "unity of powers" (*vahdet-i kuvva*). The principle of separation of powers (*taksim-i kuvva*), the progenitor of which he erroneously pointed out as Jean-Jacques Rousseau, whom Atatürk said must have come up

In my opinion, the principle of separation of powers is not fundamental. Even those who have devised the principle of separation of powers essentially acknowledge the unity of powers. However, due to their inability to establish the unity of powers, they, while taking the existing forms as a point of departure, have put forward a theory, which is the outcome of the negotiations between despots and oppressed nations. In reality, there is a unity of powers, and the primary source of this power is the nation. Therefore, the true owner of this power is the nation.[77]

In September 1924, prior to the establishment of the new opposition party, Atatürk declared that, in his opinion, Turkey was not ready for multi-party politics, as it would mean:

> Today, the committee (*heyet*) responsible for the administration of the country, in my opinion, in terms of ideal and purpose, bears the name "The People's Party", which includes the whole nation and is the party of the republic. The fundamental principle of this party is to strive for the true well-being and happiness of the country and the nation, and the path that achieves this goal, in my opinion, is clear and certain. It is to support and strengthen the republic and to ensure that the nation walks resolutely and successfully within the intellectual and social revolution (*fikri ve içtimai inkılapta*) on the path of civilization and renewal (*medeniyet ve teceddüt*). The path is certain, but undoubtedly tiring and long, and the passengers of this path may not walk in a straight line and in time from the beginning to the end, and there may be differences in their considerations and precautions. However, it is necessary for them not to deviate from the path, not to lose sight of the general goal, and not to violate the main purpose. Today, we are at the beginning of this certain path. We have not yet covered enough distance to make examinations. Points of view must be

---

with the idea in a "state of insanity" (*hali cinnet*). Despite his negative remarks, however, Atatürk also added that he had read Rousseau "from beginning to end" (*baştan nihayete kadar*), and was seemingly also highly influenced by him, for instance in relation to Rousseau's depiction of the general will and its representation in parliament (TBMM ZC, D: 1, Cilt 14, 1 December 1921, 436–440). In the interview in January 1923, Atatürk described the road from the free individual as the sole source of power to the "national will" represented in parliament, as "it is necessary for all individuals who possess that power to come together and utilize it. This is not possible in a physical sense. Therefore, there is no more practical solution than implementing this through a Parliament, which is neither too few nor too many" (Atatürk, *Eskişehir-İzmit*, 150). For a further discussion on Atatürk's views on "separation of powers", see also Demirel, *Birinci Mecliste Muhalefet*, 241.

[77] Atatürk, *Eskişehir-İzmit*, 150.

clear and useful enough to gain relevance. Otherwise, the idea of division is merely party-politics, which is not suitable in the present conditions of peace and security for the country and the nation.[78]

This did not prevent the growing opposition in parliament from continuing their works on a new party, which finally materialized in November 1924, as the Progressive Republican Party (*Terakkiperver Cumhuriyet Fırkası*), led by Mustafa Kemal's old companions-in-arms and prominent members of the resistance movement, such as Kazim Karabekir, Ali Fuat (Cebesoy), Refet (Bele), and Rauf (Orbay).[79] Not only the positions of the leaders, the first three being top generals of the Turkish army, but also the program and the political stance of the new party constituted a serious cause for worry and discontent among the People's Party leadership, Atatürk in particular.

Although later Turkish historiography mostly associated the Progressive Republicans with Unionists trying to revive the Committee of Union of Progress, in policy and rhetoric, the People's Party had much in common with the CUP on a wide range of issues, not least the national question. Indeed, it seems fair to say that while the governing People's Party laid special emphasis on the "union" (*ittihat*) part of the CUP's name, along with the preoccupation with centralism and homogenization, the PRP emphasized "progress" (*terakki*), which they associated with decentralized rule and individual rights. Similarly, when compared to the two main factions of the Young Turk movement of the late nineteenth century, the centralist and the liberal wing respectively, the PRP adopted several key issues of the liberals.[80] This could also be seen as reminiscent of the basic principles of Ottomanism, which advocated for civic rights and freedoms, including tolerance for ethnic and religious diversity. These ideas of a more liberal stock would resurface from time to time during the

---

[78] Speech delivered in Samsun, 20 September 1924. Atatürk, *Söylev ve Demeçleri*, II, 199.

[79] Tunaya, *Siyasi Partiler*, 606–622.

[80] This division within the Young Turk movement, which gained ground after the Young Turk Congress in 1902, was represented in the second constitutional period by the two main political factions: the CUP and the Liberal Alliance (*Hürriyet ve Itilaf*), respectively. During the National Struggle, the division occurred within the ranks of the resistance movement, that is among the former members of the CUP, resulting in the formation of the First Group (*Birinci Grup*) and the Second Group (*Ikinci Grup*) in the GNA.

Republican era,[81] finding expression, for instance, in the short-lived Free Republican Party (*Serbest Cumhuriyet Fırkası*) experiment in 1930.[82] It is remarkable in this regard, that the political and ideological dividing lines of the late Ottoman past, including the ideas and principles related to liberal civic Ottomanism, reappeared in various forms in the early republic as well. However, they were often overshadowed by the state-centrism dominating the political scene and state practices.

The new party, defining itself as defenders of popular sovereignty and liberalism, welcomed the idea of joining forces with others with similar standpoints.[83] Stating that the party would "strongly resist a mentality of narrow partisanship", in its manifesto[84] the PRP declared itself "vehemently opposed to arbitrariness" from an individual or an "oligarchy".[85] Contrary to Atatürk's stance on the "national will" *as* the principle of the "unity of powers" the PRP manifesto further stated:

> Although the surrender of the right to sovereignty and authority which really lies with the nation itself is born out of need, it does have its drawbacks. The most serious of these is the possibility that some form of tyranny establishes itself and takes away from the nation its rights.[86]

In addition, the manifesto stressed the importance of separation of powers, ensured by an independent judiciary and a powerful National

---

[81] For a history of liberalism in the Ottoman Empire and Turkey, see Bora & Gültekingil, *Liberalizm*. Chapters written by Ahmet Demirel (164–188) and Cem Emrence (213–231) respectively deal with the Second Group and the Free Republican Party, discussing their place within liberalism in Turkey.

[82] Tunaya, *Siyasi Partiler*, 622–635.

[83] Regarding potential allies sharing a similar standpoint with the PRP, when the latter seemed to position itself on the path of liberal decentralization, it was quite indicative that the People's Party, in response, announced in June 1924 that former members of the Liberal Alliance (*Hürriyet ve Itilaf*) would not be accepted into the People's Party.

[84] An English translation of the manifesto, program, and statutes of the Progressive Republican Party that are used here is provided by Erik J. Zürcher (EJZ) (Zürcher, *Political Opposition* 136–155). The original text in Turkish is reprinted in Tunçay, *Tek-Parti*, 385–397.

[85] Zürcher, *Political Opposition*, 138.

[86] Ibid, 136. (Translation EJZ).

Assembly (consisting if possible of two chambers) to "prevent" the executive "from exceeding its competence", and also the importance of political parties that "counterbalance each other and compete with each other"[87]:

> As is apparent from our programme, we are emphatic supporters of the collective liberties. But because in the societies of virtuous nations the liberties of the individual save social life from decay and degeneration through mutual criticism with regard to education, ethics, feelings and inclinations, we shall not hesitate to stimulate this social necessity. Personal liberty will be sacrosanct to us in all areas. We shall avoid obstructing the growing up of complete and competent human beings and blocking the development of individual skills and initiative through partizansbip and protection.[88]

Further stating that the party "shall apply a policy of great tolerance",[89] the Progressive Republican Party included in its program Article 6, stating that "The party respects religious beliefs and convictions",[90] which the People's Party used against PRP in the political purges during the turmoil created by the Sheikh Said rebellion in Eastern Anatolia (February 1925),[91] leading ultimately to the PRP's closure in June 1925.

The founding documents of the PRP, the manifesto, statutes, and programme respectively, contained very few instances of the term *Türk* (which meant both "Turk" and "Turkish"), with only one usage as

---

[87] Ibid, 136–137.

[88] Ibid, 137. (Translation EJZ).

[89] Ibid, 138.

[90] Ibid, 139.

[91] During the trials of PRP members at the Eastern Independence Tribunal (Şark İstiklal Mahkemesi) in May 1925, at the insistence of the prosecutor, the statutes of the Progressive Republican Party were read aloud. The prosecutor specifically focused on the reference "the party respects religious beliefs and convictions" (*Fırka efkar ve itikadat-ı diniyyeye hürmetkardır*), which he deemed illegal because it was now "prohibited to exploit religious sentiments for political purposes" (*hissiyat-i diniyyeyi siyasete alet etmek men edildi*) and furthermore in violation of the Treason Law (*Hiyanet-i Vataniyye Kanunu*). On the other hand, the president of the tribunal, Mazhar Müfit (Kansu), was interested in knowing whether the real intention behind this phrase was to portray the Republican People's Party as "irreligious" (*dinsiz*). Reports on this court session appeared in *Vakit* and *İkdam* (20 May 1925), reprinted in Ateş, *Türkiye Cumhuriyeti'nin Kuruluşu*, 285–295. As the minutes of the tribunals illustrate, similar accusations were directed against the PRP by the Ankara Independence Tribunal as well. See, for instance, TBMM, *İkinci Dönem Ankara İstiklal Mahkemesi*, Cilt 7/1, 33.

"Turk", used in connection with party membership. In this case, while the RPP's statutes stated that "every Turk" and those "who had embraced Turkish nationality and culture" could be members of the party, the PRP statutes formulated its requirements as:

> On the condition that he or she accepts the programme and the statutes of the party, every Turk who has reached the age of 18 who is a citizen of the Turkish Republic and is in possession of his or her full civil rights, can become a member of the party.[92]

Similar to the liberal faction of the Young Turks, the Progressive Republican Party emphasized citizenship, individual rights and duties, the strengthening of local autonomy, and reintegration based on shared economic interests and division of labour. Most of these principles went against the policies and rhetoric of the governing People's Party—for instance the Kemalist reinterpretation of "halkism" *as* unity, national, political, socioeconomic, etc., which as such rejected the existence of classes and ethnic divisions in Turkey. The realities on the ground, however, necessitated continued readjustments that often led to ambivalence and conceptual fluidity. This was especially the case regarding collective political identity, citizenship rights, and the constitution, where the People's Party often took a middle position.

It has often been pointed out that the Kemalist regime originally propagated a civic understanding of nationhood. Stanford and Ezel K. Shaw, for instance, pointed to the 1924 Constitution as the manifestation of the civic nationalism of the Kemalist republic. As a basis for their claim, they highlighted Article 88, which read "The People of Turkey, regardless of religion and race, are Turks as regards citizenship", Article 69, "All Turks are equal before the law and are expected to conscientiously abide by it. Every kind of group, class, family, and individual special privilege is abolished and prohibited", and Article 75, "Every Turk, regardless of origin, was given the same right to practice 'the philosophical creed, religion, or doctrine to which he may adhere'".[93] To quote a more recent work that confirms this observation, "the founding fathers of the Turkish Republic

---

[92] Ibid, 147. (Translation EJZ).

[93] Shaw, *History*, II, 378.

initially espoused a civic definition of citizenship and national identity. This vision was conspicuously reflected in the 1924 constitution".[94]

Perhaps this is the case at first sight, but, as Cağaptay, Üstel, and Eissenstat, among others, have rightly pointed out, there were several, often conflicting layers of meaning and implications attached to the concept of "Turk" in the new constitution, manifested particularly as a discrepancy between "citizen" and "nation".[95] When analysed further, both the text and the circumstances under which the constitution was drawn up reveal the intricacies and challenges involved. For instance, Article 88 was first formulated as the "inhabitants of Turkey" (*Türkiye ahalisi*) are "referred to as Turks, regardless of religion and ethnicity".[96] This appeared to be a formulation more in line with earlier parliamentary debates on the issue, which often led the GNA to settle on the even more vague, but, in principle, more inclusive term, *Türkiyeli* (from Turkey). In the final wording, this was changed in accordance with specific purposes and perceptions of the MPs, amongst whom there were many who saw in the first draft several inconsistencies. One MP asked whether the wording of the law referred to nationality (*milliyet*) or citizenship (*tabiiyet*).[97] When he was told that citizenship (*tabiiyet*) was meant, he warned that the word should no longer be used, as *tabiiyet* (from *tebaa* or subject) in Ottoman Turkish virtually meant allegiance. It was a relic from Ottoman times,[98] he argued, with unwelcome connotations of the sultan's subjects (*tebaa*). In a republic, he said, it should be nationality (*milliyet*)—"there is no other way" (*Başka imkanı yoktur*). Therefore, parliament must first define the nationality of the people of Turkey. He also asked what term should be used as a reference to "nationality" if "Turk" was a category of citizenship, thereby making a clear distinction between *mere* citizens and

---

[94] Kirişci, Kemal (2008). "Migration and Turkey: the dynamics of state, society and politics" in Reşat Kasaba (ed.). *Cambridge History of Turkey*. Cambridge University Press, 179.

[95] While Cağaptay characterizes this dual aspect as the Kemalists' "dilemma" between "political membership of the state" and "ethnic membership of the nation," Füsun Üstel defines it as a "republican paradox" (*cumhuriyetçi paradoks*) of "contractual nation" (*sözleşmeci ulus*) versus "organic nation" (*organik ulus*). Cağaptay, *Islam, Secularism, and Nationalism*, 14–15; Üstel, *Makbul Vatandaşın Peşinde*, 222. See also Eissenstat, "Metaphors of Race and Discourse of Nation," 249.

[96] TBMM ZC, D: 2, Cilt 8, 20 April 1924, 908.

[97] TBMM ZC, D: 2, Cilt 8, 20 April 1924, 908–910.

[98] Thus *tabiiyet-i osmaniyye* meant "Ottoman subject" as well as "Ottoman citizenship".

the, what might be labelled *full*, members of the Turkish "nation". This question was taken up by Ahmet Hamdi, who had difficulty seeing how "Turk" could designate everyone, irrespective of religion and ethnicity. Consequently, he put forth his own proposal, namely, that "those among the people of Turkey who accept the Turkish culture are called Turks".[99]

Interestingly, the strongest objections against calling everyone "a Turk, irrespective of religion and ethnicity" came from the more hard-line Turkists, among them Hamdullah Suphi, the leader of the Turkish Hearth since 1913, and formerly prominently representing the Turkist camp of the CUP.[100] Suphi reminded the Assembly of an obvious discrepancy between the attempts to devise an inclusive definition of citizenship and the actual policies implemented by the government to oust non-Muslims, for example through forced migration, or to hinder the return of those who had already left. Relating the issue to the obligations of the government under the Lausanne Treaty to secure non-Muslims minority rights and equal citizenship, Hamdullah Suphi expressed utter reluctance:

> While trying to expel those people because they are *Rum* or Armenian, if they [the foreign powers] then tell us, "No, you cannot do that, as your parliament has decided by law that those in fact are Turks", what will our answer be? ... Yes, we can pass the law with explaining amendments, but there is one truth. They cannot be Turks, not even the parliament can make the runaway *Rum*s and Armenians Turks.[101]

He then added that an Armenian had recently asked him how to become a Turk and he had answered, "It is possible for you to become a Turk ... when you have accepted the language of this country, and its schools and

---

[99] *Türkiye ahalisinden olup Türk harsini kabul edenlere Türk ıtlak olunur* (TBMM ZC, D: 2, Cilt 8, 20 April 1924, 909). The concept Ahmet Hamdi used here was *hars* (culture), following Gökalp's definition, who in turn had adopted the concept from the German *gemeinschaft*.

[100] Literally "hearth", the use of the word *ocak* here calls to mind the Unionist "Turkish Hearth" (*Türk Ocağı*) movement, founded in 1912 by Unionist writers and thinkers, including founding members Ahmet Ferit (president), Yusuf Akcura (vice-president), Mehmet Emin, Ahmet Ağaoğlu, and Fuat Sabit (the two latter being the discussants of *the three policies* in Chapter Two). In 1932 the Turkish Hearth—allegedly with over 30,000 members in 1931—was converted by Atatürk's order to his "national culture" institution, Halkevleri (People's Houses) (Üstel, *Türk Ocakları*, 344–362).

[101] TBMM ZC, D: 2, Cilt 8, 20 April 1924, 909.

education as your own".[102] He admitted, however, that the Armenians of Anatolia once had in fact "almost" become Turks.

> They had no separate education system, no separate upbringing, no separate language. They wrote their poems in Turkish, they sang their songs in Turkish, they shared the same basic habits and temperament with Turkey, it was possible even to call them Christian Turks. But then propaganda entered the stage, so did dissension. Literature, music, churches, and schools managed to separate the Armenians, whom the centuries had Turkified. Now they have their own language, own schools, and something different in their hearts. (...) Now, passing a law calling them Turks, will it remove the existing differences, I wonder? Whom among us will it satisfy to name them Turks? ... Like the Jews of France, who gave up separate schooling, do not speak another language, and have embraced France as their own, likewise you close down your schools, give up your Armenian-ness, accept Turkish culture. Then we will call you Turks. ... Otherwise, when you resist like this, I cannot help you, for there is no way my soul will believe you. (Shouts of "True!").

Celal Nuri, head of the parliamentary commission charged with preparing the new constitution, declared his full endorsement of Suphi's statements; however, he said, there were other things at stake that tied the hands of the Turkish state.

> In the past, there was this all-inclusive concept, "Ottoman". We are abolishing this concept. In its place there is a republic. However, the individuals in this republic are not all Turk and Muslim. What are we going to do with them? There are the *Rum*s, the Armenians, the Jews, all kinds of elements. Thank God they are minorities. If we don't grant them the name of "Turks", what then to call them? (Shouts of "Türkiyeli!" I am sorry to say it, but the word "Türkiyeli" signifies nothing.

In Celal Nuris' opinion, making a distinction between *Türk* (Turk) and *Türkiyeli* (from Turkey) would ultimately lose all practical meaning, as the foreign powers—with reference to Article 37 of the Lausanne Peace Treaty on securing the rights of minorities—would demand that both *Türk* and *Türkiyeli* enjoy the same civic and political rights as Muslims. More importantly, Celal Nuri's explanation revealed that *Türk* in this

[102] Ibid.

case meant Muslims, while *Türkiyeli* in its constitutionally civic inclusivity meant Muslims and non-Muslims alike. As such, *Türkiyeli* was comparable with Tanzimat version of Ottomanism, both in its usage, as well as its strengths and weaknesses. Mazhar Müfit, a close adjutant of Mustafa Kemal, seemed to have a solution:

> **Mazhar Müfit Bey**: Sir, how about we add "insofar as citizenship is concerned" to "irrespective of religion and ethnicity"?
>
> **Celal Nuri Bey**: As I have mentioned earlier, the word *tabiiyet* signifies allegiance to an overlord.
>
> **Suleyman Sırrı Bey**: This nation is the overlord. There you have it.

According to Celal Nuri, however, it was simply impossible to add something like *Türk tebaası* into the text (which could mean "Turkish citizens", "Turkish subjects", or "subjects of the Turks"), however convenient that might be, because "this is a republic". It is thought-provoking, nonetheless, that this discussion of citizenship also caused the implicit reappearance of the old Ottoman notion of *millet-i hakime* (dominant nation)—in itself a strong reminder of the Ottoman legacy—underlining that the republican elite was trying to adapt old concepts and experiences to new realities, while also continuing old habits and building upon past experiences. Thus, according to some parliamentarians, constitutional-civic membership of Turkishness formed a second tier comprising non-Muslims in relation to the membership of the Turkish "nation", as *millet*, which somehow assumed the role of the Ottoman sultan, thereby creating a master-subject relationship between the "national" groups. To complicate matters even further, the frequent emphasis on Turkishness in ethnic terms in official and public discourse it became increasingly blurred whether this only meant domination by Muslims as a whole, or domination by Muslim Turks over non-Muslims as well as non-Turkish Muslims, such as the Kurds.

In the end, the solution was sought and found in ambiguity, by providing a two-part definition: "The people of Turkey are referred to as Turks regardless of religion or ethnicity insofar as citizenship is concerned" (*vatandaşlık itibarıyle Türk ıtlak olunur*). Therefore, instead of the usual Ottoman term for citizenship (*tabiiyet*), a more recent word was chosen, *vatandaşlık* (which literally meant "sharing the same homeland"). Now *Türk* meant to belong to the same homeland, but only "insofar as citizenship is concerned". Thus, there would be Turks as nationals and Turks as citizens, the former truly belonging to the Turkish nation, and the latter only labelled as such because they had to be called something in terms of citizenship. A distinction, which has persisted to the present day.

A Question of Saying or Not Saying?

The civic-constitutional version of Turkishness was epitomized by Atatürk's famous statement in 1933: "*Ne mutlu Türküm diyene!*" ("How happy the one who says: 'I'm a Turk'"). Since then scholars have produced several derivations of the concepts to provide an interpretation of what this formulation also could mean besides the more obvious, that Turkishness was something to be celebrated with pride and joy.[103] Of particular interest is the "one who says", which often is described as an expression of a voluntarist, inclusive kind of nationalism. In that case, Turkishness was something one could ascribe to by mere self-declaration. The long list of further conditions attached made it far from as accessible as it seemed, however. As Recep Peker, the general secretary of the Republican Peoples party stated, the person should really mean it when saying "I am a Turk", and also show it in thought, feeling, and deed. Even more challenging to comply with, however, was the cultural definitions of Turkishness, which, as discussed by Zürcher, made membership in the nation highly restricted. Given the ambiguous nature of Kemalist nationalism, though, these definitions were never fully applied and both the inclusive and exclusive features coexisted.

Atatürk himself, as the main figure of the regime, had a composite concept of Turkishness. In his opinion, for example, the Turkish nation was made up of the following elements: (a) political union; (b) common language; (c) shared territory; (d) the same ethnic origin (*ırk ve menşe birliği*); (e) historical kinship; (f) kinship in morality.[104] Thus what might be called the civic-constitutional aspects of nationhood are listed as a-c, and those pertaining to a more ethnic categorization as d-f. This emerges clearly from one of the most striking sources on Mustafa Kemal's thoughts

---

[103] See, for instance, Brockett, *How Happy to Call Oneself a Turk*; Yıldız, *Ne Mutlu Türküm Diyebilene;* see also Philliou, Turkey, 17.

[104] Afetinan, A. (ed.) (2000[1931]). *Medeni Bilgiler ve M. Kemal Atatürk'ün El Yazıları*, 455.

and assumptions on issues like the nation, state, religion, and modernization: his handwritten commentaries of about 200 pages in length (dated 1931) to Afet Inan's *Medeni Bilgiler* ("civic knowledge"). This was a citizen's handbook, part of which Kemal had dictated to his adopted daughter.[105] Unsurprisingly, the first point of his commentary on the nation concerned the state. To Kemal, as had been the case with the Ottoman ruling elite, when talking about the nation (*millet*), the first association was with the state. Point 1 thus read, "The Turkish nation is a state, ruled by people under a republican government".[106] Further, in the section pertaining to the state, Kemal repeated the phrase, heavily underlining the text, that the Turkish nation "is a state" (*bir devlettir*).[107] The second emphasis he added was to the reference to Turkish, "the most beautiful [language] in the world", as the sole language of the nation.

Before long, Atatürk began encountering problems when listing the characteristics of the nation, and had to admit that there were some dissimilarities in physical appearance among the "Turkish" population of Anatolia. He tried to reduce the magnitude of the problem by questioning whether such homogeneity was, in any case, possible for a nation as ancient as the Turkish—exposed throughout history to all sorts of climates, ranging from the harsh weather of the Central Asian steppes, the Siberian winter, the warmth of the Mediterranean, and the hot deserts of Egypt and Mesopotamia. Then there was the fact, he added, that Turks had lived side by side with "all kinds of indigenous races" (*başka başka cinsten yerlilerle*), further contributing to the variety in physical appearance.

Although he refrained from making a direct connection between the variations in physical appearances and the multiethnic imperial past, Atatürk had to admit that ethnic intermixing had been at play.[108] Still, he

---

[105] A professor of history, Afet Inan (1908–1985) was entrusted with providing scientific arguments and research suitable for utilization as part of the new nationalist wave of the 1930s, revolving around the Turkish History Thesis and the Sun Language Theory. According to these "theories", Turks were the ancient source of civilization, and Turkish the mother of all languages. (see *Türk Tarih Kurultayı; Türk dil Kurultayı*).

[106] Afetinan, *Medeni Bilgiler*, 436.

[107] Ibid, 468.

[108] Not to mention the diverse ethnic makeup of the Kemalist elite itself stemming from the immediate imperial background. The annually updated lists on the "leading personalities in Turkey" during Ataturk's presidency (1923–1938), for instance, depict a Kemalist top leadership whose members had different ethnic origins, such as "Turk",

avoided explaining how, then, the "Turkish nation" had kept itself intact despite such lengthy interaction with so many people. Only implicitly did he define these influences as peripheral and superficial, not effecting the main body of the nation. "Anyway", he said, "even when the members of a small family do not appear fully identical, how reasonable is it then to expect such a quality from the whole nation?".

According to Kemal, the essential character of the Turkish nation was its common history, "which has created a particular Turkish archetype" (*muayyen Türk tipi*) with an exalted morality. In nation-building, he argued, morality was of paramount importance, and "the morals of the Turks are more or less always identical" (*Türklerin ahlakları aşağı yukarı hep birbirlerine benzer*), the hallmark of which was the Turk's unparalleled willingness to sacrifice himself:

> When I say morality, I mean that which transcends the individual. The kind of morality that makes the individual put aside his own interests, sacrifice his life for his nation if necessary. This is the kind of morality in which the Turkish nation excels. This morality is sacred ... The purpose of all teaching and upbringing of the nation's children is endlessly and tirelessly to instil this morality and national feeling.

He declared that those who emphasized the importance of shared religion to the national character were completely wrong vis-à-vis the Turkish case (*Türk millet tablosu*), observing, "Turks constituted a great nation prior to their acceptance of the religion of the Arabs".[109] Islam had no influence on the formation of nations, least of all the Turks. On the contrary, he argued, what Islam in fact did "was to loosen the national ties of the Turkish nation, numbing its national feelings and excitement".[110] To Kemal "the religion that Muhammad founded" (*Muhammed'in kurduğu din*) represented "Arab nationalism" (*Arap milliyeti siyaseti*) under the name of *ummah*. Those who accepted the "religion of the Arabs" then "forgot themselves" and were forced to work for the exaltation of "the

---

"Kurd", "Circassian", "Laz", "Albanian", "Jewish" etc. These lists consistently describe Atatürk as "son of an Albanian father and Turkish mother. Brought up totally Turkish". FO 371/398/44; FO 371/247/44; FO 371/1251/44; FO 371/649/44; FO 371/438/44; FO 371/259/44; FO 371/234/44; FO 371/127/44.

[109] *Türkler Arapların dinini kabul etmeden evvel de büyük bir millet idi* (p. 448).

[110] *Bilakis Türk milletinin milli rabıtalarını gevşetti, milli hislerini, milli heyecanını uyuşturdu*—p. 448).

word Allah" (*Allah kelimesini yükseltmesine*)[111] and to serve a religion that encouraged the desire in its members to die as soon as possible in order to obtain the delights of the everlasting afterlife.[112] In place of national languages, Arabic was imposed on non-Arabic peoples. This highly critical, even hostile, approach and choice of words about Islam was also repeated in official textbooks, as God underwent nationalization and became a Turk.

> The Turkish God [*Tanrı*] was not an unattainable, all-superior *Allah* - too proud and indifferent to the lamenting cries of his creation. He liked to fight and appreciated acts of courage. In this we see the Turkish soul .... This God was a national deity, a Turkish God.[113]

Thus, Kemal wrote, had the Turkish nation wandered without knowledge and purpose for centuries (*bir çok asırlar ne yaptığını ne yapacağını bilmeksizin*). Now, he claimed, the hold of this religion on the hearts of the Turks had been broken, and its adherents had left the country for "the Arab deserts which are the enemy of the Turks" (*Türk düşmanları olan Arap çöllerine gitti*). As the Turkish national fire had now been lit in its "home" (*ocak*)—"the last Turkish homeland" (*son Türk elleri*), Anatolia—the Turkish nation would no longer devote itself to the attainment of paradise, but to the defence and preservation of "this sacred heritage of the forefathers". Therefore, Kemal said, it was the greatest of achievements that the Turkish nation had managed, "against all the odds" (*her şeye rağmen*), to maintain its national unity, thanks above all to nearly constant engagement in war; likewise, he argued, the national unity and strength forged during the National Struggle was caused by the war situation. "According to one account", he said, "war is the most important factor in uniting tribes",[114] thus echoing Ibn Khaldun's theories wherein tribal, warlike *asabiyya* (social solidarity) was assigned the attributes of special cohesion, strength, and zeal.

---

[111] Afetinan, *Medeni Bilgiler*, 449.

[112] *Bir an evvel ölüm niyaz ederek ahiret hayatına kavuşmak telkin eden din* (p. 448).

[113] *Türk Tanrısı öyle herkesten yüksek, kendisine erişilmez, yarattıklarının isyanlarına gülümser mağrur bir Allah değil. Muharebe, kahramanlıktan hoşlanıyor. İşte burada Türk ruhunu görüyoruz. ... Bu Tanrı milli bir mabuttu, Türk Tanrısıydı* (p. 94 & 100).

[114] *Bir malumata göre, muharebe kavimlerin birleşmesinde en kuvvetli amildir.*

Although there was propaganda, according to Kemal, that promoted ideas of separate Kurdish, Circassian, Laz, and Bosnian identity, these were merely leftovers from the past age of despotism, and would have no effect besides giving rise to some minor grievances among "the few enemy instruments, and some brainless reactionaries". In Kemal's opinion, Kurds, Circassians, Laz, and Bosnians were to be regarded as members of the greater Turkish community (*camia*), as they "share the same past experiences, history, morality, legal rights and obligations". Kemal's wording here is interesting, as *umumi Türk camia* (general community of Turks) rather than "nation" implies some sort of invisibly drawn rings of Turkishness, expanding outwards in relation to the ethnic Turkish Muslim inner core. At the outer edge stood the Christians and Jews, towards whom Kemal adopted a very cautious approach indeed. Opening the door slightly, he thought they could be accepted as fellow citizens (*vatandaş*) if they declared their allegiance "from the heart" and made common cause with Turkish nationality. Ultimately, however, Kemal was more interested in the image of his modern, secular, and civilized republic than in categorizing its inhabitants. Thus, he asked himself, when their ties of loyalty and devotion were firmly established, "would it not be wrong (of us) and incompatible with noble Turkish morals, to look at them with hostile eyes and as something alien".[115]

Fully outside the national rings were the Arabs, who met with Kemal's scorn and resentment. "I wonder if the Arabs who refused to form a nation through union with Turks—even though we had accepted their religion—on the grounds that they already constituted a separate and great community, are content with their current state of slavery".[116] This was the official stance of the Turkish Republic. As a textbook produced by the Ministry of Education proclaimed, "The Arabs betrayed us by uniting with our enemies in WWI, even though we share the same religion, and the Albanians founded a separate kingdom. We then understood clearly,

---

[115] ... *mukadderatını ve tabilerini Türk milliyetine vicdani arzularıyla rapt ettikten sonra kendilerine yan gözle yabancı nazarıyla bakılmak Türk milliyetinin asıl ahlakından beklenebilir mi?*

[116] *Ayrı ve kesretli cemiyetlere malik olduklarını iddia etmiş ve bu yüzden Türklerle birleşip bir millet teşkil etmemiş olan Araplar—hem de dinlerini kabul ettiğimiz halde— acaba bugünkü esaretlerinden memnun mudurlar?* (p. 461).

the Turk has no friend other than himself. So, we embraced Turkism with heart and soul".[117]

However, some of Kemal's statements were quite revealing in that they disclosed underlying tensions and uncertainties. He argued that from now on (i.e., 1931) the goal should be to bring about and deepen national feeling in every individual, thereby implicitly admitting that this had not yet been done. Further, he said, "let us adopt a definition of nation [that is] as wide as possible, applicable to every nation".[118] Such an inclusive definition, he stressed, required a civic understanding of nationalism based on citizenship and a voluntarist approach, whereby the nation is made up of those "who are willing to live together, with equal rights and obligations, united in patriotic attachment". Yet, along with this, he again promoted the importance of the Turkish language, the innate national character, and the unique Turkish morality, making inclusion anything but easy, even impossible, to attain if one were not brought up with Turkish culture from an early age, a conundrum he failed to explicate.

True to his statement that writing history is as important as making it, from the early 1930s Mustafa Kemal turned his attention firmly to the writing and teaching of history. He had already authored the most influential history book of the republic, the *Nutuk* (Speech), narrating therein the republic's creation myth. History was assigned the role of locomotive for the new nationalist wave, resonating with similar trends in Europe. Under Kemal's auspices and supervision, a number of official history books were produced and used in schools. Among these, *Tarih IV*—the culmination of attempts to write a fully national history—was particularly influential.

Tarih IV claimed that Turkish nationalism had not obtained a distinct character before the War of Independence. The Ottoman Empire, it said, had tried to create an Ottoman nation out of different population elements, but this "policy of Ottomanness" had resulted in total failure. Depicting the Kemalist Republic as the final break with the Ottoman past, *Tarih IV* was especially critical of the CUP government for its indecisive nationalist policies. It then moved on to unfold the classic Turkish

---

[117] *Cihan harbinde Araplar Müslüman oldukları halde bize hainlik etmişler, düşmanlarımızla birleşmişlerdi; Arnavutlar ayrı bir krallık kurmuşlardı. Biz de artık anladık ki Türk'e Türk'ten başka dost yoktur. Onun için Türkçülüğe dört elle sarıldık* (Türk Tarihi Tetkik Cemiyeti, *Tarih IV*, 159).

[118] ... *mümkün olduğu kadar her millet uyabilecek bir tarifi bizde alalım.*

account of the historical process. Identifying the Balkan Wars as a turning point and a "national disaster" (*milli felaket*), the textbook also saw them as the beginning of national awakening at the popular level, as they aroused the general feeling that the time was ripe for a "national policy" (*milli siyaset*). However, *Tarih IV* claimed, the CUP had hesitated to throw itself fully into this national "stream" (*cereyan*) and, until the very end, had wandered around "wobbling between the policies of Ottomanness, Islamism and Turkism".[119]

> Turkism sometimes became Ottomanism, sometimes Turanism, sometimes a policy of Islamic union, and at times a mixture of them all. Consequently, there was no clarity or firmness in their ideas and currents of thought. In political life in particular, the impact of these ideas was minimal at best.[120]

According to *Tarih IV*, Turkish nationalism only became supreme with the republic. The state, the nation, and the army had been called "Ottoman" under the empire, causing the Turkish national character to be forgotten and Turkish history to be rejected.[121] With the republic, all this was corrected. Now that everything Ottoman was eradicated, the republic "has reunited the Turkish nation and the Turkish homeland with its proper name. From now on this homeland is called Turkey, the state 'the Turkish Republic', our army is no longer the 'Ottoman', it is 'the Turkish army.'"[122] Echoing Mustafa Kemal's definition of a "Turk", *Tarih IV* formulated it as "every individual who lives within the borders of Turkey, uses the Turkish language [i.e., does not just "speak Turkish"—*Türkçe konuşmak*—but uses it when speaking—*Türk dili ile konuşmak*—implicitly making it compulsory in daily speech], is brought up with Turkish culture, has embraced the Turkish ideal, is, irrespective of religion, a Turk".[123]

---

[119] *Osmanlılık, İslamcılık, Türkçülük siyasetleri arasında bocalayıp durmuştur* (Türk Tarihi Tetkik Cemiyeti, *Tarih IV*, 181).

[120] Türk Tarihi Tetkik Cemiyeti, *Tarih IV*, 181.

[121] Ibid, 182.

[122] Ibid, 182.

[123] *Türkiye Cumhuriyeti dahilinde Türk dili ile konuşan Türk kültürü ile yetişen, Türk mefkuresini benimseyen her fert, hangi dinden olursa olsun Türk'tür* (Türk Tarihi Tetkik Cemiyeti, *Tarih IV*, 183).

The Turkish History Thesis and the arguments of *Tarih IV* were taught in concentrated form in the primary schools of the republic. The outlines of Turkish national history were provided in "My Child's History Book" (*Yavrumun Tarih Kitabı*),[124] published by the Ministry of Education, and stretched from Europe to China, from the earliest known history to the present. In this narrative, Turks were the origin and propagator of all civilization. The "Sumerian Turks" (*Somer Türkleri*) had founded civilization in Mesopotamia,[125] and had spread the light of civilization and "civilized government" (*medeni hükümetler*) to all corners of the world. Those Turks who went to Anatolia embraced it as their own, thus Anatolia became a "Turkish homeland" (*Türk yurdu*).[126] Contrary to *Tarih IV*, which claimed that the Ottomans had made Turks forget their national identity, "My Child's History Book" argued that Turks "never forgot their nationality, language, and traditions. They were always proud of being Turks".[127] Confusingly, however, despite the textbook's claim that the Sumerian Turks had been the "light of civilization", it goes on to say that, after founding civilization as such in Mesopotamia, they had passed it on to the Chaldeans (in this case not depicted as Turks), merged with them, and vanished.

---

[124] Esat & Abdulbaki, *Yavrumun Tarih Kitabı: İlkmektep Dördüncü Sınıf*; Esat & Abdulbaki, *Yavrumun Tarih Kitabı: İlkmektep Beşinci Sınıf.*

[125] Esat & Abdulbaki, *Yavrumun Tarih Kitabı: İlkmektep Beşinci Sınıf,* 89–90.

[126] Ibid, 91.

[127] Ibid, 91–92.

CHAPTER 8

Conclusion

In 2019, President Erdoğan issued a signed statement under the heading, "one nation, one flag, one homeland, one state", wherein he defined *millet* as "everyone, who lives in this country, whether they are Turks, Kurds, Arabs, Circassians, Bosniaks, Georgians, or Roma, regardless of their ethnic descent, are part of the same nation. This is our understanding of the nation".[1] It is notable that, while saying "everyone" (*herkes*), Erdoğan only mentioned the Muslim population of Turkey, even including an otherwise often stigmatized and excluded group as the Roma. The non-Muslims were not included, or if they were, it was hidden between "everyone" and "whether" (in this case given as a suffix attached to the components listed (*-üyle, -ıyla, -iyle*)). For after all, the "nation" (*millet*) was "regardless of ethnic descent", but evidently not regardless of religion. Interestingly, the latter framing was mentioned by Erdogan in connection with "citizenship". In 2015 on the commemoration of "1915 events" (*1915 olayları*), Erdoğan described the "Turk, Kurd, Arab, Armenian" (*Türk, Kürt, Arap, Ermeni*) as "Ottoman citizens" (*Osmanlı vatandaşı*) "regardless of religion and ethnic descent" (*hangi din ve etnik*

---

[1] *Bu ülkede yaşayan herkes Türküyle, Kürdüyle, Arabıyla, Çerkeziyle, Boşnağıyla, Gürcüsüyle, Romanıyla, etnik kökenine bakılmaksızın aynı millettir. Bizim millet anlayışımız işte budur.* Erdoğan, Recep Tayyip (@RTErdogan), 11 March 2019, (https://twitter.com/RTErdogan/status/1105007951109148672).

kökenden olursa olsun).² These conceptualizations of the "nation" and the underlying mindset and nuances of meaning cannot be understood without their historical background and the processes studied in this book.

It has dealt with a period of radical change in Ottoman Turkish history, where the boundaries of meaning were constantly shifting, presenting various possibilities and trajectories for the individuals involved, while the subsequent processes of adaptation, reinterpretation, and reimagining shaped the characteristics of national identity. Building upon the fundamental theoretical assumption that nations and national identities are constructed phenomena, the central objective here has been to identify the elements of continuity and change during the construction process, focusing in particular on the flow of the notions of the "Ottoman nation" within different circumstances and contexts taking place during this crucial period. Hence, the study has highlighted the conceptual fluidity and the multi-layered nature of national identity formation in the late Ottoman Empire and the early Republic of Turkey. It has argued that focusing the analysis on possibilities rather than predetermined paths, ambiguities rather than certainties, and flexible boundaries rather than fixed positions, is better suited to comprehending the complex processes at hand.

Such a processual, non-teleological approach requires to examine the matter over a longer time span, meaning, in this case, bridging the conventional divide between the empire and the republic, which explains the periodization here. While most works on Turkish nationalism still present the republic as the dividing line, the study suggests an alternative periodization by analysing the late Ottoman and early republican periods as one unit. Such an approach is arguably better suited to capturing the ongoing transformations of meaning and vocabulary that continued, regardless of the fact that the state in Anatolia was now called the Republic of Turkey. Therefore, the late Ottoman period is presented here as the very foundation and an integral part of the same process, rather than a mere historical background to the republic, as it has often been depicted in historiography.

In addition, the book has problematized some of the core concepts related to nation and nationalism in the Ottoman Turkish context, such as

---

² https://www.mfa.gov.tr/basbakan-sayin-recep-tayyip-erdogan-1915-olaylarina-iliskin-bir-mesaj-yayimladi.tr.mfa.

"Ottoman" and "Turk", and the types of nationalism attributed to them. Thus, although the term "Ottoman" is generally seen as an older form of identification compared to "Turk", with the implication that Ottoman nationalism was outdated, and therefore had no chance of success, in comparison to Turkish nationalism, this book has highlighted the complex relationship between what is considered "old" and "new" forms of identification. The argument that Turkish nationalism was genuine and meaningful while Ottoman nationalism was artificial, hollow, and insincere is challenged. As illustrated, both "Ottoman" and "Turk" underwent similar conceptual transformations as markers of national identity during the period under study. They were associated with similar themes and vocabulary and tasked with similar goals. However, they also encountered comparable difficulties, often arising from internal contradictions and the involvement of various complex interests and actors.

Furthermore, what is generally known in historiography as "Ottomanism", and often described as patriotism rather than nationalism per se, is framed here as "Ottoman nationalism" However, the term "Ottomanism" is retained and used interchangeably here to illustrate the point that Ottoman nationalism also could hold such meaning and function as an –ism. In the Ottoman usage, however, it was a –ness instead of an –ism, that is *osmanlılık* instead of *osmanlıcılık*, which in fact was the term coined by later writers to bring a closer alignment with "Ottomanism". The designation "Ottoman nationalism" is justifiable by the fact that there were many identifiable key features to qualify it as such, including the conceptualization of "Ottomans" as a "nation" and as a political collective with the right to representation in parliament and government. Moreover, it provided the imagining and the vocabulary of a shared national identity, education and language, entailing different degrees of homogenization of the population. "Patriotism" therefore often falls short in describing the multi-layered and complex notions of "the Ottoman nation" (*millet-i osmaniye*) encountered in the source material of this study. Also, while trying to delineate the language of Ottoman-Muslim-Turkish nationalism(s) in historical analysis, it has become clear that we cannot speak of one single category of "Ottoman" or "Turkish" nationalism.

Consequently, it is just as misleading to speak of a clear-cut, unilinear movement from Ottomanism, through Islamism, to finally Turkish nationalism, as it is evident that the interactions between different forms of national identity were highly complex and not always in competition with each other. In the "Ottoman" and later the "Turkish" case, instead of competition, there was a continuous, multi-layered restructuring and compliance that endowed Ottoman and Turkish national identity formation with a highly ambiguous and flexible character, which was translated by the political elites as contextual fluidity and instrumentalist pragmatism. As such, it was rather a multidimensional and multi-actor phenomenon, able for example to function simultaneously as an ideology, a discourse, and a political strategy. Hence, there were different modes of Ottoman nationalism, readjusted to changing circumstances since its beginnings during the first half of the nineteenth century.

While the Ottoman nationalism of the Tanzimat, climaxed at the beginning of Abdulhamid II's rule with the proclamation of the Ottoman constitution in 1876, exhibited principles for national unity based on equal citizenship regardless of religious and ethnic affiliation, the Ottoman nationalism of the Hamidian regime emphasized Muslimness as the fundamental element of Ottoman national identity. Then, with the advent of the second constitutional revolution, the inclusive civic, constitutional, Tanzimat-like interpretations of Ottomanness regained currency, to be replaced yet again by an Ottoman Muslim nationalism during the National Struggle, while the early republic providing a combination, as well as parallel usages, of abovementioned elements. What we witness is therefore the broadening or narrowing of the boundaries of Ottomanness accompanied closely by changing circumstances, most drastic of which were brought about by defeats in the devastating wars and the following loss of territory and population.

Therefore, following the historical events and their effects on national identity discourses, it is possible to trace three major reorientation and adaptation attempts. First, the crucial four years between 1908 and 1912, were characterized by a political systemic shift caused by the Unionist takeover in 1908. In an atmosphere of hope for the future in the immediate aftermath of the Young Turk revolution, and the ensuing pluralist political setting as the Hamidian regime's firm grip on state and society loosened, the rhetoric and public re-imaginings of Ottoman unity gained broad currency. Revitalizing the Tanzimat-modelled, secular, civic conceptions of the Ottoman nation, this period witnessed a highly vivid political life and the general public engaged in debates on the boundaries, conditions, and content of Ottoman national identity.

8 CONCLUSION 221

During these years, far from being the dead letter, it is often portrayed as, the concept "Ottoman" as a general marker of identity across ethnic and religious divides manifested itself as a highly dynamic, adaptable, and inclusive category. The intensity and energy involved in the parliamentary debates illustrate the seriousness attached to the matter. The lengthy negotiations involved political actors, who represented not only different population elements but also the vastly diverse sociopolitical, economic, and local interests at play. As shown in Chapter 5, the main issue during these debates was not whether to reject Ottoman national identity or Ottoman unity as such, but to define the components thereof. Hence, members of parliament, Muslim and non-Muslim alike, frequently and forcefully underlined their commitment to "Ottomanness", as each particularly understood it.

The points of contention, however, revolved around issues of a more concrete, but also more difficult, nature. Non-Muslims protested against the dominance of Muslims within the Ottoman polity, Muslims demanded greater support from the non-Muslim elements for the defence of the empire in terms of money and manpower. Both Muslims and non-Muslims demanded a just and effective administration. While some, especially those MPs belonging to the governing Committee of Union and Progress, called for greater integration between the imperial centre and the provinces, including a higher degree of homogenization in terms of education and language, others requested the strengthening of local elements and the Ottoman state's recognition and respect for ethnic, religious, and cultural identities.

Unfortunately, these experimentations with parliamentary party politics and the pluralist atmosphere brought about by the revolution came to an abrupt end following the dramatic events of the Balkan Wars, leading, among other things, to the CUP's virtual one-party dictatorship. The next ten years of almost uninterrupted war (1912–22) gave particular impetus to the fact that nationalism in this period was primarily formed by events and historical contingencies, rather than ideology. The reaction of the governing Unionist elite involved redefining the boundaries of the nation in accordance with circumstances. Thus, while war raged on, Ottomanness was increasingly conceptualized as the unity of Ottoman Muslims, while the more inclusive interpretations envisioned by the constitution of 1876, which above all required the willingness of the Muslim Ottoman elites to include non-Muslims in an Ottoman national framework, received a hard blow. At the same time, Ottoman non-Muslims became a central part of the Unionist regime's construction work, fuelled by conditions and sentiments of warfare, on establishing the image of outer and inner enemies, effectively excluding the Ottoman Armenians and *Rum*s from the imagined nation.

This process of exclusion was finalized during the National Struggle 1918–22, when Ottoman national unity was defined exclusively as a community of Ottoman Muslims. The nation, still regarded as Ottoman, was exclusively imagined and represented in religious terms, best illustrated by the decision of the resistance movement to only allow Muslims as members. At the same time, MPs tried very hard to preserve solidarity and unity within the assembly, taking great care not to delve too much into the ethnic differences of the Muslim components of the resistance movement when discussing the nationality question. For the Ottoman non-Muslims, delineated as the "other", the exclusion was unequivocal: as with the membership criteria of the resistance movement, only Muslims were allowed in the parliament in Ankara.

Furthermore, the strategies for survival following the defeat in 1918 coupled with the introduction of president Wilson's "Fourteen Points", gave Ottoman nationalism a new dimension it had not had before: the idea of self-determination, and thus the invocation of the right to self-rule and legitimacy based on the convergence between the ruling element and the ruled. This marked a significant discursive shift in relation to the prevailing mindset of Ottoman Turkish history, where, as is often pointed out by historians, the state typically took precedence in the policies and rhetoric of the Ottoman political elites. Therefore, Ottoman nationalism had characterized a state looking for, or seeking to construct its nation. Among the Ottoman political elites, this state-centredness, in turn, had led to a basic understanding of nation-building, which ultimately saw the loss of territory and people as secondary to the state, which Namık Kemal had dramatically problematized, asking whether Silistra was mere territory or indeed "homeland" (*vatan*). The Ottoman defeats during the nineteenth century and the early twentieth showed an attitude that even though vast territories and populations were lost to the Ottomans, the state, duly called "the everlasting state" (*devlet-i ebed müddet*), had to endure at all costs. As long as it endured, according to this approach, there was hope for the nation as well, which brought about a preoccupation with the preservation of the Ottoman state as a key theme of nationalism.

For a brief moment at the beginning of the National Struggle, the roles and rhetoric shifted into a nation looking for its state/government. As the imperial centre was bypassed because of occupation and turmoil, followed by the sultan and his government in Istanbul took a hostile attitude towards the resistance movement, the backbone of which was the Ottoman army and the Unionist cadres, who in turn was in desperate need of legitimacy and support, Ottoman nationalism underwent a popular turn. While broadening the possibilities for a nationalist discourse more detached from the usual state-centred framework, this popular turn, whereby the "people" or "nation" now came before the state, brought about more ethnicized, religious-cultural interpretation of Ottoman national identity. This trend was intensified by the prevailing idea in the early stages of the resistance that the Ottomans had to define and present themselves in Wilsonian terms in order to obtain the right to national existence in the eyes of the world, meaning American and European audiences. While trying to produce the right arguments to convince said audiences that the Ottoman Muslims of Anatolia qualified according to such terms (e.g. demographic majority, historical, cultural, ethnic rights, etc.), the content and vocabulary of Ottoman nationalism underwent a change. With Muslimness as the focal point, the Muslim population was reframed as one "people" with a political will and the right to self-determination within its "homeland", which was redefined in terms of a vastly diminished territory in size and population.

Hence, Anatolia was reimagined and conceptualized as the homeland and national core territory—a trend that had already begun during the World War I, but subsequently reached its climax with the War of Independence (1919–22). As one MP pointed out, however, the new "national" borders were more "political" than "national" as the "homeland" designated the territory that the resistance forces had been able to retake and hold militarily. Mosul, for instance, populated mostly by Kurds, although included in the National Pact as part of the "national" borders to be reclaimed, was nonetheless relinquished in the face of British opposition. The territory thus defined the composition of the nation in the Turkish Republic, leaving, for instance, the Ottoman Arabs outside the boundaries of Anatolia and its "nation".

The newly established republican regime viewed the Muslim population as the primary building block for shaping the "Turkish" nation, a process that was facilitated by the fact that Anatolia had lost nearly all its non-Muslim population, leaving it demographically more Muslim than ever before in history. This higher level of homogeneity bolstered the republic's notion and rhetoric as a nation-state. However, the actual realities on the ground presented significant challenges to this characterization. Most importantly, the republic inherited an ethnically diverse population that included Turks, Kurds, Circassians, Laz, and others. Moreover, Anatolia remained a society deeply affected by mass migrations and the displacement of people due to the preceding decade of Ottoman war losses. Consequently, national homogeneity remained more of an ideal and a rhetorical concept rather than a fact.

Yet, it is important to note that the republic did exhibit characteristics and objectives of a nation-state. As part of its nation-building endeavours, it early on implemented several top-down policies aimed at homogenization. These were very much in line with the ideas and rhetoric expressed by the Unionist regime, especially echoing some of the basic principles propagated by the government during the parliamentary discussions on the Law on Associations in 1909. These debates had primarily revolved around the contentious issue of permitting ethnic and racial-based associations. The government had essentially questioned the viability of alternative formulations of national identity parallel to "Ottomanness". In essence, the critical issue revolved around the state's willingness to recognize and uphold diverse ethnic, religious, sectarian, and cultural distinctions that deviated from the official stance.

In the Kemalist republic, the response to this question was most severely manifested through the outright denial of distinct ethnic identities, particularly that of the Kurds. The "Kurdish question", which has emerged as one of the most persistent and contentious issues throughout the century-long history of the republic, presented significant challenges to Kemalist nation-building efforts, highlighting all the elements of ambiguity and contradictions of Ottoman-Turkish national identity formation. For the Kurds were in different settings conceptualized as *both* self and other, and thus, ultimately, *neither*. During the National Struggle, the Kurds had been considered a part of the "Ottoman Muslim nation" *as* "Kurds". However, the term "Ottoman" had become increasingly problematic, primarily for political and diplomatic reasons, as the resistance movement found itself in conflict with the imperial centre while simultaneously attempting to present the Muslim population of Anatolia as a nation in Wilsonian terms. *Türk* or *Türkiyeli* was then uneasily introduced as an alternative general marker of national identity to designate Ottoman Muslims, Kurd and Turk alike, while explicitly recognizing their ethnic identities - a crucial difference compared to the policies and discourses of the republic.

From the beginning, the term "Turk" faced considerable contestation and disagreement. Yet, as shown by this study, the concept was ambiguous enough to allow its users to present it in inclusive terms, as had been the case with "Ottoman". Also, similar to "Ottoman", which it finally replaced as an official marker of national identity and designation of nationality, "Turk" conveyed different meanings in different settings. When it was perceived as being used in exclusive terms, for example, the GNA witnessed intense debates akin to those in the Ottoman parliament, 1908–12, when MPs saw the use of "Ottoman" as meaning "Muslim" only. To ease the tensions, both assemblies resorted to a well-known remedy: emphasizing the inclusive meaning of "Turk" and "Ottoman", respectively.

In the first Grand National Assembly (1920–23), "Turk" was often claimed to mean Ottoman Muslims of Anatolia and Thrace (not unlike the contemporary European usage, where the Ottoman Empire was called "Turkey", and "Turk" meant "Ottoman Muslim")[3]. In this usage, "Turk" would be nothing more than an adaptation of "Ottoman" in the face of new realities. Unlike "Ottoman", however, "Turk" was evidently more prone to ethnic connotations as its usage continued to cause dissatisfaction and suspicion in the GNA, leading MPs to demand time and again its meaning defined by its users. Ultimately, the MPs found the issue of defining "Turk" in exact terms too difficult and the assembly chose repeatedly to shelve it to be resolved at an unspecified future date, which arguably never came, as how to define "Turk" still remains a highly contested issue.

As the usage of the term "Ottoman" had become problematic during the National Struggle, with the founding of the republic in 1923, Muslimness, another main component of Ottoman nationalism forged during this period, became problematic as well. This timing, as highlighted by Mete Tunçay, was particularly peculiar. For a regime that emphasized national unity, Tunçay argues, it was surprising to witness the adoption of policies and rhetoric that jeopardized the solidarity achieved during the National Struggle. According to Tunçay, if the primary

---

[3] Karpat, *Ottoman population*, 55. See for example also *The Concise Oxford Dictionary of Current English* (1919), which defines "Turk" as "Ottoman", "Osmanli", and "Mohammedan".

concern was the formation of a nation, it would have been more logical for the Kemalist regime to continue fostering Muslim nationalism. By doing so, they could have increased their chances of successfully shaping the Anatolian population into a cohesive nation.

Tunçay argues that Atatürk's departure from Muslim nationalism can be attributed to his modernization project, which placed a strong emphasis on sociocultural reform and secularism with a strong Western orientation. While it is undeniable that Atatürk's reform policies and secularist ideas played a significant role in shaping the new direction of the country, these factors alone do not fully explain the radical methods employed in the process. They especially fell short in accounting for the uncompromising approach taken, which was directed even against other reformist and secularist interpretations, such as those advocated by the Progressive Republican Party.

At this point, as argued here, it is crucial to consider the aspects related to the regime itself, which include issues surrounding the construction of legitimacy, political group identity, coherence, and the consolidation of power. Of particular importance are the sociopolitical structures, some of which were intertwined with religious themes, symbols, and discourses, which had the potential to challenge the Kemalist regime and its overarching master narrative, thus perceived and confronted as a threat. At this point, the political process, power politics to be more exact, in the early Republic proved crucial for the further course of modernization and national identity construction.

While the vocabulary and principles laid down by Ottoman nation-building attempts continued in new forms in the aftermath of the empire, discrepancies soon emerged, when state-building—motivated above all by legitimacy, loyalty, security, and stability—met nation-building, which emphasized collective political identity, homogeneity, unity, culture, language, and history. As pointed out in recent scholarship, Kemalist nationalism was highly ambiguous and laden with tensions and contradictions. Yet, these characteristics were, to a wide extent, a reflection of the basic features of Ottoman nationalism during the late empire. Evidently, the conceptual ambiguity of the late Ottoman Empire, characterized as "confusion" by Niyazi Berkes, who claimed it to have finally ended with the Kemalist republic (which, allegedly, had unequivocally chosen the way of modern, secular, nationalist, Western civilization), still trailed behind the Kemalist elites as a legacy of their imperial past.

Similar ambiguity and tensions can be traced in the works of leading Kemalist politicians and intellectuals, including Atatürk, who figured prominently in producing the official version of Turkish history and the Kemalist principles of Turkish nationalism. In his handwritten commentary to Afet Inan's *Civic Knowledge*, Atatürk himself presented different formulations of nationalism: pragmatic, civic, and voluntarist, but also laden with strong ethnic nationalist elements in its references to an ancient Turkish nation with a glorious history, the progenitor of civilizations and founder of great states. Here, he almost echoed the ambiguity of Akcura when the latter proclaimed his national identity as Muslim Ottoman Turk. As shown in Chapter 7, Atatürk's formulation reflected a similar tripartite composition for the nation: Muslim raw material, coupled with a Western-oriented, civic, secular civilizational ideal, and Turkish nationalism in name, language, and history.

Atatürk's very critique against the Ottoman past gave him away, however. He blamed the empire for causing to forget and hindering the Turks in awakening as a nation, obviously ignoring the implication of such a claim: that the Turks had not yet become a nation, or, if they once had been, they no longer were, but had to be "reminded" thereof. Atatürk also seemed to ignore the fact that those he accused of preventing the national revival, the Ottoman political elites, were also the same group to which he himself had belonged. Unfortunately, though, he did not discuss the reasons why his generation had talked and acted the way they did while in the imperial setting, and why the same ruling elite took on itself bringing to life the "Turkish nation" when entering the new settings of the republic. Neither did he mention why the same military-bureaucratic leadership that founded the republic were only a few years prior defending the empire with their lives on several warfronts under the banner of Ottoman unity.

Bibliography

Archives

Başbakanlık Cumhuriyet Arşivi (BCA).
Foreign Office Papers (FO), The National Archives.

Official Publications

Düstur
Meclis-i Mebusan Zabıt Ceridesi (MM ZC). Türkiye Büyük Millet Meclisi Basımevi, 1982–1991.
Türkiye Büyük Millet Meclisi Zabıt Ceridesi (TBMM ZC). TBMM Matbaası, 1942–1981.
Türkiye Büyük Millet Meclisi Gizli Celse Zabıtları (TBMM GCZ). Vol. 1–4. TBMM Basımevi, 1985.
Türk Tarih Kongresi. (1932). *Birinci Türk Tarih Kongresi: Konferanslar Müzakere Zabıtları*. T.C. Maarif Vekaleti.
Türk Dili Kurultayı. (1933). *Birinci Türk Dili Kurultayı: Tezler, Müzakere Zabıtları*. T.C. Maarif Vekaleti.
Türk Tarihi Tetkik Cemiyeti. (1934). *Tarih IV: Türkiye Cumhuriyeti*.
Türkiye Cumhuriyeti Maarif Vekaleti. (1931). *Türk Tarihinin Ana Hatları*.
Türkiye Cumhiriyeti Başvekalet Istatistik Umum Müdürlüğü. (1930). *Istatistik Yıllığı*.

Newspapers & Periodicals

Cumhuriyet (Istanbul).
Hakimiyet-i Milliye (Ankara).
Ikdam (Istanbul).
Tanin (Istanbul).
Tasvir-i Efkar or *Tevhidi Efkar* (Istanbul).
Sabah
Türk Hayatı (Istanbul).
Türk Yurdu (Istanbul).

Memoirs & Other Contemporary Sources

Abbott, G. F. (1909). *Turkey in Transition*. Arnold.
Adil, S. (1982). *Hayat Mücadeleleri: Selahattin Adil Paşanın Hatıraları*. Zafer Matbaası.
Adıvar, H. E. (1926). *Memoirs of Halide Edib*. John Murray.
Adıvar, H. E. (1930). *Turkey Faces West*. Yale University Press.
Adıvar, H. E. (1935). *Conflict of East and West in Turkey*. Jamia Press.
Afetinan, A. (2000 [1931]). *Medeni Bilgiler ve M. Kemal Atatürk'ün el Yazıları*. Atatürk Araştırma Merkezi.
Ağaoğlu, A. (1927). *Üç Medeniyet*. Türk Ocakları Merkez Heyeti Matbaası.
Ahmed, C. P. (1980). *Maruzat*. Çağrı Yayınları.
Ahmet, I. P. (1993). *Feryadım*. (eds. S. I. Furgaç &. Y. Kanar). Vol. II. Timaş Yayınları.
Akçura, Y., & Fehmi, I. (1981). Yusuf Akçura's Üç Tarz-ı Siyaset ('Three Kinds of Policy'). *Oriente Moderno*, 61(1/12), 1–20.
Akçura, Y. (1976). *Üç Tarz-ı Siyaset*. Türk Tarih Kurumu Basimevi.
Akman, E. H. (1936). *Türk Ulusallığı*. Izmir Cumhuriyet Basimevi.
Akseki, A. H. (1944). *Askere Din Kitabı*. İdeal Matbaa.
Altay, F. (1970). *10 Yıl Savaş ve Sonrası, 1912–1922*. İnsel Yayınları.
Amca, H. (1958). *Doğmayan Hürriyet*. Akın Yayınları.
Apak, R. (1988). *Yetmişlik Bir Subayın Hatıraları*. Türk Tarih Kurumu Basimevi.
Arar, I. (1969). *Atatürk'ün İzmit Basın Toplantısı: (16–17 Ocak 1923)*. Burçak Yayınevi.
Arslan, Ş. (2005). *İttihatçı Bir Arap Aydının Anıları*. Klasik.
Atatürk, M. K. (1993). *Eskişehir-İzmit Konuşmaları (1923)*. Kaynak Yayınları.
Atatürk, M. K. (1997). *Atatürk'ün Söylev ve Demeçleri*, vol. I–III. Türk Tarih Kurumu Basimevi.
Atatürk, M. K. (2004). *Atatürk'ün Bütün Eserleri*. Kaynak Yayınları.
Atatürk, M. K. (1969 [1927]). *Nutuk*. Vol. I–III. Milli Eğitim Basımevi.
Baring, M. (1913). *Letters from the Near East 1909 and 1912*. Smith, Elder.
Başar, A. H. (1946). *Hürriyet Buhranı*. İstanbul Yayın İstihlak Kooperatifi.

Başar, A. H. (1981). *Atatürk'le Üç Ay ve 1930'dan sonra Türkiye*.
Bayar, C. (1997). *Ben de yazdım: Milli mücadele'ye gidiş, vol. I-VIII*. Sabah kitapları.
Bleda, M. Ş. (1979). *İmparatorluğun Çöküsü*. Remzi Kitabevi.
Buxton, C. R. (1909). *Turkey in Revolution*. Fisher Unwin.
Cami. (1331 [1915]). *Osmanlılığın Atisi, Düşmanları ve Dostları*. İfham Matbaası.
Cebesoy, A. F. (2000). *Milli Mücadele Hatıraları*. Temel Yayınları.
Cebesoy, A. F. (2002). *Siyasi Hatıralar*, Vol. I–II. Temel Yayınları.
Cemal Paşa (1922). *Hatırat, 1913–1922*.
Cemaleddin, Efendi (1978). *Siyasi Hatıralar* (1908-1913). Tercüman.
Deliorman, M. N. (1944). *Meşrutiyetten Önce Balkan Türkleri: Makedonya Şarki Rumeli meseleleri*. Balkan Neşriyat ve Gazetecilik Yurdu.
Dursunoğlu, C. (1946). *Milli Mücadelede Erzurum*.
Efimyanidi, Y. (1324 [1908]). *Sevgili Türk Kardeşlerimize Takdim: Rum Kardeşleriniz*. Matbaa-i Kütüphane-i Cihan.
Emirzade, M. Ş. (1913). *Milleti Ikaz ve Ihya Yolunda Alem-i Insaniyete Hizmet, Yahut, Acı Acı Figanların Vediği Dersler*. Hurşid Matbaası.
Enver, P., & Cengiz, H. E. (1991). *Enver Paşa'nın Anıları: 1881–1908*. İletişim Yayınları.
Ertürk, H. (1996). *İki Devrin Perde Arkası*. Sebil Yayınevi.
Esat, S., & Abdulbaki. (1930). *Yavrumun Tarih Kitabı. İlkmektep—Dördüncü Sınıf*. Şirketi Mürettibiye Matbaası.
Esat, S., & Abdulbaki. (1930). *Yavrumun Tarih Kitabı. İlkmektep – Beşinci Sınıf*. Şirketi Mürettibiye Matbaası.
Fatınoğlu, A. N. (1977). *Yılların İçinden*. Gözlem Yayınları.
Fazlı, N. (2007 [1925]). *Rumeli'yi Neden Kaybettik?* Örgün Yayınevi.
Galanti, A. (2000). *Vatandaş Türkçe Konuş*. Kebikeç Yayınları.
Gökalp, Z. (1918). *Türkleşmek, Islâmlaşmak, Muasırlaşmak*. Yeni Matbua.
Gökalp, Z. (1339 [1923]). *Türkçülüğün Esasları*. Matbuat ve İstihbarat Matbaası.
Gölpınarlı, A. (2005). *Cumhuriyet Çocuğunun Din Dersleri: Atatürk Dönemi Ders Kitabı*. Kaynak Yayınları.
Günday, A. F. H. (1960). *Hayatım ve Hatıralarım*. Çelikcilt Matbaası.
The American-Hellenic Society. (1919). *Memorandum Presented by the Greek Members of the Turkish Parliament to the American Commission on Mandates over Turkey*.
Hilmi, I. (1329 [1913]). *Türkiya Uyan: Millet-i Osmaniyenin Intibahına, Genclerimizin Terbiye-i Istikbaline Hadim Ahlaki ve Ictimai Müfid Bir Rehberdir*. Dersaadet/İstanbul: Kitabhane-i İslam ve Askeri.
Hilmi, I. (1927). *Türk Çocuğunun Din Kitabı*. Orhaniye Matbaası.

Hilmi, I. (1931). *Millet Mekteplerine ve Halka Mahsus Yurt Bilgisi*. Marifet Matbaası.
Hüseyin, K. K. (1991). *Meşrutiyet'ten Cumhuriyet'e Hatıralarım*. İletişim Yayınları.
Hüseyin, K. K. (1992). *Türkiye'nin Çöküşü: II Meşrutiyetin Perde Arkası Ve Makedonya, Arnavutluk, Ermenistan ile Suriye'nin Elden Çıkışı*. Hikmet Neşriyat.
Hüseyin, K. K. (2003). *Balkanlardan Hicaz'a Imparatorluğun Tasfiyesi: 10 Temmuz İnkılabı ve Netayici*. Pınar Yayınları.
Hüseyin, K. K. (1943). *Türk lugati*. Dördüncü Cilt. Cumhuriyet Matbaası.
Iğdemir, U. (1986). *Sivas Kongresi Tutanakları*. Türk Tarih Kurumu Basımevi.
Ihsan, A. (1931). Matbuat Hatıralarım, 1888-1923: Vol. II; Meşrutiyetin ilanından umumî muharebeye kadar. Ahmet İhsan Matbaası.
Ismail, K. (1920). *The Memoirs of Ismail Kemal Bey*. Constable.
Karabekir, K. (1995). *Istiklal Harbimizin Esasları*. Emre Yayınları.
Karabekir, K. (1995). *Ittihat ve Terakki Cemiyeti 1896-1909*. Emre Yayınları.
Karaosmanoğlu, Y. K. (1968). *Politikada 45 yıl*. Bilgi Yayınevi.
Kırzıoğlu, M. F. (1993). *Bütünüyle Erzurum Kongresi*. Kültür Ofset.
Knight, E. F. (1909). *The Awakening of Turkey: A History of the Turkish Revolution*. John Milne.
Lermioğlu, O. N. (1976). *Halkın İstemediği İnkılap, Meşrutiyet*. Sabah Gazetesi.
Lütfi, F. (1326-1910). *Selanik'te Bir Konferans: Bizde Fark-ı Siyasiye; Hal-ı Hazırı*. Matbaa-i Ahmet İhsan.
Martin, L. (1924). *The treaties of peace, 1919-1923* (Vol. II). Carnegie Endowment for International Peace.
Mehmed, B. T. (1346 [1927]). *Yeni Türkçe Lügat*. Evkâf-ı İslâmiye Matbaası.
Menteşe, H. (1986). *Osmanlı Mebusan Meclisi Reisi Halil Menteşe'nin Anıları*. Hürriyet Vakfı Yayınları.
Meray, S. L., & Olcay, O. (1977). *Osmanlı İmparatorluğunun Çöküş Belgeleri: Mondros Bırakışması, Sevr Andlaşması, Ilgili Belgeler*. Ankara Üniversitesi Siyasal Bilgiler Fakültesi.
Meray, S. L. (1993). *Lozan Barış Konferansı: Tutanaklar belgeler*. Yapı Kredi Yayınları.
Miller, W. (1923). *The Ottoman Empire and Its Successors, 1801-1922*. University Press.
Muallim, N. (1318 [1902]). *Lugat-ı Naci*. K. Faik - Asır Matbaa Kütübhane ve Mücellithanesi.
Mustafa, H. (1324 [1908]). *Efrad-ı Şahaneye Mahsus İlmihal Kitabı*.
Müstecebizade, I. (1325 [1909]). *Rehber-i Ittihad: Mekatib-i Ibtidaiyye Çocukları İçin Kıraat Risalesi*. Köylü Matbaası.
Naim, A. (1332 [1916]). *Islamda Dava-i Kavmiyyet*. Tevzi-i Tabiat Matbaası.
Namık, K. (2004 [1889]). *Vatan Yahut Silistre*.

Necati, A., & Emiroğlu, K. (2010 [1912]). *İttihad'ın İç Yüzü; Cinayat-ı İttihadiyeden bir Nebze; 1912 Yılında Yolsuzluk, Baskı ve Hukuk Mücadelesi*. Heyamola Yayınları.
Niyazi, R. (1326 [1910]). *Hatırat-ı Niyazi*. Sabah Matbaası.
Okyar, A. F. (1980). *Üç Devirde bir Adam*. Tercüman Yayınları.
Orbay, R. (2000). *Cehennem Değirmeni*, Vol. I-II. Emre Yayınları.
Peker, R. (1984). *Inkilap Dersleri*. İletişim Yayınları.
Rıza, N. (1335 [1919]). *Hürriyet Ve İtilaf Nasıl Doğdu, Nasıl Öldü*. Akşam Matbaası.
Rıza, N. (1991). *Lozan Hatıraları*. Boğaziçi Yayınları.
Ramsay, W. M. (1909). *The Revolution in Constantinople and Turkey*. Hodder and Stoughton.
Redhouse, J. W. (1987 [1890]). *A Turkish and English Lexicon: Shewing in English the Significations of the Turkish Terms*. Librairie du Liban.
Karabekir, K. (2005). *Paşaların Kavgası: İnkılap Hareketlerimiz*. Emre Yayınları.
Sabahaddin, Prens (1999 [1334]). *Türkiye Nasıl Kurtarılabilir? Ve Izahlar*. Ayraç Yayınevi.
Sabahaddin, Prens (1327 [1911]). *İttihad Ve Terakki Cemiyetine Açık Mektublar: Mesleğimiz Hakkında Üçüncü Ve Son Bir Izah*. Mahmud Bey Matbaası.
Sabahaddin, Prens (1324 [1908]). *Teşebbüs-ü şahsi ve adem-i merkeziyet hakkında ikinci bir izah*. Mahmud Bey Matbaası.
Selek, S. (2000). *Anadolu Ihtilali*. Vol. I-II. Kastaş Yayınevi.
Şehabeddin, S. (1332 [1916]). *Osmanlılıkta Vahime-i Mesuliyet*. Cemiyet Kütüphanesi.
Şerif, P. (1990). *Bir Muhalifin Hatıraları: İttihat Ve Terakkiye Muhalefet*. Nehir Yayınları.
Stationary Office, H. M. (1920, August 10). *Treaty of Peace with Turkey: Signed at Sevres*.
Süleyman, S. (2011). *Üç Devirde Gördüklerim: Hakayıkü'l-beyan Fi Eşkali'l-Ezman Yahut ne Derekeye Inmiştik Ne Dereceye Çıktık*. Türk Tarih Kurumu.
Tansu, S. N. (1960). *Ittihad Ve Terakki İçinde Dönenler*. Inkilap Kitabevi.
Tekin, A. (1928). *Türkleştirme*. Resimli Ay Matbaası.
Tekin, A. (1936). *Kemalizm*. Cumhuriyet Gazete ve Matbaası.
Temo, I. (1939). *Ittihad Ve Terakki Cemiyetinin Teşekkülü Ve Hidematı Vataniye Ve Inkılab-ı Milliye Dair Hatıratım*. Mecidiye/Medgidia.
Tunalı, H. (1318 [1902]). *Onbirinci Hutbe: Türkiyelilik Osmanlılıktır, Osmanlılık Türkiyeliliktir*. Geneva.
Tunalı, H. (1327 [1911]). *Onuncu Hutbe: Bir Geçmişin Yadigarı. Namık Kemal Hazretlerinin Ruhuna, Türbesine Bir Armağan*. 2nd printing, Kahire/Cairo.
Tunalı, H. (1337 [1921]). *Istanbul'da Mebuslar Meclisi Kapısında*. Ikaz Matbaası.

Türkiye Büyük Millet Meclisi. (1338 [1922]). *23 Nisan Takvimi.* T.B.M.M. Matbaası.
Türkiye Büyük Millet Meclisi. (2020). *İkinci Dönem Ankara İstiklal Mahkemesi (1925–1927)*, Cilt 7 / 1–3. TBMM Basımevi.
Uran, H. (1959). *Hatıralarım.*
United States Congress. (1928). *Papers Relating to the Foreign Relations of the United States, 1915, Supplement: The World War.* United States Government Printing Office Washington.
Us, H. T. (1939). *Meclis-i Meb'usan Zabıt Ceridesi, 1293–1877.* Ed. Hakkı Tarık Us. Vakit.
Us, A. (1964). *Gördüklerim, Duyduklarım, Duygularım.* Vakit Matbaası.
Yalçın, H. C. (1976). *Siyasal Anılar.* Türkiye İş Bankası Kültür Yayınları.
Yalman, A. E. (1997). *Yakın Tarihte Gördüklerim ve Geçirdiklerim)*, Vol. I-II. Pera Turizm ve Ticaret.

Secondary Works

Aboona, H. (2008). *Assyrians, Kurds, and Ottomans: Intercommunal Relations on the Periphery of the Ottoman Empire.* Cambria Press.
Adanır, F. & Faroqhi, S. (2002). *The Ottomans and the Balkans: A Discussion of Historiography.* Brill.
Afetinan, A. (1973). *Türkiye Cumhuriyeti ve Türk Devrimi.* Başbakanlık Basımevi.
Ağaoğlu, A. (2013). *Üç medeniyet.* Doğu Kitabevi.
Ahmad, F. (2003). *Turkey: The Quest for Identity.* London Oneworld.
Ahmad, F. (2014). *The Young Turks and the Ottoman Nationalities: Armenians, Greeks, Albanians, Jews, and Arabs, 1908–1918.* The University of Utah Press.
Ahmad, F., & Rustow, D. (1976). Ikinci Meşrutiyet Döneminde Meclisler, 1908–1918. *Güneydoğu Avrupa Araştırmaları Dergisi, 4–5*, 247.
Ahmad, F. (1969). *The Young Turks. The Committee of Union and Progress in Turkish Politics 1908–1914.* The Clarendon Press.
Akçam, T. (2003). *From Empire to Republic: Turkish Nationalism and the Armenian Genocide.* Zed Books.
Akçam, T. (2012). *The Young Turks' Crime against Humanity: The Armenian Genocide and Ethnic Cleansing in the Ottoman Empire.* Princeton University Press.
Akçam, T. (2013). The Young Turks and the Plans for the Ethnic Homogenization of Anatolia. In O. Bartov & E. D. Weitz (Eds.), *Shatterzone of Empires: Coexistence and Violence in the German, Habsburg, Russian, and Ottoman Borderlands.* Indiana University Press.

Akkoyunlu, K. (2017). Electoral Integrity in Turkey: From Tutelary Democracy to Competitive Authoritarianism. In B. Başer & A. E. Öztürk (Eds.), *Authoritarian Politics in Turkey: Elections, Resistance and the AKP*, 47–63.
Aksan, V. H. (2006). Ottoman to Turk: Continuity and Change. *International Journal, 61*(1), 19–38.
Akşin, S. (1980). *100 soruda Jön Türkler ve İttihat Terakki*. Gerçek.
Akşin, S. (1998). *Istanbul Hükümetleri ve Milli Mücadele*, Vol 1–2. Türkiye İş Bankası Kültür Yayınları.
Aktar, A., Kizilyürek, N., & Özkırımlı, U. (2010). *Nationalism in the Troubled Triangle: Cyprus*. Palgrave Macmillan.
Aktürk, S. (2009). Persistence of the Islamic Millet as an Ottoman Legacy: Mono-Religious and Anti-Ethnic Definition of Turkish Nationhood. *Middle Eastern Studies, 45*(6), 893–909.
Alkan, M. O., Belge, M., & Bora, T. (2009). *Cumhuriyet'e Devreden Düşünce Mirası: Tanzimat ve Meşrutiyet'in Birikimi*. İletişim Yayınları.
Anderson, B. (1983). *Imagined Communities: Reflections on the Origin and Spread of Nationalism*. Verso.
Anderson, M. S. (1966). *The Eastern Question: 1774–1923: A Study in International Relations*. Macmillan.
Anscombe, F. F. (2014). *State, Faith, and Nation in Ottoman and Post-Ottoman Lands*. Cambridge University Press.
Arıburnu, K. (1975). *Milli Mücadelede İstanbul Mitingleri*. Yeni Desen Matbaası.
Ateş, N. Y. (1998). *Türkiye Cumhuriyeti'nin Kuruluşu ve Terakkiperver Cumhuriyet Fırkası*. Der Yayınları.
Aviv, E. (2017). *Antisemitism and Anti-Zionism in Turkey: From Ottoman Rule to AKP*. Routledge.
Aybars, E. (1998). *İstiklâl Mahkemeleri 1920–1927*, Vol. I–II. İzmir.
Ayni, M. A. (1943). *Milliyetçilik*. Marifet Basımevi.
Baer, M. D. (2010). *The Dönme: Jewish Converts, Muslim Revolutionaries, and Secular Turks*. Stanford University Press.
Bali, R. N. (2005). *Cumhuriyet Yıllarında Türkiye Yahudileri: Bir Türkleştirme Serüveni, 1923–1945*. İletişim.
Balistreri, A. E. (2016). A Provisional Republic in the Southwest Caucasus: Discourses of Self-Determination on the Ottoman–Caucasian Frontier, 1918–19. In Y. T. Cora, D. Derderian & A. Sipahi (Eds.), *The Ottoman East in the Nineteenth Century: Societies Identities and Politics*, 62–87. I.B. Tauris.
Barkey, K., & Hagen, M. V. (1997). *After Empire: Multiethnic Societies and Nation-Building: The Soviet Union and the Russian, Ottoman, and Habsburg Empires*. Routledge.
Barkey, K. (2008). *Empire of Difference: The Ottomans in Comparative Perspective*. Cambridge University Press.

Bartov, O., & Weitz, E. D. (2013). *Shatterzone of Empires: Coexistence and Violence in the German, Habsburg, Russian, and Ottoman Borderlands*. Indiana University Press.

Bayar, Y. (2014). *Formation of the Turkish Nation-State, 1920–1938*. Palgrave Macmillan.

Bein, A. (2007). A "Young Turk" Islamic Intellectual: Filibeli Ahmed Hilmi and the Diverse Intellectual Legacies of the Late Ottoman Empire. *International Journal of Middle East Studies, 39*(4), 607–625.

Ben-Bassat, Y. (2009). Rethinking the Concept of Ottomanization: The Yishuv in the Aftermath of the Young Turk Revolution of 1908. *Middle Eastern Studies, 45*(3), 461–475.

Ben-Bassat, Y., & Ginio, E. (2011). *Late Ottoman Palestine: The Period of Young Turk Rule*. I.B. Tauris.

Berger, S., & Miller, A. I. (Eds.) (2015). *Nationalizing Empires*. Central European University Press.

Berkes, N. (1998). *The Development of Secularism in Turkey*. Hurst and Company.

Bloxham, D. (2005). *The Great Game of Genocide: Imperialism, Nationalism, and the Destruction of the Ottoman Armenians*. Oxford University Press.

Blumi, I. (2003). Contesting the Edges of the Ottoman Empire: Rethinking Ethnic and Sectarian Boundaries in the Malësore, 1878–1912. *International Journal of Middle East Studies, 35*(2), 237–256.

Blumi, I. (2011). *Reinstating the Ottomans: Alternative Balkan Modernities 1800–1912*. Palgrave Macmillan.

Bora, T., & Gültekingil, M (Eds.) (2005). *Modern Türkiye'de Siyasi Düşünce Cilt 7: Liberalizm*. İletişim Yayınları.

Bora, T. (2003). Nationalist Discourses in Turkey. *South Atlantic Quarterly*, Vol. 102.

Boyar, E. (2007). *Ottomans, Turks and the Balkans: Empire Lost, Relations Altered*. I.B. Tauris.

Braude, B., & Lewis, B. (Eds.). (1982). *Christians and Jews in the Ottoman Empire: The Functioning of a Plural Society*. Holmes and Meier.

Brockett, G. D. (2011). *How Happy to Call Oneself a Turk: Provincial Newspapers and the Negotiation of a Muslim National Identity*. University of Texas Press.

Brown, L. C. (Ed.) (1996). *Imperial Legacy: The Ottoman Imprint on the Balkans and the Middle East*. Columbia University Press.

Brubaker, R. (1996). *Nationalism Reframed: Nationhood and the National Question in the New Europe*. Cambridge University Press.

Bruinessen, M. (1992). *Agha, Shaikh and State: The Social and Political Structures of Kurdistan*. Zed Books.

Brummett, P. (2000). *Image and Imperialism in the Ottoman Revolutionary Press, 1908–1911.* State University of New York Press.
Çağaptay, S. (2006). *Islam, Secularism, and Nationalism in Modern Turkey: Who is a Turk?* Routledge.
Çağaptay, S. (2017). *The New Sultan: Erdogan and the Crisis of Modern Turkey.* I.B. Tauris.
Campos, M. U. (2010). *Ottoman Brothers: Muslims, Christians, and Jews in Early Twentieth-Century Palestine.* Stanford University Press.
Çetinkaya, Y. D. (2014). *The Young Turks and the Boycott Movement: Nationalism, Protest and the Working Classes in the Formation of Modern Turkey.* I.B. Tauris.
Çevik, S. (2021). Ottomanism and Varieties of Official Nationalism. In J. Chovanec, & O. Heilo (Eds.), *Narrated Empires: Perceptions of Late Habsburg and Ottoman Multinationalism,* 59–64. Springer International Publishing AG.
Cohen, J. P. (2014). *Becoming Ottomans: Sephardi Jews and Imperial Citizenship in the Modern Era.* Oxford University Press.
Cora, Y., Derderian, T. D., & Sipahi, A. (2016). *The Ottoman East in the Nineteenth Century: Societies, Identities and Politics.* I.B. Tauris.
Criss, Nur Bilge (1999). *Istanbul under Allied Occupation, 1918–1923.* Brill.
Darendelioğlu, I. E. (1977). *Türkiye'de Milliyetçilik Hareketleri: Toplantılar, Mitingler, Nümayişler, Bildiriler, Cemiyetler, Basın.* Toker Yayınları.
Davison, R. H. (1963). *Reform in the Ottoman Empire: 1856–1876.* Princeton University Press.
Davison, R. H. (1990). *Essays in Ottoman and Turkish History, 1774–1923: The Impact of the West.* University of Texas Press.
Demirel, A. (1995). *Birinci Mecliste Muhalefet. İkinci Grup.* İletişim Yayınları
Der Matossian, B. (2014). *Shattered Dreams of Revolution: From Liberty to Violence in the Late Ottoman Empire.* Stanford University Press.
Derek, H. (1994). *National Self-Determination: Woodrow Wilson and his Legacy.* Palgrave Macmillan.
Deringil, S. (1993). The Invention of Tradition as Public Image in the Late Ottoman Empire, 1808 to 1908. *Comparative Studies in Society and History* 35(1): January, 3–29.
Deringil, S. (1999). *The Well-protected Domains: Ideology and the Legitimation of Power in the Ottoman Empire 1876–1909.* Tauris.
Deringil, S. (2007). *Simgeden Millete: II. Abdülhamid'den Mustafa Kemal'e Devlet ve Millet.* İletişim Yayınları.
Derrida, J. (1978). *Writing and Difference.* Routledge & Kegan Paul.
Der Matossian, B. (2011). From Bloodless Revolution to Bloody Counterrevolution: The Adana Massacres of 1909. *Genocide Studies and Prevention,* 6(2), 152–173.

Doumanis, N. (2012). *Before the Nation: Muslim-Christian Coexistence and its Destruction in Late Ottoman Anatolia*. Oxford University Press.
Dündar, F. (2001). *İttihat ve Terakki'nin Müslümanları İskan Politikası (1913-1918)*. İletişim Yayıncılık.
Dündar, F. (2008). *Modern Türkiye'nin Şifresi: İttihat ve Terakki'nin Etnisite Mühendisliği (1913-1918)*. İletişim Yayıncılık.
Eissenstat, H. (2007). *The Limits of Imagination: Debating the Nation and Constructing the State in Early Turkish Nationalism*. University of California.
Eissenstat, H. (2003). History and Historiography: Politics and Memory in the Turkish Republic. *Contemporary European History, 12*(1), 93–105.
Eissenstat, H. (2005). Metaphors of Race and Discourse of Nation: Racial Theory and State Nationalism in the First Decades of the Turkish Republic. In P. Spickard (Ed.), *Race and Nation: Ethnic Systems in the Modern World* (pp. 239–256). Routlege.
Eissenstat, H. (2015). Modernization, Imperial Nationalism, and the Ethnicization of Confessional Identity in the Late Ottoman Empire. In S. Berger & A. I. Miller (Eds.), *Nationalizing Empires* (pp. 429–459). Central European University Press.
Emrence, C. (2008). Imperial Paths, Big Comparisons: The Late Ottoman Empire. *Journal of Global History, 3*(3), 289–311.
Emrence, C. (2011). *Remapping the Ottoman Middle East: Modernity, Imperial Bureaucracy, and the Islamic State*. I.B. Tauris.
Eraslan, C. (1992). *II. Abdülhamid ve İslam Birliği: Osmanlı Devleti'nin İslam Siyaseti 1856–1908*. Ötüken.
Ergül, F. A. (2012). The Ottoman Identity: Turkish, Muslim or Rum? *Middle Eastern Studies, 48*(4), 629–645.
Erol, E. (2015). 'Macedonian Question' in Western Anatolia: The Ousting of the Ottoman Greeks before World War I. In H. Kieser (et al.) (Eds.), *World War I and the End of the Ottoman Empire: From the Balkan Wars to the Turkish Republic*. I.B. Tauris.
Erol, E. (2016). *The Ottoman Crisis in Western Anatolia: Turkey's Belle Époque and the Transition to a Modern Nation State*. I.B. Tauris.
Evered, E. O. (2012). *Empire and Education under the Ottomans: Politics, Reform, and Resistance from the Tanzimat to the Young Turks*. I.B. Tauris.
Ezherli, I. (1992). *Türkiye Büyük Millet Meclisi (1920–1992) ve Osmanlı Meclisi Mebusanı (1877–1920)*. TBMM Kültür, Sanat ve Yayın Kurulu.
Fahrenthold, S. D. (2019). *Between the Ottomans and the Entente: The First World War in the Syrian and Lebanese Diaspora, 1908–1925*. Oxford University Press.
Farah, C. E. (2002). *The Sultan's Yemen: 19th-Century Challenges to Ottoman Rule*. I.B. Tauris.

Faroqhi, S. (2005). *Subjects of the Sultan: Culture and Daily Life in the Ottoman Empire*. I.B. Tauris.

Findley, C. V. (1980). *Bureaucratic Reform in the Ottoman Empire: The Sublime Porte, 1789–1922*. Princeton University Press.

Findley, C. V. (1989). *Ottoman Civil Officialdom: A Social History*. Princeton University Press.

Fisch, J. (2016). *The Right of Self-Determination of Peoples*. Cambridge University Press.

Fortna, B. C. (2002). *Imperial Classroom: Islam, the State, and Education in the Late Ottoman Empire*. Oxford University Press.

Fortna, B. C., Katsikas, S., Kamouzis, D., & P. Konortas (eds.) (2013). *State-Nationalisms in the Ottoman Empire, Greece and Turkey: Orthodox and Muslims, 1830–1945*. Routledge.

Fortna, B. C. (2016). *The Circassian: A life of Eşref Bey, late Ottoman Insurgent and Special Agent*. Oxford University Press.

Frangoudaki, A. (2007). *Ways to Modernity in Greece and Turkey: Encounters with Europe: 1850–1950*. Tauris.

Gawrych, G. W. (2006). *The Crescent and the Eagle: Ottoman Rule, Islam and the Albanians, 1874–1913*. I.B. Tauris.

Gellner, E. (1994). *Encounters with Nationalism*. Blackwell.

Gellner, E. (1996). The Coming of Nationalism and its Interpretation: The Myths of Nation and Class. In G. Balakrishnan (Ed.), *Mapping the Nation* (pp. 98–145). Verso.

Georgeon, F. (1986). *Türk Milliyetçiliğinin Kökenleri: Yusuf Akçura (1876–1935)*. Yurt Yayınevi.

Getachew, A. (2019). *Worldmaking after Empire: The Rise and Fall of Self-Determination*. Princeton University Press.

Gingeras, R. (2009). *Sorrowful Shores: Violence, Ethnicity, and the End of the Ottoman Empire, 1912–1923*. Oxford University Press.

Gingeras, R. (2016). *Fall of the sultanate: The Great War and the end of the Ottoman Empire 1908–1922*. Oxford University Press.

Ginio, E. (2005). Mobilizing the Ottoman Nation during the Balkan Wars (1912–1913): Awakening from the Ottoman Dream. *War in History*, 12(2), 156–177.

Göçek, F. M. (1996). *Rise of the Bourgeoisie, Demise of Empire: Ottoman Westernization and Social Change*. Oxford University Press.

Göçek, F. M. (2011). *The Transformation of Turkey: Redefining State and Society from the Ottoman Empire to the Modern Era*. I.B. Tauris.

Göçek, F. M. (1996). *Rise of the Bourgeoisie*. Ottoman Westernization and Social Change. Oxford University Press.

Gövsa, I. A. (1946). *Türk Meşhurları Ansiklopedisi*. Yedigün Neşriyat.

Gondicas, D., & Issawi, C. P. (1999). *Ottoman Greeks in the Age of Nationalism: Politics, Economy, and Society in the Nineteenth Century*. Darwin Press.

Gramsci, A. (1992 [1971]). *Selections from the Prison Notebooks of Antonio Gramsci* (ed. and trans. Q. Hoare and G. N. Smith), International Publishers.

Grandits, H. et al. (2011). *Conflicting Loyalties in the Balkans: The Great Powers, The Ottoman Empire and Nation-Building*. I.B. Tauris.

Grigoriadis, I. N. (2013). *Instilling Religion in Greek and Turkish Nationalism*. Palgrave Macmillan US.

Gül, A., & Gökçen, S. (2010). *Son Dönem Osmanlı Nüfusu ve Ecnebiler Meselesi*. Cedit Neşriyat.

Gürpınar, D. (2013). *Ottoman Turkish Visions of the Nation, 1860–1950*. Palgrave Macmillan.

Hall, R. C. (2000). *The Balkan Wars 1912–1913: Prelude to the First World War*. Routledge.

Hanioğlu, M. S. (1985). Osmanlıcılık. In M. Belge & F. Aral (Eds.), *Tanzimat'tan Cumhuriyet'e Türkiye Ansiklopedisi*, 5. Cilt (pp. 1389–1393). İletişim Yayınları.

Hanioğlu, M. S. (1995). Tunalı Hilmi Bey'in 'Devlet Modeli.' *İstanbul Üniversitesi İktisad Fakültesi Mecmuası*, 2, 107–144.

Hanioğlu, M. S. (1995). *The Young Turks in Opposition*. Oxford University Press.

Hanioğlu, M. S. (2001). *Preparation for a Revolution: The Young Turks, 1902–1908*. Oxford University Press.

Hanioğlu, M. S. (2002). Turkish Nationalism and the Young Turks, 1889–1908. In F. M. Göcek (Ed.), *Social Constructions of Nationalism in the Middle East* (pp. 85–97). State University of New York Press.

Hanley, W. (2017). *Identifying with Nationality: Europeans, Ottomans, and Egyptians in Alexandria*. Columbia University Press.

Hechter, M. (2004). *Containing Nationalism*. Oxford University Press.

Helmreich, P. C. (1974). *From Paris to Sèvres: The Partition of the Ottoman Empire at the Peace Conference of 1919–1920*. Ohio State University Press.

Heper, M. (2000). The Ottoman Legacy and Turkish Politics. *Journal of International Affairs*, 54(1), 63–82.

Heyd, U. (1950). *Foundations of Turkish Nationalism: The Life and Teachings of Ziya Gökalp*. Luzac and the Harvill Press.

Hirschon, R. (2003). *Crossing the Aegean: An Appraisal of the 1923 Compulsory Population Exchange between Greece and Turkey*. Berghahn Books.

Hobsbawm, E. J. (1990). *Nations and Nationalism Since 1780: Programme, Myth*. Cambridge University Press.

Hobsbawm, E. J. (1996). *The Age of Revolution 1789–1848*. 1st Vintage (Books). Vintage Books.

Howard, H. N. (1959). *The Partition of Turkey: A Diplomatic history, 1913–1923*. H. Fertig.

İçduygu, A., Toktas, S., & Soner, B. A. (2008). The Politics of Population in a Nation-Building Process: Emigration of Non-Muslims from Turkey. *Ethnic and Racial Studies, 31*(2), 358–389.
Isom-Verhaaren, C., & Schull, K. F. (2016). *Living in the Ottoman Realm: Empire and Identity, 13th to 20th Centuries.* Indiana University Press.
Jacobson, A. (2008). Negotiating Ottomanism in Times of War: Jerusalem during World War I through the Eyes of a Local Muslim Resident. *International Journal of Middle East Studies, 40*(1), 69–88.
Jäschke, G. (1972). *Yeni Türkiye'de İslamlık.* Bilgi Yayınevi.
Kadıoğlu, A., & Keyman, E. F. (2011). *Symbiotic Antagonisms: Competing Nationalisms in Turkey.* University of Utah Press.
Kansu, A. (1995). *1908 Devrimi.* İletişim Yayınları.
Kansu, A. (2000). *Post-Revolutionary Politics in Turkey, 1908–1913.* Brill.
Karal, E. Z. (1944). *Türkiye Cumhuriyeti Tarihi: 1918–1944.* Millî Eğitim Basımevi.
Karpat, K. H. (1985). *Ottoman Population 1830–1914: Demographic and Social Characteristics.* University of Wisconsin Press.
Karpat, K. H. (1974). *The Ottoman State and Its Place in World History.* Brill.
Karpat, K. H. (2001). *The Politicization of Islam: Reconstructing Identity, State, Faith, and Community in the Late Ottoman State.* Oxford University Press.
Kars, H. Z. (1997). *1908 Devrimi'nin Halk Dinamiği.* Kaynak Yayınları.
Kasaba, R. (2010). *A Moveable Empire: Ottoman Nomads, Migrants, and Refugees.* University of Washington Press.
Katsikas, S. (2009). Millets in Nation-States: The Case of Greek and Bulgarian Muslims, 1912–1923. *Nationalities Papers, 37*(2), 177–201.
Kayalı, H. (1995). Elections and the Electoral Process in the Ottoman Empire, 1876–1919. *International Journal of Middle East Studies, 27*(3), 265–286.
Kayalı, H. (1997). *Arabs and Young Turks: Ottomanism, Arabism and Islamism in the Ottoman Empire, 1908–1918.* University of California.
Kayalı, H. (2021). *Imperial Resilience: The Great War's End, Ottoman Longevity, and Incidental Nations.* University of California Press.
Keyder, Ç. (1987). *State and Class in Turkey: A Study in Capitalist Development.* Verso.
Kezer, Z. (2015). *Building Modern Turkey: State, Space, and Ideology in the Early Republic.* University of Pittsburgh Press
Kieser, H. L., Öktem, K., & Reinkowski, M. (eds.) (2015). *World War I and the End of the Ottoman Empire: From the Balkan Wars to the Turkish Republic.* I.B. Tauris.
Kieser, H. L., Anderson, M. L., Bayraktar, S., & Schmutz, T. (2019). *The End of the Ottomans: The Genocide of 1915 and the Politics of Turkish Nationalism.* I.B. Tauris.
Kili, S. (1995). *Türk Devrim Tarihi.* Tekin Yayınevi.

Klein, J. (2007). Kurdish Nationalists and Non-Nationalist Kurdists: Rethinking Minority Nationalism and the Dissolution of the Ottoman Empire, 1908–1909. *Nations and Nationalism*, 13(1), 135–153.
Koloğlu, O. (1992). *Osmanlı'dan Günümüze Türkiye'de Basın.* İletişim Yayınları.
Köroğlu, E. (2007). *Ottoman Propaganda and Turkish Identity: Literature in Turkey during World War I.* I.B. Tauris.
Koselleck, R. (2004). *Futures Past: On the Semantics of Historical Time (Translated and with an Introduction by Keith Tribe).* Columbia University Press.
Kuehn, T. (2011). *Empire, Islam, and Politics of Difference: Ottoman Rule in Yemen, 1849–1919.* Brill.
Kuran, A. B. (1945). *Inkilap Tarihimiz ve Ittihad ve Terakki.* Tan Matbaası.
Kushner, D. Z. (1977). *The Rise of Turkish Nationalism, 1876–1908.* Cass.
Kutlu, S. (2008). *Didar-ı Hürriyet: Kartpostallarla Ikinci Meşrutiyet (1908–1913).* İstanbul Bilgi Üniversitesi.
Ladas, S. P. (1932). *The Exchange of Minorities: Bulgaria, Greece, and Turkey.* The Macmillan Company.
Landau, J. M. (1990). *The Politics of Pan-Islam: Ideology and Organization.* Clarendon Press.
Landau, J. M. (1995). *Pan-Turkism: From Irredentism to Cooperation.* Indiana. University Press.
Lerner, D. (1958). *The Passing of Traditional Society: Modernizing the Middle East.* Free Press.
Lévy, Noémı & François Georgeon. (2016). *The Young Turk Revolution and the Ottoman Empire: The Aftermath of 1908.* I.B. Tauris.
Lewis, B. (1968). *The Emergence of Modern Turkey.*
Liebich, A. (2023). *Cultural Nationhood and Political Statehood.* Routledge.
Macfie, A. L. (1998). *The End of the Ottoman Empire, 1908–1923.* Routledge.
MacMillan, Margaret (2003). *Paris 1919: Six Months That Changed the World.* Random House Inc.
Makdisi, U. (2000). *The Culture of Sectarianism: Community History and Violence in 19th-Century Ottoman Lebanon.* University of California Press.
Makdisi, U. S. (2002). After 1860: Debating Religion, Reform, and Nationalism in the Ottoman Empire. *International Journal of Middle East Studies*, 28, 601–617.
Manela, Erez (2007). *The Wilsonian Moment: Self-Determination and the International Origins of Anticolonial Nationalism.* Oxford University Press.
Mango, A. (1999). *Atatürk.* John Murray.
Mansfield, P. (1973). *The Ottoman Empire and Its Successors.* Macmillan.
Mardin, Şerif (2000 [1962]). *The Genesis of Young Ottoman Thought: A Study in the Modernization of Turkish Political Ideas.* Syracuse University Press.
Mardin, Ş. (2006). *Religion, Society, and Modernity in Turkey.* Syracuse University Press.

Mardin, Ş. (2008 [1964]). *Jön Türklerin Siyasi Fikirleri 1895–1908*. İletişim Yayınları.

Masters, B. (2011). *Christians and Jews in the Ottoman Arab World, the Roots of Sectarianism*. Cambridge University Press.

McCarthy, J. (1995). *Death and Exile: The Ethnic Cleansing of Ottoman Muslims, 1821–1922*. The Darwin Press.

Meeker, M. E. (2001). *A Nation of Empire: The Ottoman Legacy of Turkish Modernity*. University of California Press.

Meyer, J. H. (2015). *Turks across Empires: Marketing Muslim Identity in the Russian-Ottoman Borderlands, 1856–1914*. Oxford University Press.

Motyl, A. J. (2001). *Imperial Ends: The Decay*. Columbia University Press.

Nielsen, J. S. (ed.) (2011). *Religion, Ethnicity and Contested Nationhood in the Former Ottoman Space*. Brill.

O'Byrne, D. J. (2003). *The Dimensions of Global Citizenship: Political Identity Beyond the Nation-State*. Routledge.

Olson, R. (1989). *Emergence of Kurdish Nationalism and the Sheikh Said Rebellion, 1880–1925*. Univeristy of Texas Press

Ortaylı, İ. (2016) *İmparatorluğun En Uzun Yüzyılı*. Timaş Yayınları.

Özavcı, H. O. (2015). *Intellectual Origins of the Republic: Ahmet Ağaoğlu and the Genealogy of Liberalism in Turkey*. Brill

Özbek, N. (2007). Defining the Public Sphere during the Late Ottoman Empire: War, Mass Mobilization and the Young Turk Regime (1908–18). *Middle Eastern Studies, 43*(5), 795–809.

Özkırımlı, U. (2017). *Theories of Nationalism. A Critical Introduction* (3rd ed.). Palgrave.

Özkırımlı, U., & Sofos, S. A. (2008). *Tormented by History: Nationalism in Greece and Turkey*. Hurst & Co.

Özoğlu, H. (2001). 'Nationalism' and Kurdish Notables in the Late Ottoman-Early Republican Era. *International Journal of Middle East Studies, 33*, 383–409.

Özoğlu, H. (2004). *Kurdish Notables and the Ottoman State: Evolving Identities, Competing Loyalties, and Shifting Boundaries*. State University of New York Press.

Panayi, P. (2012). *Refugees and the End of Empire: Imperial Collapse and Forced Migration in the Twentieth Century*. Palgrave Macmillan.

Parla, T. (1985). *The Social and Political Thought of Ziya Gökalp: 1876–1924*. Brill.

Philliou, C. M. (2021). *Turkey: A Past Against History*. University of California Press.

Pichler, R., Clayer, N., & Grandits, H. (2011). *Conflicting Loyalties in the Balkans: The Great Powers, the Ottoman Empire and Nation-building*. I.B. Tauris.

Polat, G. (2012). Changes in State-Society Relations from the First World War to the National Independence Struggle (1914–1923). *Turkish Historical Review, 3*(1), 19–41.

Poulton, H. (1997). *The Top Hat, the Grey Wolf, and the Crescent: Turkish Nationalism and the Turkish Republic.* NYU Press.

Prott, V. (2016). *The Politics of Self-determination: Remaking Territories and National Identities in Europe, 1917–1923.* Oxford University Press.

Provence, M. (2017). *The Last Ottoman Generation and the Making of the Modern Middle East.* Cambridge University Press.

Quataert, D. (1997). Clothing Laws, State, and Society in the Ottoman Empire, 1720–1829. *International Journal of Middle East Studies, 29*(3), 403–425.

Quataert, D. (2005). *The Ottoman Empire, 1700–1922.* Cambridge University Press.

Ramsaur, E. E. (1957). *The Young Turks: Prelude to the Revolution of 1908.* Princeton University Press.

Reinkowski, M. (2005). The State's Security and the Subjects' Prosperity: Notions of Order in Ottoman Bureaucratic Correspondence (19th Century). In H. T. Karateke & M. Reinkowski (Eds.), *Legitimizing the Order: The Ottoman Rhetoric of State Power* (pp. 195–212). Leiden.

Reynolds, M. A. (2011). *Shattering Empires: The Clash and Collapse of the Ottoman and Russian Empires 1908–1918.* Cambridge University Press.

Roshwald, A. (2001). *Ethnic Nationalism and the Fall of Empires: Central Europe, Russia and the Middle East, 1914–1923.* Routledge.

Rustow, D. A., & Ward, R. E. (1964). *Political Modernization in Japan and Turkey.* Princeton University Press.

Safi, P. (2012). History in the Trench: The Ottoman Special Organization—Teşkilat-ı Mahsusa Literature. *Middle Eastern Studies, 48*(1), 89–106.

Şapolyo, E. B. (1943). *Atatürk.* Cumhuriyet Matbaası.

Sarinay, Y. (2011). The Relocations (tehcir) of Armenians and the Trials of 1915–16. *Middle East Critique, 20*(3), 299–315.

Sciarcon, J. (2009). Unfulfilled Promises: Ottomanism, the 1908 Revolution and Baghdadi Jews. *International Journal of Contemporary Iraqi Studies, 3*(2), 155–168.

Segal, D. A., & Handler, R. (2006). Cultural Approaches to Nationalism. In G. Delanty & K. Kumar (Eds.), *The Sage Handbook of Nations and Nationalism* (pp. 57–65). Sage.

Sencer, E. (2004). Balkan Nationalisms in the Ottoman Parliament, 1909. *East European Quarterly, 38*, 41–64.

Şenışık, Pınar (2011). *The Transformation of Ottoman Crete: Revolts, Politics and Identity in the Late Nineteenth Century.* I.B. Tauris,

Shaw, S. J. (2000). *Studies in Ottoman and Turkish History: Life with the Ottomans.* Isis Press.

Shissler, A. H. (2003). *Between Two Empires: Ahmet Agaoglu and the New Turkey.* I.B. Tauris.
Simon, R. (1987). *Libya between Ottomanism and Nationalism: The Ottoman Involvement in Libya during the War with Italy (1911–1919).* K. Schwarz.
Sohrabi, N. (2011). *Revolution and Constitutionalism in the Ottoman Empire and Iran.* Cambridge University Press.
Spencer, P., & Wollman, H. (2002). *Nationalism: A Critical Introduction.* Sage Publications.
Sterio, M. (2012). *The Right to Self-determination under International Law: Selfistans, Secession, and the Rule of the Great Powers.* Routledge.
Strauss, J. (1995). The Millets and the Ottoman Language: The Contribution of Ottoman Greeks to Ottoman Letters (19th-20th Centuries). *Die Welt Des Islams, 35*(2), 189–249.
Suny, R. G. (2006b). Nationalism, Nation Making, & the Postcolonial States of Asia, Africa, & Eurasia. In L. Barrington (Ed.), *After Independence: Making and Protecting the Nation in Postcolonial and Postcommunist States.* The University of Michigan Press.
Suny, R. G., Naimark, N. M., & Göçek, F. M. (2015). *A Question of Genocide: Armenians and Turks at the End of the Ottoman Empire.* Oxford University Press.
Tanör, B. (1997). *Osmanlı-Türk Anayasal Gelişmeleri.* Yapı Kredi Yayınları.
Thomas, D. S. (1992) (transl.). Akcura's Uc Tarz-i Siyaset. In H.B. Paksoy (Ed.) *Central Asian Monuments* (pp. 133–150). Isis Press.
Tilly, C. (1999). Conclusion: Why Worry About Citizenship. In M. P. Hanagan & C. Tilly (Eds.), *Extending Citizenship, Reconfiguring States.* Rowman and Littlefield.
Tilly, C. (1998). *Durable Inequality.* University of California Press.
Todorova, M. N. (2003). *Balkan Identities: Nation and Memory.* New York University Press.
Tokay, G. (1996). *Makedonya Sorunu: Jön Türk Ihtilalinin Kökenleri, 1903–1908.* AFA Yayınları.
Toprak, Z. (2006). Bir Hayal Ürünü: 'İttihatçıların Türkleştirme Politikası.' *Toplumsal Tarih, 146,* 14–22.
Toprak, Z. (2012). Balkan Harbi, İntikam ve 'Ötekileştirme' Süreci. *Toplumsal Tarih, 228,* 42–53.
Toprak, Z. (1982). *Türkiye'de Milli Iktisat, 1908–1918.* Yurt Yayınları.
Toprak, Z. (1995). *Milli Iktisat - Milli Burjuvazi: Türkiye'de Ekonomi Ve Toplum; 1908–1950.* Tarih Vakfı Yurt Yayınları.
Topuz, H. (2003). *II. Mahmut'tan Holdinglere Türk Basın Tarihi.* Remzi Kitabevi.
Tunaya, T. Z. (1952). *Türkiye'de Siyasi Partiler, 1859–1952.* Arba Yayınları.
Tunaya, T. Z. (1989). *Medeniyetin Bekleme Odasında.*

Tunaya, T. Z. (1996). *Hürriyet'in Ilanı. Ikinci Meşrutiyetin Siyasi Hayatına Bakışlar.* Arba Yayınları.

Tunaya, T. Z. (1998). *İslamcılık Cereyanı: İkinci Meşrutiyetin Siyasi Hayatı Boyunca Gelişmesi ve Bugüne Bıraktığı Meseleler*, vol. I–III. Cumhuriyet Yayınları.

Tunaya, T. Z. (2000). *Türkiye'de Siyasal Partiler: vol. I-III.* İletişim Yayınları.

Tunçay, M., & Zürcher, E. J. (1994). *Socialism and Nationalism in the Ottoman Empire, 1876–1923.* British Academic Press.

Tunçay, M. (1981). *Türkiye Cumhuriyeti'nde Tek-Parti Yönetimi'nin Kurulması: 1923-1931.* Yurt Yayınları.

Tuncer, E. (2003). *Osmanlı'dan günümüze seçimler: 1877–1999.* Topumsal ekonomik ve siyasal araştırmalar vakfı.

Türesay, Ö. (2016), Political Victims of the Old Regime under the Young Turk Regime (1908–11). In Noémi Lévy-Aksu & François Georgeon (Eds.), *The Young Turk Revolution and the Ottoman Empire: The Aftermath of 1908.* I.B. Tauris.

Turfan, N. N. (2000). *Rise of the Young Turks: Politics, the Military and Ottoman Collapse.* I.B. Tauris.

Ülker, E. (2005). Contextualising 'Turkification': Nation-Building in the Late Ottoman Empire, 1908–18. *Nations and Nationalism, 11*(4), 613–636.

Ünal, H. (1998). Ottoman Policy during the Bulgarian Independence Crisis, 1908–9: Ottoman Empire and Bulgaria at the Outset of the Young Turk Revolution. *Middle Eastern Studies, 34*(4), 135–176.

Üngör, U. U. (2011). *The Making of Modern Turkey: Nation and State in Eastern Anatolia: 1913–1950.* Oxford University Press.

Üstel, F. (1997). *Imparatorluktan Ulus-Devlete Türk Milliyetçiliği: Türk Ocakları (1912–1931).* İletişim Yayınları.

Üstel, F. (2008). *"Makbul Vatandaş"ın Peşinde: II. Meşrutiyet'ten Bugüne Vatandaşlık Eğitimi.* İletişim Yayınları.

Uyanık, N. (2015). *Dismantling the Ottoman Empire: Britain.* Routledge.

Uzer, U. (2016). *An Intellectual History of Turkish Nationalism: Between Turkish Ethnicity and Islamic Identity.* University of Utah Press.

Vovchenko, D. (2016). *Containing Balkan Nationalism: Imperial Russia and Ottoman Christians, 1856–1914.* Oxford University Press.

Weiker, W. F. (1973). *Political Tutelage and Democracy in Turkey: The Free Party and its Aftermath.* E. J. Brill.

Weismann, I., & Fruma, Z. (2005). *Ottoman Reform and Muslim Regeneration.* I.B. Tauris.

Yavuz, M. H., & Blumi, I. (2013). *War and Nationalism: the Balkan Wars, 1912-1913, and Their Sociopolitical Implications.* The University of Utah Press.

Yavuz, M. H., & Feroz, A. (2016). *War and Collapse: World War I and the Ottoman State*. The University of Utah Press.
Yerasimos, S. (2000). *Kutuluş Savaşında Türk-Sovyet İlişkileri*. Boyut Yayın Grubu.
Yetkin, Ç. (1996). *Başlangıçtan Atatürk'e Türk Halk Eylemleri Ve Devrimler*. Ümit Yayıncılık.
Yıldız, A. (2001). *Ne Mutlu Türküm Diyebilene: Türk Ulusal Kimliğinin Etnoseküler Sınırları (1919 - 1938)*. İletişim Yayınları.
Yılmaz, H. (2013). *Becoming Turkish: Nationalist Reforms and Cultural Negotiations in Early Republican Turkey, 1923–1945*. Syracuse University Press.
Yosmaoğlu, I. K. (2006). Counting Bodies, Shaping Souls: The 1903 Census and National Identity in Ottoman Macedonia. *International Journal of Middle East Studies, 38*(1), 55–77.
Yosmaoğlu, I. K. (2013). *Blood Ties: Religion, Violence and the Politics of Nationhood in Ottoman Macedonia, 1878–1908*. Cornell University Press.
Zürcher, E. J. (1984). *The Unionist Factor: The Role of the Committee of Union and Progress in the Turkish National Movement, 1905–1926*. Brill.
Zürcher, E. J. (1991). *Political Opposition in the Early Turkish Republic: The Progressive Republican Party, 1924–1925*. Brill.
Zürcher, E. J. (1993). *Turkey: A Modern History*. I.B. Tauris.
Zürcher, E. J. (2010). *The Young Turk Legacy and Nation Building: From the Ottoman Empire to Atatürk's Turkey*. I.B. Tauris.

Index

A

Abdulaziz, sultan (r. 1861–1876), 29
Abdulmecid, sultan (r. 1839–1861), 29
   and Islamic conservatism, 40
   and Tanzimat, 40, 44, 47, 220
   legitimacy, 41, 42
Action Army (*Hareket Ordusu*), 87
Adıvar, Halide Edip, 70, 71
ADR. *See* Association for the Defence of Rights of Anatolia and Rumelia—ADR (*Anadolu ve Rumeli Müdafaa-i Hukuk Cemiyeti*), the
Ağaoğlu, Ahmet, 46
Ahrar Fırkası. *See* Ottoman Freedom Party (*Osmanlı Ahrar Fırkası*)
Akçura, Yusuf, 15, 18, 47–60, 135, 168, 205, 227. *See also* Three Kinds of Policy (*Üç Tarz-ı Siyaset*), the

Albania/Albanians, 32, 46, 76, 81, 102, 108, 110–114, 118, 172, 173, 212
Ali, Kemal, 54, 55, 58
Amasya Circular (*Amasya Tamimi*), 136
Anatolia, 8, 16, 19, 27, 40, 53, 69, 95, 108, 117, 119, 122–124, 128–130, 132–140, 142, 144, 145, 147–152, 154, 156, 161, 162, 169–171, 173, 177, 182–184, 186, 193, 194, 197, 206, 209, 211, 215, 218, 223–225
Anderson, Benedict, 106
Ankara, 3, 17, 55, 126, 127, 139, 140, 155–160, 164–166, 172, 178, 187, 198, 222
Anti-imperialism, 145
Arab provinces, 16, 76, 111
Arab revolt (1916), 168
Arabs, 46, 168, 172, 173, 185, 210, 212, 217, 223

Armenia/Armenians, 25, 46, 55, 56, 73, 102, 122–124, 127, 130–133, 143, 144, 146–152, 156, 175, 177–180, 182–184, 205, 206, 217, 222
Army of the Caliphate, The (*Hilafet Ordusu*), 156
Assembly of Deputies (*Meclis-i Mebusan*), 17, 37, 39, 54, 96, 98, 139, 155, 160, 192
Association for the Defence of Rights of Anatolia and Rumelia—ADR (*Anadolu ve Rumeli Müdafaa-i Hukuk Cemiyeti*), the, 140
Atatürk, Mustafa Kemal, 3–5, 10, 29, 32, 79, 83, 87, 117, 126, 127, 132, 135, 136, 144, 145, 154, 156, 167, 170, 171, 180–182, 187, 191, 194–201, 205, 208, 209, 226, 227
Atatürk revolution, 194–198
Austria-Hungary, 9, 65, 80
Avlonya (Valona), 76
Ayni, Mehmet Ali, 44, 46

B

Babıali baskını (Raid on the Sublime Porte), 116
Balkans. *See* Rumelia/*Rumeli*
Balkan Wars (1912–1913), 9, 14, 19, 82, 95, 108, 114, 115, 117, 123, 147, 214, 221
Bayar, Celal, 119–121, 124
Berlin, Treaty of (1878), 80
Bitlis, 130, 152
Bleda, Mithat Şükrü, 132, 133
Bolshevik revolution, 134
Bonaparte, Napoleon, 103
Bosnia-Herzegovina/Bosnians, 9, 46, 80, 81, 212
Boycott movement, 81

Bulgaria/Bulgarians, 25, 32, 33, 46, 55, 58, 64, 67, 71, 72, 80, 81, 91, 102, 109, 110, 116, 123
Büyük Millet Meclisi. *See* Grand National Assembly (GNA)

C

Caliphate, the Ottoman, 3
Capitulations, 121
Cebesoy, Ali Fuat, 133, 134, 136, 200
Celal Nuri (İleri), 206, 207
Cemal Pasha, 112
Central Committee (*Merkezi Umumi*), 80, 85, 88, 93, 132
Centralization/centralism, 26, 27, 93, 94, 108, 200
Citizen/citizenship
 and the 1924 constitution, 203, 204
 and the Ottoman constitution, 35, 36, 38, 63, 70, 103, 107, 159, 166, 220
 Ottoman citizenship law of 1869, 35
Committee of Union and Progress—CUP (*İttihat ve Terakki Cemiyeti*), 55, 67–70, 74–76, 78–88, 93–96, 100–102, 105, 107–110, 112–119, 121, 124, 128, 131, 132, 134, 153, 157, 190, 194, 200, 205, 213, 221
Committee of Union and Progress—CUP (*İttihat ve Terakki Cemiyeti*), 13, 19, 44, 59, 63, 65, 67, 69
Constitution
 Law on Fundamental Organization, 158, 159
 of 1876, 35, 63, 68, 70, 107, 159, 166, 220, 221
 of 1924, 203, 204

INDEX 251

Constitutional clubs, 101, 109, 110
Counterrevolution attempt, of 1909, 86, 87, 157
Crete, 64, 80, 108
Crimean War (1853–1856), 29, 31
Cumhuriyet Halk Fırkası. See Republican People's Party
Cyprus, 182, 183

D
Democracy, 3, 121, 189
Diyarbekir, 130, 151, 161

E
Eastern Question, the, 26
Edirne, 66, 75, 76, 116, 117, 130, 143, 184
Education, 6, 19, 24, 29, 36, 40, 78, 83, 91, 92, 95, 104, 202, 206, 219, 221
Egypt, 182, 183, 209
Elections
  of 1908, 78
  of 1912, 115
  of 1919, 155
  of 1923, 198
Entente powers, 130, 134, 135, 139, 141, 146, 147, 155–157
Enver Pasha, 116, 119, 132, 134
Erdoğan, R.T., 217
Ertürk, Hüsamettin, 131–133
Erzurum, Congress of, 19, 137, 139, 141–144, 146–149, 151, 154, 157
Ethnic cleansing, 19
Ethnicity, 2, 6, 24, 31, 37, 49, 60, 73, 97–99, 102, 103, 108, 142, 170, 192, 204, 205, 207
Ethnic nationalism, 15, 33, 44, 50, 149
Ethniki Etairia, 120

F
Ferid Pasha, Damat, 98, 129, 153
Ferit, Ahmet, 54–59, 135, 205
Fez, 28, 29, 198
Fourteen Points, the, 125, 140, 143, 148, 222
Franz Joseph, emperor of Austria-Hungary, 65
Free Republican Party (*Serbest Cumhuriyet Fırkası*), 201
French Revolution, the, 25, 31, 70, 99, 100, 196
Fuad Pasha, 29, 37, 71

G
Gellner, E., 25, 169
Germany, 5, 31
Gökalp, Ziya, 2, 46, 190, 191, 197, 205
Grand National Assembly of Turkey—GNA (*Türkiye Büyük Millet Meclisi*), the, 20, 126, 155, 158–160, 162, 164–166, 172, 173, 175, 182, 186, 187, 189, 194–196, 198, 200, 204, 225
Great Britain, 64
Great Powers, 20, 26, 29, 34, 41, 52, 67, 68, 81, 118, 121, 166. See *also* Entente powers
Greece, 28, 53, 64, 80, 93, 116, 123, 127, 135, 146, 156, 164, 175, 179
Greek Orthodox Ottomans. See *Rum*
Greek War of Independence (1821–32), 26
Gülhane Reform Decree (1839), 30

H
Habsburg Empire. See Austria-Hungary

Hakimiyet-i milliye (national sovereignty), 140, 157, 188, 190
Halaskar Zabitan (Savior Officers), 115
Halkism/halkists, 188–191, 203
Hamdullah Suphi (Tanrıöver), 205
Hamidian regime, the, 6, 16, 41, 77, 78, 83, 84, 104, 220
Hanioğlu, Şükrü, 4
Historiography, the revisionist, 12
Historiography, the traditional Turkish, 127
Hürriyet ve Itilaf Fırkası. See Liberal Alliance Party (*Hürriyet ve Itilaf Fırkası*)
Hüseyin Avni (Ulaş), 182

I
Ikinci Grup (The Second Group), 200
Ilinden uprising, the, 64
İlmihal kitabı (Catechism Manual), 104
Inan, Afet, 209, 227
Independence Tribunals (*Istiklal Mahkemeleri*), 198
Internal Macedonian Revolutionary Organization (IMRO), 64
Iraq, 53, 143, 170, 171, 181
irtica (religious reaction), 86, 193
Işkodra (Scutari), 76
Islahat Fermanı. See Reform Edict (*Islahat Fermanı*) (1856)
Islam, 3, 9, 28, 49, 51, 52, 54, 56, 96, 102, 104, 112, 114, 151, 165, 210, 211
Islamism/Pan-Islamism, 14, 18, 41, 42, 47, 49–51, 55, 56, 214, 219
Ismail, Kemal, 81, 85
Istanbul, 53, 58, 59, 66, 67, 70, 72, 73, 76, 82, 93, 98, 108, 112, 116, 129–131, 133, 135, 136, 153, 154, 156, 157, 160, 165, 166, 170, 172, 177, 178, 180, 223
Italy, 5
Ittihad ve Terakki Cemiyeti. See Committee of Union and Progress—CUP (*İttihat ve Terakki Cemiyeti*)
Izmir, 60, 98, 119–121, 127, 134, 135, 143, 146, 156, 179, 180
Izzet Pasha, 133, 134

J
Jews, 46, 72, 161, 179, 180, 206, 212

K
Kamil Pasha, 84, 85, 116
Kansu, Mazhar Müfit, 202, 207
Karabekir, Kazım, 74, 87, 131, 133, 136, 137, 156, 159, 198, 200
Kara, Kemal, 133
Karakol, 132, 133
Kars, Islamic National Council of (*Kars Milli Islam Şurası*), 141
Kemalism, 165. See also Six Arrows (*Altı Ok*), the
Kemalists, the, 4, 13, 20, 194, 204
Kemal, Mustafa. See Atatürk, Mustafa Kemal
Kemal, Namık, 35, 58, 71, 106, 168, 182, 222
Khaldun, Ibn, 211
King-Crane Commission, 142
Konya, 39, 73, 76, 179, 187
Kosovo, 64, 112
Kurds, 46, 144, 148–152, 163, 181–187, 207, 212, 217, 223, 224
Kusçubaşızade Eşref, 119

L

Language, 1, 19, 32, 38, 41, 48, 95, 99, 104, 110, 111, 135, 142, 145, 149–151, 153, 169, 176, 182, 205, 206, 208, 209, 211, 213–215, 219, 221, 226, 227
Lausanne, Treaty of (1923), 121, 156, 175, 176, 179, 205
Law on Associations (*Cemiyetler Kanunu*), 96, 98, 101, 103, 109, 192, 224
Law on Fundamental Organization (*Teşkilatı Esasiye Kanunu*), 158, 159
Law on General Offsetting (*Mahsubu Umumi Kanunu*), 176, 179
Laz, 46, 161–163, 210, 212, 224
League of Nations, 183
Lebanon, 64
Legitimacy, 27, 28, 41, 42, 49, 56, 67, 95, 105, 112, 113, 125, 137, 141, 157, 166, 188, 193, 194, 196, 222, 223, 226
Lewis, Bernard, 4, 9, 10, 25, 47
Liberal Alliance Party (*Hürriyet ve Itilaf Fırkası*), 55, 93, 115
Liberals, 19, 87, 93, 99, 117, 200
Libya, 108

M

Macedonia, 41, 64, 65, 67, 69, 71, 72, 74, 80, 109, 110, 118, 171
Mahmud II, sultan (r. 1808–1839), 28, 29, 82
Mahmud Şevket Pasha, 87
Manastır, 64, 67, 69, 74, 76
Mardin, Şerif, 28, 31, 34, 95, 96, 151, 197
Meclis-i Mebusan. *See* Assembly of Deputies (*Meclis-i Mebusan*)
Medeni Bilgiler (Civic Knowledge), 209

Megali Idea, 120
Mehmed VI Vahideddin, sultan (r. 1918–1922), 166
Midhat Pasha, 29, 71
Millet-i hakime (the ruling nation), 8
Millet-i mahkume (the ruled nation), 8
Millet system, 24, 25
Misak-ı Milli. *See* National Pact (*Misak-ı Milli*), the
Modernity, 2–4, 6, 9–11, 18, 23, 24, 27, 29, 32, 40, 86, 195, 197, 209, 226
Modernization paradigm, the, 9–11
Montenegro, 116
Mosul, 143, 163, 173, 181–185, 223
Mudanya, armistice of (1922), 165, 170
Mudros, Armistice of (1918), 126, 127, 129
Muslims, 1, 25, 31, 34, 38, 39, 46, 49, 52–54, 60, 72, 73, 76, 86, 100, 102, 104, 110, 113, 118, 122–124, 133, 143–147, 150–152, 154, 156, 160, 163, 167, 175, 177–179, 206, 207, 221–225
Mustafa Reşit Pasha, 29

N

National economy (*milli iktisat*), the, 81, 122
National forces (*kuva-i milliye*), the, 135
National Pact (*Misak-ı Milli*), the, 127, 155, 156, 161, 184, 223
National Struggle (*Milli Mücadele*), the, 42, 74, 125, 127, 146, 166, 170–172, 175, 181, 187, 190, 193, 194, 196, 200, 211, 220, 222–225

Nation-building, 2, 3, 5, 7, 8, 13–18, 24, 25, 32, 36, 42, 46, 95, 197, 210, 222, 224, 226
Nation-state, 3, 4, 10–12, 14, 15, 32, 44, 45, 224
Nicholas II, Tsar of Russia, 64, 65
Niyazi of Resne, 65, 113
Non-Muslims, 28, 31, 33, 34, 38, 44, 46, 49, 52, 53, 60, 86, 112, 118–120, 122, 123, 148, 151, 158, 167, 176–180, 205, 207, 217, 221, 222
Nutuk (The Speech), 196, 213

O

Ottoman Freedom Party (*Osmanlı Ahrar Fırkası*), 54, 55, 79, 93
Ottomanism, 6–8, 10, 11, 14, 18, 19, 28, 30, 33–35, 39, 41–44, 47, 48, 50–52, 56, 57, 59, 60, 92, 95, 96, 102, 105, 108, 168, 169, 189, 200, 201, 207, 219
Ottoman-Italian War, 9
Ottoman public, the, 5, 41, 71, 118
Ottoman-Russian War (1877–78), 117

P

Paris Peace Conference (1919), the, 142, 153
Pasha, Ali, 29, 37
Pasha, Talat, 133
Patriarchate, the Greek Orthodox, 180
Peker, Recep, 208
Periodization, 5, 13, 218
Population exchange, 123, 148, 175, 178, 180, 198
Populism. *See Halkism/halkists*

Progressive Republican Party—PRP (*Terakkiperver Cumhuriyet Fırkası*), 191, 200–203, 226

R

Rıza, Ahmet, 92
Race, 2, 49, 75, 97, 98, 102, 103, 150, 192, 203
Reform Edict (*Islahat Fermanı*) (1856), 31, 34
Rehber-i Ittihad (Guide to Unity), 104, 105
Renewal Party (*Teceddüt Fırkası*), 132
Representative Committee (*Heyeti Temsiliye*), 138
Republican People's Party—RPP (*Cumhuriyet Halk Fırkası*), 79, 125, 191, 192, 202, 203, 208
Republic, proclamation of the, 6, 126, 166
Reşad (Mehmed V), sultan (r. 1909–1918), 88
Reval meeting, 65, 107
Rum, 25, 60, 102, 122, 123, 134, 146, 147, 177, 179, 205
Rumelia/*Rumeli*, 12, 16, 25, 39, 53, 67, 69, 82, 83, 87, 101, 102, 108, 112, 113, 116, 124, 142, 143, 145, 183
Ruşen Bey, 74
Russia, 29, 34, 39, 47, 53, 64, 65. *See also* Soviet Russia

S

Sabahaddin, Prince, 54, 93, 94
Said Pasha, 84
Salonica, 64, 69, 70, 72, 74–77, 82, 85, 88, 93, 118
Sarıkamış, 123
Secularism, 4, 10, 194, 195, 226

INDEX   255

Self-determination, national, 139, 145, 186
Serbia/Serbs, 53, 55, 64, 116
Sevres, Treaty of (1920), 152, 160
Sheikh Said rebellion (*Şeyh Said İsyanı*) (1925), 202
Sivas, Congress of, 19, 125, 137–141, 143, 144, 146–149
Six Arrows (*Altı Ok*), the, 191
Soviet Russia, 159
Special Organization (*Teşkilatı Mahsusa*), the, 119, 124, 132
Sultanate, the Ottoman, 3, 19, 195
Sun Language Theory (*Güneş Dil Teorisi*), 48, 209
Syria, 108, 112, 143, 170–173

T
Tanin, 74, 89, 93
Tanzimat, 18, 24, 27, 29, 31, 32, 34, 35, 37, 40, 41, 44, 47, 55, 57, 71, 105, 197, 207, 220
Tarih IV, 10, 168, 213–215
Tekin Alp (Moise Cohen), 43, 47, 165
Thrace, 8, 118, 123, 136, 138, 140, 143, 171, 183, 184, 225
Three Kinds of Policy (*Üç Tarz-ı Siyaset*), the, 18, 47–49, 57, 59
Tönnies, Ferdinand, 197
Tunalı Hilmi, 167, 188, 189
Tunaya, Tarık Zafer, 30, 40, 44–46, 55, 86, 93, 107, 110, 117, 131, 200, 201
Turk/Turks, 4, 14, 20, 42–46, 49, 51–53, 56, 57, 59, 60, 96, 100, 119, 128, 129, 143, 148–153, 160–165, 168, 170, 173–176, 180, 183–185, 187, 192, 202–215, 217, 219, 224, 225, 227

Turkey, 2–7, 9, 10, 12, 16, 21, 32, 45, 46, 48, 56, 63, 68, 70, 81, 94, 129, 131, 137, 152, 158–160, 166, 168–171, 173–176, 181, 184, 186, 188, 192–194, 199, 201, 203–208, 214, 217, 218, 225
Turkification, 14, 95
Turkish Hearth (*Türk Ocağı*), the, 135, 205
Turkish History Thesis (*Türk Tarih Tezi*), the, 48, 209, 215
Turkism/Pan-Turkism, 18, 43, 47, 48, 50, 51, 55, 59, 95, 96, 190, 214
Türk Yurdu, 48, 215

U
Unity of elements (*ittihad-ı anasır*), the, 6, 28
Unity of powers (*vahdeti kuvva*), the, 198, 199, 201
Üsküb (Skopje), 72

V
Van, 130, 152
Vasıf, Kara, 127, 133, 148
Vatan (homeland), 35, 51, 58, 71, 95, 105, 106, 170, 222
Vatan Yahut Silistre (Homeland or Silistra), 35, 58, 106
Venizelos, Eleftherios, 179

W
War of Independence (*İstiklal Savaşı*), 19, 56, 67, 82, 176, 177, 213, 223
Wilson, Woodrow, 125, 129, 139, 140, 142, 143, 149, 152, 181, 222

World economic crisis, 5
World system theory, 11
World War I, 3, 13, 16, 19, 61, 80, 82, 96, 117, 119, 121, 123, 126, 129, 139, 147, 173, 176, 178, 179, 212, 223

Y

Yalçın, Hüseyin Cahit, 89
Yemen, 108, 109, 112, 170, 173
Young Ottomans, 34, 35, 197
Young Turk Revolution (1908), 5, 18, 19, 59, 63–65, 69, 80, 108, 220

Young Turks, 6, 13, 16, 19, 21, 42–48, 51, 54, 55, 58, 63, 64, 66, 67, 69, 71, 79–84, 86–89, 92, 94–96, 100, 104, 105, 107–110, 113, 115–119, 122, 123, 130–134, 166, 174, 189, 190, 200, 203, 205, 220, 222–224

Z

Zürcher, Erik Jan, 13, 26, 30, 64, 84, 87, 113, 118, 124, 128, 134, 136, 156, 166, 191, 193–195, 197, 201, 208

Printed in the United States
by Baker & Taylor Publisher Services